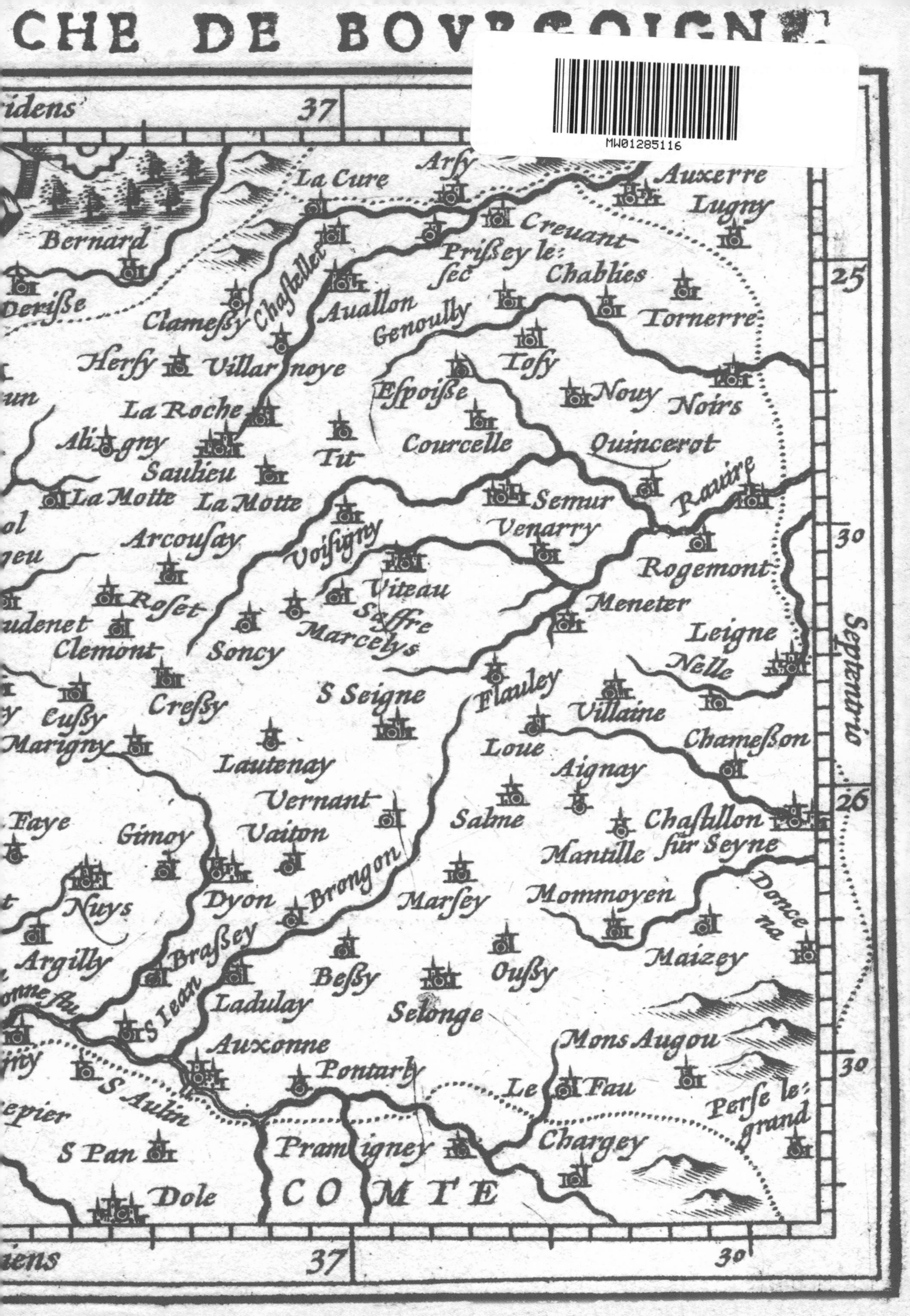

...idens 37

La Cure Arly Auxerre Lugny

Bernard Creuant Lugny

Priſſey le ſec Chablies

Clameſſy Chaſtellet Auallon Genoully Tornerre

Herſy Villar noye Eſpoiſſe Toſy Nouy Noirs

La Roche Courcelle Quincerot Rauire

Aligny Tit Semur

Saulieu La Motte Venarry Rogemont

La Motte Voiſigny Meneter

Arcouſay Viteau Leigne

Roſet Seſſre Nelle

Clemont Soncy Marcelys

audenet Villaine

Creſſy S Seigne Flauley Chameſſon

Cuſſy Loue

Marigny Lautenay Aignay 26

Faye Vernant Salme Chaſtillon ſur Seyne

Gimoy Vaiton Mantille Donce na

Nuys Dyon Brongon Marſey Mommoyen Maizey

Argilly Braſſey Beſſy Ouſſy

S Iean Ladulay Selonge

Auxonne Mons Augou

Pontarly Le Fau Perſe le grand

epier S Aulin

S Pan Pram igney Chargey

Dole COMTE

...iens 37 30

THE 100
BURGUNDY

For my mother, wish you were here.

THE 100
BURGUNDY

EXCEPTIONAL WINES TO BUILD A DREAM CELLAR

JEANNIE CHO LEE
MASTER OF WINE

ASSOULINE

CONTENTS

PREFACE

This book was born from my growing admiration and love for the wines from this region, and the good fortune of living in a city where great Burgundy is generously shared and enjoyed on a regular basis. I have been a visitor to the region for nearly two decades, but a keen buyer and consumer for far longer.

Intended for those discovering Burgundy and those already smitten with the region's seductive wines, this book is an informative guide to the greatest masterpieces that should be not just tasted but *experienced* with friends and family! In narrowing the list, I had my daughter in mind, to create a dream cellar for her to understand and appreciate Burgundy by tasting its benchmark wines as well as some of its rising stars.

Within the book I tried to capture the context, the people, and the history that allows for the creation of these masterpieces, timeless expressions that are more in the realm of art than the world of drink. Rather than going into the microscopic details of Burgundy's terroir, viticulture, fragmented vineyard holdings, or winemaking choices, this book aims to provide an "impressionistic" portrait of Burgundy's greatest wines. Great Burgundy doesn't come cheap and most have hefty price tags, with highly contentious opinions of their relative values, but if one considers them as artistic, emotional, and sometimes spiritual experiences, the price one is willing to pay varies widely by individual.

The 100 wines selected for this book, focusing on the Côte d'Or, have been chosen specifically to celebrate their "live performances" as artistic expressions—classic masterpieces or potential masterpieces that I would want my daughter to experience one day. These are the most memorable wines that I have had the privilege of experiencing over the past thirty years. The most important factors considered for inclusion were the wine's inherent quality, its timeless expression, its proven ability to evolve and improve over several decades, and its ability to evoke emotion. Ultimately I asked myself, would I want my daughter to experience these wines and would I want them for her cellar?

Wishing you an emotional, pleasure-filled journey with Burgundy,

Jeannie Cho Lee MW

FOREWORD

In this book, Jeannie Cho Lee invites readers to appreciate and discover the greatest Burgundy wines for their dream cellar. While there are numerous books on the terroir and vineyards of Burgundy, this book offers a fresh consumer's perspective by a dedicated professional who visits the region regularly and clearly recognizes the greatest wines of Burgundy. I admire her commitment to educating and to communicating wine's pleasures and mystery, not just to her strong followers in Asia, but also to a global community that appreciates fine wine. Having tasted with Jeannie for many years, I am delighted to be writing this Foreword for her latest book—it is essential reading for all fine wine enthusiasts, especially those who love great Burgundy wine.

What is great Burgundy wine? The best, in Burgundy, must not only be a well made, well vinted, well balanced wine, it must also have essential qualities of its own AOC as well as those unique to the particular vintage. It must have in its very essence—engraved within it, if you will, in its very soul—a mark of the earth and the plant itself.

In comparing wines from the same AOC and vintage, a wine is the best, in my opinion, if it has the perfume, a sublime and precise "nose" of the vine at the moment of its flowering. It is this captivating scent that it will keep and develop throughout its lifetime.

It is better still if it evokes the flesh of the well-ripened grape when we taste it just before harvesting. The wine must keep this flavor and profound density.

And finally, the wine is the best if it evokes the structure of the world around it—the ancient homes of the winemakers or the soaring spires of the village church where the vineyards thrive.

Indeed, to coax such great wines from the vineyards, the soil, and the plants, it is essential to truly understand that the vineyards, the soil, and the plants are all living beings. They are living beings just as we are, because, in fact, there is only one life. It is imperative to respect this life and to stop killing with herbicides, fungicides, pesticides, insecticides, and all other -icides so akin to homicide.

The next step is to really care for the vines, and in doing this you will get to know them

better and better. You must remember that the vine that gives us such beautiful wines was once a wild, free rebel plant that man tamed and domesticated some 8,000 years ago. In order to get from her what you want, you must live with her, understand her, heal her when she is hurting from the pruning and constant cutting, always giving her more and still more love and care.

The vine becomes, for the true winemaker who comes to love his or her vines, much more than a plant. As a dear pet, so close to the heart, she is always there, grateful for this constant attention with surely some small bud of consciousness. She gives each year more perfect and aromatic grapes, thus returning, in her own way, all the love and care she has received.

In such grapes—though unimaginable, in fact we can already perceive the wine as it will one day become—there are countless strong and vigorous living yeasts. These yeasts, during the course of the fermentation for which they are completely responsible, will deconstruct the grapes in transforming the sugar into alcohol and then die with them, killed by this same alcohol, thus giving their lives to their creation, the wine. Year after year, this mysterious alchemy takes place and gives to us a lesson to live by.

This glorious liquid, this wine which has just been created, if it is also treated as a living being—respected, raised, well-kept, loved—will unveil all throughout its long life, as a medium, the secrets of its origin and its profound identity. It will enchant with its song, an intimate and sublime music for those who have the patience and inner silence to hear it.

Lalou Bize-Leroy

BURGUNDY THEN AND NOW

HISTORY

Along the Côte d'Or in the heart of Burgundy, there are no grand châteaux, no impressive cellars designed by famous architects; rather, what stands out in the landscape of rolling hillsides and small villages along the Route des Grands Crus are church steeples and crosses. The visual landscape tells part of the region's rich history, which is inextricably tied to its unique winemaking and grape-growing culture.

Evidence such as recent archaeological excavations in Gevrey-Chambertin confirms that grapes were cultivated during the Roman times, but it likely began much earlier. From a geological and topographic view, the foundations were laid hundreds of millions of years ago, when the soil's unique combinations were formed. Burgundy's culture of winegrowing from archaeological and literary evidence dates back over 1,700 years[1]; from a religious-historical perspective, the culture spans over a thousand years. All of these influences have shaped the Burgundy we know today.

As a wine-producing region, it is tiny, representing only 3.7% of the total vineyards in France[2], yet nearly a quarter of the *appellations* are based in Burgundy. This extreme fragmentation—with hundreds of place names and thousands of producers—is part of the reason why Burgundy is so difficult to understand. At the heart of this minute region is the Côte d'Or—just fifty kilometers north to south, and barely one kilometer wide. Nearly all the wines covered in this book come from this center.

Only two major grape varieties dominate—Pinot Noir and Chardonnay—and yet the expressions they offer are seemingly limitless. Even within one Grand Cru, an appellation such as Échezeaux, with only 37 total hectares[3], there is a dizzying array of options, with over 80 owners, more than 60 of whom bottle under their own estate label[4]! In Bordeaux, 35 hectares in the Médoc is someone's expansive garden or modest-sized property, while in Burgundy it is a considerable domaine or a large Grand Cru appellation.

The huge variation created by different winegrowers owning tiny parcels and making a Grand Cru labeled "Échezeaux" or "Clos Vougeot" is further complicated by vintage and quality differences brought on by microclimate conditions and vine material as well as winemaking decisions, all contributing to the diversity and fascination—or confusion—for many Burgundy lovers.

GEOLOGICAL FORMATION

Côte d'Or soils mainly date to the Jurassic period, 200 to 150 million years ago. During the early Jurassic, when dinosaurs roamed the land, most of France was submerged under the sea. Over hundreds of thousands of years, the remains of coral, shellfish, and other marine life created a seabed of calcareous rock, or limestone. This, mingled with other layers, such as silts and clays, created a type of sedimentary rock called marl. These calcified submarine layers eventually emerged to form France and the Côte d'Or.

The movement and collision of the Adriatic and Eurasian continental plates, known as the Alpine orogeny, created the Alps around 35 to 40 million years ago, and contributed to the creation of the Côte d'Or's unique topography. The shifting of the earth's deep layers created many cracks and faults in this region, leading to the formation of hillsides and contributing to a wide range of soil types that can vary from one vineyard row to another.

The main geological fracture in the Côte d'Or is the north-south fault along which erosion from the slopes created irregular and diverse soil mixtures. The chalkiest areas lie in the north from Dijon to Nuits-Saint-Georges, referred to as the Côte de Nuits. The best vineyards have rocky limestone subsoil interladen with strips of marl, are sloped and east-facing, with good sun exposure and ideal microclimate: A vineyard on a hillside facing east enjoys maximum morning and afternoon sun, allowing more reliable ripening conditions— perfect for Pinot Noir. Thus nearly all the 550 hectares of Grand Cru vineyards within the Cote d'Or are on east-facing slopes.

In comparison, Côte de Beaune to the south, from Ladoix-Serrigny to Santenay, has more marl than limestone, and the orientation is not fully east-facing. Here, the clay, grainy silt, and marl over limestone, with cooler site conditions, finds its partner in the Chardonnay grape. Whenever there is a higher proportion of limestone, Pinot Noir pops up, especially in the southern part of Côte de Beaune such as Santenay and Maranges.

The Corton hill is unique in that both Grand Cru red and white wines, Corton and Corton-Charlemagne, respectively, are produced. Following the geological formula in line with the rest of the Côte d'Or, the upper slope, richer in marl and generally cooler, is planted with Chardonnay, while the lower slope on late Jurassic soil, made of red marl, richer in iron and silt, is planted with Pinot Noir.

This soil diversity is the result of weathering from 300 meters of Jurassic limestone and marls with variations in strata occurring vertically and horizontally, as geologist James Wilson points out[5]. Over thousands of years, minor faulting and tilting added to the gradations and topography of the region. So when walking from one vineyard to another, one could be crossing through soils with millions of years of difference between them.

MONASTIC INFLUENCE

Archaeological evidence of wine production in Burgundy dates back nearly 2,000 years. During this time, the region was the territory of the Celts, also known as Gauls, and then it came under control of the Roman Empire in 51 BC until its demise. Although there is limited evidence of the Romans greatly expanding viticulture in Burgundy, we can assume that their influence must have been quite profound. The Romans treated wine as a necessity and made it available to everyone, even slaves, peasants, and women, and not just to soldiers and aristocrats. Vineyard planting on hillside terrain near rivers and towns, as was their custom, was likely encouraged, and the seeds for viticulture and winemaking were thus planted.

With the disintegration of the Roman Empire, the region went through a period of conflict, with different Germanic tribes fighting to establish their presence. Around this time the kingdom of Burgundy was becoming defined as a territory and given the name from a tribe originating in Bornholm[6] (modern Denmark). By the sixth century, the Franks occupied the region and added it to their growing empire across western continental Europe. When the Franks lost their grip on the territories by the ninth century, Burgundy became divided into Upper, Lower, and Duchy of Burgundy (modern Côte d'Or and its environs).

By the early fourth century, the Roman Catholic monastic order was starting to take a foothold in Burgundy. The towns of Autun, Langres, and Auxerre had their own bishops[7]. By the sixth century, Chalon-sur-Saône, Nevers, and Mâcon also came under monastic influence. However, it took several centuries, around the turn of the millennium, for monastic communities to dig deep roots in Burgundy. During this period the Benedictine order dominated northern and western Europe—monks lived communally, following the texts written by Saint Benedict of Nursia. The rules of conduct for monastic life written in the sixth century were strict and detailed, encouraging monks to devote their lives to prayer, work, and solitary piety. The Abbey of Cluny, located northwest of Mâcon, established in 910 by the Benedictines, became immensely influential. By the early twelfth century, Cluniac abbeys multiplied throughout France and abroad and contributed two Cluniac popes: Urban II and Pascal II[8].

Cluny's success bred ostentation, decadence, and ultimately corruption. It brought material wealth and political power, and the abbots and senior church members were not shy about wielding it. The monks were no longer urged to engage in manual labor and were encouraged instead to pray. One of the reformist groups who left the Benedictine fold in 1098 were the Cistercians. This group became instrumental in delineating and discovering the future Grand Cru sites of Burgundy. In history books about Burgundian viticulture, it is the Cistercians who are credited with having the greatest influence on grape cultivation and focus on quality in the region.

Cistercians rejected ostentation and the material world and chose to follow the strict rule of Saint Benedict by returning to manual labor, penitence, humility, and remaining "poor with the poor Christ."[9] Based at the Abbey of Cîteaux, just south of Dijon, the Cistercian order was founded under the auspices and the protection of the Pope in Rome and the powerful dukes of Burgundy.

Agricultural work was part of every monk's duty, since each monastery had to be independent and self-sufficient. The Cistercians were provided with land donations, especially vineyards, by dukes and wealthy landlords, thus allowing them to grow food for sustenance and also to grow grapes to make wine for religious ceremonies, for daily consumption in moderation, and for guests.

One of the key leaders and saints of the Cistercian order was Bernard of Clairvaux, who wrote about the inextricable link between spiritual life and the vineyard in a text titled *The Mystical Vineyard*[10], a treatise on viticulture and winemaking with religious references. Saint Bernard describes

Michel Charlat

Engraving of medieval Burgundian monks cultivating vines, by Louis Figuier, *Les merveilles de l'industrie*, 1873.
PREVIOUS PAGES Cistercian monks at the winepress.

the importance of healthy soil, pruning, trellising, observing the maturity of the grapes and of harvest. Winemaking is a holy task, and monks are encouraged to care for the vines with all their religious fervor and love. By the end of the twelfth century, hundreds of Cistercian abbeys were spread across Europe, from Sweden to Portugal.

From 1363 to 1477, the ecclesiastic influence was tempered by the four Valois dukes who ruled Burgundy[11]. Philippe le Hardi and his grandson Philippe le Bon contributed to the growth of viticulture and quality wine production: Philippe le Hardi, or the Bold, sent out an edict in 1395 that banned the production of the Gamay grape in Burgundy, instead encouraging the noble Pinot Noir. He considered Gamay an overproductive, insipid grape variety, calling it "evil and disloyal" and "harmful to humans"[12]. He also cautioned against abandoning good vineyard sites and the use of fertilizers to increase yields. His grandson Philippe le Bon, the Good, also condemned Gamay for its inferior quality.

By 1477, however, Burgundy lost its independence due to Philippe the Good's son Charles' aggressive expansion plans, which

ultimately failed and led to the region's incorporation into France. Just as twenty-four years earlier, in 1453, Bordeaux had also returned to the French monarchy after three centuries under English rule.

THE FRENCH REVOLUTION

The monastic influence steadily declined during the three centuries of the Bourbon monarchy's reign in France. Vineyard ownership was divided among the nobility, the church, and the growing wealthy middle class. Burgundy wines were favored, along with the still wines of Champagne during the reign of Louis XIV. The royal physician is said to have "prescribed" Burgundy wine for the king's health, and wines were starting to be transported in glass bottles with cork seals.

The French Revolution resulted in the dissolution of power in the hands of the monarchy and landlords in 1789, which essentially changed all land and vineyard ownership. Land held by the church was sold to pay off the public debt, and redistributed. The Revolution dragged on for a decade, culminating in the National Convention abolishing the monarchy, establishing the Republic, and executing the royal family. Political chaos prevailed until Napoleon Bonaparte brought the country together (briefly) with his military victories.

After declaring himself Emperor in 1804, Napoleon established the Napoleonic Code that streamlined the legal system, abolishing all previous laws that discriminated between classes and attempting to place equality at the center. Inherited assets and estates were to be divided equally among heirs— meaning large estates became ever smaller over subsequent generations, resulting in highly fragmented vineyards in an already modest region. The high inheritance tax structure exacerbated this problem, and vineyards were further subdivided into tiny parcels or sold to new owners to pay the taxes.

PHYLLOXERA DEVASTATION

The nineteenth century brought a stream of difficulties for Burgundian farmers: In the 1840s it was fungal diseases such as powdery mildew, also called oidium, which could be controlled with sulphur sprays. This was followed by downy mildew, which required copper sprays, and the devastating *Phylloxera vastatrix*, an aphid that appeared in France in the 1860s and reached Burgundy's vineyards by the 1870s. This root pest was an American import that ravaged European vineyards, leaving dead or unproductive vines in its wake. Until the solution of grafting vines onto phylloxera-resistant American rootstock was discovered in the 1880s, farmers were at a loss for how to cope with the destruction.

Before the phylloxera infiltration in France there were nearly 2.5 million hectares of vines, and currently there is only about one-third that amount, almost 800,000 hectares[13]. Many different grape varieties had been in use; despite Philip the Bold banning Gamay, it was more widely planted in the 1850s than Pinot Noir. Viticulture was overhauled, with systematic replanting of clearly known varieties on neat rows of trellises, which we recognize today. Mechanization and modernization began and was made possible partly as a result of this massive national replanting from the 1880s to the 1920s.

From the 1870s to the late 1880s, vineyards were being replanted or

Manuscript illustration from Cîteaux.

even abandoned, as the grafting solution was only permitted in 1887. Those who could afford it kept phylloxera at bay with an insecticide of carbon disulfide (CS_2). This highly flammable solution was injected into the soil near the trunk using a large syringe-like device. It was expensive, and its efficacy depended on so many variables that small peasant farmers were left to find other solutions. After the French Revolution, vineyards that once belonged to the Church or the nobility were divided among numerous small owners. When phylloxera decimated the Burgundian vineyards, many small landowners opted to plant more lucrative crops or use the land for other purposes.

The last vineyards in Burgundy to be replanted were the Romanée-Conti and Richebourg vineyards, owned by Domaine de la Romanée-Conti, in 1945[14].

AOC CLASSIFICATION SYSTEM

Prior to phylloxera, many grape varieties existed besides Pinot Noir and Chardonnay, including Aligoté, Pinot Gris, and Gamay. However, Gamay

turned out to be more sensitive to the pest than Pinot Noir[15], contributing to its decline. Given the high cost coupled with low revenue and returns, only the best vineyards were considered worth replanting with Pinot Noir.

By this time the best Burgundian vineyards were already identified, by reputation and experience as well as from well-documented books from the eighteenth and nineteenth centuries. Mapping out the best vineyards before the French appellation systems were created can be credited to authors such as Claude Arnoux (1728), Andrew Jullien (1815), Dr. Denis Morelot (1831), and Dr. Jules Lavalle (1855). Most of the books, except for Jullien's, were not fully translated into English until 2014, when Charles Curtis MW wrote *The Original Grands Crus of Burgundy,* in which he translated key passages from the authors. The Beaune Committee of Agriculture, together with Dr. Jules Lavalle, devised the three classifications, and most of the vineyards identified in the first class became Grands Crus in the INAO (Institut National de l'Origine et de la Qualité) classification of Burgundy in the 1930s.

The need for the classifications and legal protection was due to the problem of fraud and adulteration. By the 1850s, when the railroad linked Burgundy with Paris in the north as well as Lyon and the Mediterranean cities in the south, wine fraud was rampant. Many wines arriving from the south were bottled as "Burgundy" or were adulterated with darker, fruitier, more alcoholic wines from the south. This enraged the landowners, who demanded protection for their vineyard and regional names. Local authorities and committees made efforts to provide some form of protection, but it was only with the 1936 law creating the hierarchical system of Appellation d'Origine Contrôlée (AOC) that place names received legal protection.

Four broad designations were created: At the top of the pyramid is the Grand Cru, making up only 1.5% of the total production of Burgundy (excluding Beaujolais); Premier Cru is 10%; the Village

Historical reports on wine production in Burgundy.

level is 38%; and at the bottom of the pyramid is Bourgogne, or generic Burgundy wines[16]. Within the much smaller Côte d'Or, translated as the "hillside of gold," the pyramid becomes flatter and the spread less dramatic: Grand Cru makes up 4.2%, Premier Cru is 21.3%, the Village level 39.2%, and basic Bourgogne 35.3%[17].

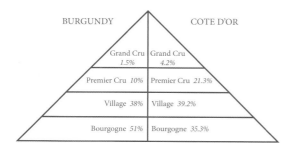

Since 2012, the French classification was amended to simplify quality levels to align with those of the European Union. For Burgundy, not much has changed, since most of the wines fall within the four AOC levels above. However, the wines are now also recognized as being an *appellation d'origine protégée* (AOP), or protected designation of origin (PDO) in English.

On the surface, the classification seems straightforward: Basic, everyday wines at the regional Bourgogne level; Village (*commune*) wines at a higher level, with distinguishable characteristics; Premier Cru wines, subject to lower yields and fine quality; and at the very top, Grand Cru wines. However, the classification is often trumped by producers who enjoy a reputation for excellence and command prices for their regional and Village wines that are the same as other producers' Premier Cru and Grand Cru wines. On the other hand, a mediocre producer's Grand Cru wines may trade at the same price as a top producer's Village-level wine.

What the AOC and the classification system provides are base standards with strict guidelines for the producers: All classified wines have restrictions for grape variety, yield, sourcing, minimum ripeness levels, and labeling, with stricter limits as one moves up the ranks. Even if one producer's Village is superior to another's Premier Cru wine, at least it is assured that the minimum standards set out by the AOC were followed by the producers, if the classification is written on the label. For many wine lovers who are unfamiliar with Burgundy producers, the system provides guidance and some assurance of quality.

FROM NÉGOCIANTS TO DOMAINE BOTTLING

Redistribution of land from the Church and nobility to local growers left a gap for the *négociants* to fill. While the Church and aristocrats had ready access to the market, small farmers knew nothing about marketing, selling, and bringing their wines to consumers. Négociants and cooperatives began to play an important role in post-Revolutionary France. During the 1800s until the early 1900s, négociants monopolized winemaking, bottling, and sales simply because they could afford to. Small landowners sometimes did not even have enough grapes from a single vineyard plot to fill one barrel, nor did they have the means to buy winepresses, tanks, bottling equipment, and employ a sales team.

Many successful Burgundy négociants were established during this period—Bouchard Père et Fils in 1731, Louis Latour in 1798, Joseph Faiveley in 1825, Louis Jadot in 1859, and Joseph Drouhin in 1880. Founded in 1868, Maison Leroy, with numerous entries in this book, is testament to the quality level that négociant wines can achieve. In the 1930s, domaine bottling was rare everywhere in France. In Burgundy, three pioneers of this movement were Armand Rousseau, Jacques d'Angerville, and Henri Gouges, who had accused the large shippers of adulterating wines,

Engraving of the Burgundy countryside, 19th century

and so their wines were no longer distributed by the négociants. Partly out of necessity and partly to protect themselves from fraud, the three domaines started the trend to bottle at the estate.

There was cause for the domaine owners to be concerned. From 1880 to 1930, Algeria was the largest wine exporter and the fourth largest wine producer in the world. Even as late as 1960, Algeria exported more wine than France, Italy, and Spain combined[18]. As a French colony from 1830 to 1962, Algerian wine was freely imported and used widely by the wine trade. The peak of Algerian wine production was in the 1930s, surpassing 20 million hectoliters (equivalent to 220 million twelve-bottle cases) per annum[19]. This is the period when Burgundy *vignerons* as well as government officials started to react against the widespread adulteration and fraudulent labeling of their wines; it was common knowledge that shippers were adding southern French and, more often than not, Algerian wines before bottling.

Following the end of Prohibition in the United States in 1933, top Burgundy wines started to trickle in. But America was still quite a small market for Burgundy, and domaine bottling still rare; only a tiny handful of domaines found overseas outlets. Wine merchants like Frank Schoonmaker, Frederick Wildman, and Alexis Lichine, who became leading wine influencers of their times, started during this time and opened the U.S. markets to Burgundy. It took another generation, when importers and agents like Becky Wasserman, Martine Saulnier, and Kermit Lynch came onto the scene in the 1970s, for Burgundy to catch the attention of serious buyers.

In Asia during the 1970s, wine importation was dominated by spirits companies who carried a handful of wine brands just to broaden their portfolio—spirits were most profitable, especially VSOP and XO Cognac, which was in vogue. In Hong Kong, Rémy retail shops dominated the consumer scene for decades; other small retail operations open and shut every few years, pushed out by exorbitant and ever-increasing rental costs. In China, the market was still not yet open, and the only Asian city with a thriving wine scene was Tokyo.

The estate bottling movement began in earnest in Burgundy in the 1970s and 1980s, coinciding with America's increasing interest. The 1980s brought a new wave of Burgundy importers who demanded quality, and domaine bottling was one of their requirements, in addition to temperature-controlled shipping and transportation, barrel selection, and unfined, unfiltered wines, all leading to Burgundy's "modern renaissance"[20].

CONTEMPORARY BURGUNDY

From the 1980s, rising exports and demand meant an increase in prices, but this was not the only factor that led to the perception of Burgundy as a beverage for the elite, it was also the difficulty in understanding the hundreds of appellations, *lieux dits* (traditional, distinctive vineyards that can fall outside the appellation), and thousands of growers producing minute quantities of wine. Burgundy requires time, and only those with the time, interest, and inclination became well versed and confident enough to navigate the region and the wines.

In Asia, wine was initially a beverage reserved for the colonial powers or the ruling class, then trickled down to the wealthy who could afford the imported prices. By the time wine reached the shores of Tokyo, Singapore, Hong Kong, or Shanghai, the cost often made it more expensive than the price of a filling meal at a top local restaurant. Thus, unlike Europe, where wine was often part of a meal, wine in Asia acquired the status of an aspirational, luxury product from the onset.

During the 1980s and 1990s, the rise of wine critics who rate and score wines helped to attract a new generation of consumers, first in the United States and later in markets around the world. Their influence was greatest in Bordeaux and in emerging wine regions. In Burgundy, the consumer market ultimately dictated prices and popularity, rather than critics. Prices for Roumier's Les Amoureuses has long been higher than most producers' Grands Crus, not because a critic rated it 20/20 or 100 points, but because the market simply thought it was worth it. The same can be said about numerous wines from top Burgundy producers that defy critics' low ratings, poor vintage assessments, and even Grand Cru classifications. In Burgundy, the consumer market rules.

Also starting in the 1980s, the quality revolution in Burgundy led to a transformation in the vineyard. After two world wars, vignerons were struggling, thus favoring rootstocks and clones that offered quantity and consistency over quality; pesticides, herbicides, and fertilizers were liberally used. Microbiologist Claude Bourguignon's declaration in 1989 that Burgundy's vineyards were devoid of living organisms was a wake-up call for many Burgundian growers. Some opted to lower their chemical use and follow *lutte raisonnée*, a form of sustainable farming, while others chose organic cultivation, and a select handful decided to become biodynamic growers.

BIODYNAMIC VITICULTURE

Biodynamics deserves a special mention here because so many of the top Burgundian domaines have become devotees. A pioneer in Burgundy, Lalou Bize-Leroy, at her namesake domaine, started out as biodynamic in 1988. Domaine de la Romanée-Conti experimented with biodynamics in the 1990s and converted fully in 2007. Anne Claude Leflaive became convinced of biodynamics after slowly experimenting with it in the 1990s, eventually converting totally by 1997. Other notable Burgundy biodynamic growers include Comtes Lafon, Pierre Morey, and Domaine de la Vougeraie.

The unusual preparations and strict calendar that need to be followed led some to consider biodynamics to be "voodoo"-style grape growing. But the biodynamic farming calendar is nearly 100 years old. According to Monty Waldin in *Biodynamic Wines,* it is the oldest organic agricultural movement, founded by Rudolf Steiner in 1923. Even in Bordeaux, where huge vineyards make organic and biodynamic farming challenging and expensive, there are now believers such as Château Latour, Château Palmer, and Château Pontet Canet.

But what does the moon, alignment of planets, and microorganisms have to do with making quality wine? While scientific explanations are lacking, the results of biodynamic farming, which definitely increases the health of the vineyard and can produce more refined and flavorful grapes, continue to convince many Burgundian growers to adopt this costlier and more labor-intensive method. However, simply becoming a biodynamic grower does not improve wine quality significantly, it helps the grower become a more conscientious farmer who aims to prevent rather than merely treat problems as they arise in the vineyard. Biodynamic and organic farming certainly do improve soil health and microbial activity.

Below is a list of select Burgundy producers, many of whom are featured in this book, that practice biodynamic viticulture:

- Domaine Arlaud
- Domaine Bonneau du Martray
- Domaine d'Auvenay
- Domaine de la Romanée-Conti
- Domaine de la Vougeraie
- Domaine des Comtes Lafon
- Domaine du Comte Liger-Belair
- Domaine Leflaive
- Domaine Leroy
- Domaine Michel Lafarge
- Domaine Michel Magnien
- Domaine Pierre Morey
- Domaine Rossignol-Trapet
- Trapet Père et Fils

PREMATURE OXIDATION

An important and ongoing contemporary Burgundian challenge is the issue of premature oxidation, or "premox," which has plagued top white wines since the 1990s. Wines less than a decade old can become amber-brown and flat, devoid of freshness and nuanced flavors. In many cases the wine is undrinkable, while in milder cases the wines may taste a decade or two advanced. It can strike wines randomly, even within the same case: One bottle might be pristine while another bottle looks and tastes fifteen to twenty years older. While some growers and collectors say the problem is no longer a serious issue, we still see premox in collectible white Burgundy from 2007, 2008, and 2009 vintages. It is difficult to say if more recent vintages suffer from premox, since it is not apparent until seven to ten years after bottling.

The issue was brought to light in the early 2000s by wine writers such as Steven Tanzer and Allen Meadows as well as collectors exchanging experiences in online forums. The 1996 vintage

had serious problems, as well as 1999, 2000, and 2002. As for my own personal experience with 2008 and 2009 vintages, premox seems much less widespread than with wines from the mid-1990s. By 2005, many producers were responding to the alarm.

The potential causes of premox are so diverse—and still not fully understood—that producers are grasping in all directions for the source and the solutions. Some say that later harvests combined with lower sulfur dioxide levels provide insufficient protection against oxidation; others suggest the trend toward protective winemaking, with pneumatic presses and use of clean juice with very little solids, has removed the natural protection against oxidation; yet others point to the trend toward less sulfur, about half the amount used in the 1980s, which may cause the oxidation; still others suggest that the culprit is the cork. Poor quality cork was rampant in the 1990s, as were silicone-treated corks, which consumed the free sulfur, effectively reducing the key antioxidant in the wine. The problem seems to be less of an issue now, but smart buyers should be aware that the problem has not been completely eliminated or solved. When buying white Burgundy, do your research, and review forums that discuss certain producers and vintages that are flagged for premox by collectors, writers, and merchants.

FAKE WINES

A serious concern for Burgundy lovers is the increasing number of fake wines. My personal experience with wines in Asia shows that we need to be more vigilant than ever. Authentication experts Michael Egan and Maureen Downey also note the rising trend of fraudulent Burgundy wines, not just older vintages but new ones as well. Only a handful of domaines, such as Romanée-Conti (DRC) and Ponsot, have serious antifraud measures in place on their packaging; however, this is recent, only since around 2010—a reactive move after discovering millions of dollars' worth of their wines faked by Rudy Kurniawan, nicknamed "Dr. Conti," who was arrested in 2012 was released from jail in 2021.

Other counterfeits currently circulating include Roumier, Vogüé, Henri Jayer, and Leroy, and as prices increase for all Burgundy wines, fakes will expand quickly. Small domaines will have to consider if the cost of anticounterfeit measures are worthwhile if their wines are targeted by fraudsters. For buyers, the best way to avoid fakes is to buy the wines young, two years after harvest when official distributors allocate wines direct from the domaine. While fakes can be distributed through this *primeur* channel, it is highly unlikely if you buy from the official distributor.

Burgundy is an easy target for fraudsters because the bottles are usually standard, as are the labels, making them easy to replicate. The riskiest purchases are older vintages of collectible wines from auctions and fine wine brokers,

especially if the seller is not named and the provenance or receipts are not forthcoming. Be sure to buy from trustworthy sources and retailers, and demand proof of how and where they sourced the wines.

TERROIR

Only a few generations ago, *terroir* was a pejorative term, referring to wines that were rustic and tasted of the earth. In modern usage, terroir has transformed to become a positive, used most often by the French to refer to a special plot of land that is distinctive both in taste as well as its geological makeup. Some New World growers pay homage to it, while consumers pay a premium for what they perceive as "terroir wines," or as Matt Kramer calls it, wines with "somewhereness."[21] Proponents claim that terroir and its unique site-specific conditions endow a wine with its distinctive voice expressed in particular flavors and aromatic profile. Jacques Perrin goes so far as to say that "at the heart of terroir, we find the mystery of man and of continuance."

A key problem is that the term is vague, and critics question whether terroir can really be tasted. Often it is dismissed as an elusive term exploited for marketing purposes. How does one taste the land or identify a vineyard through a wine? How can one attribute a wine's sensorial characters to the land, soil, aspect, and microorganisms? Most Burgundy lovers, however, don't need to be convinced of the existence of terroir; we have tasted it manifested in Musigny, Montrachet, or Richebourg. Taste Armand Rousseau's Chambertin and Clos de Bèze from the same vintage side by side—the vineyards are just steps away, and the wines are made with exactly the same method, yet the two wines are a world apart. Chambertin is majestic and fine while Clos de Bèze is more expressive, powerful, taking the concentration one notch higher.

When great terroir marries with the right variety and is looked after by a skilled winegrower (*vigneron*), then wines express typicity. The rose petal aromas and delicacy typical of Chambolle-Musigny, for example, is very different from the firm tannins and black cherries of Nuits-Saint-Georges. Burgundy lovers may refer to a perfumed, elegant Nuits as being Chambolle-like, or when a Puligny-Montrachet is fuller with a more creamy texture, it may be referred to as Meursault-like in character. So spending time understanding the typicity of Burgundy's terroir is the first step toward speaking the common language of Burgundy fans.

Vintage posters touting Burgundy wines.

The wines included in this book unequivocally express terroir. Each wine comes from a unique plot of land and designated appellation, and has a reputation for producing a consistent style and flavor profile appreciated by Burgundy aficionados for decades. A well-known terroir confers automatic credentials to the wine—a sense of historical reputation and a documented track record.

The human element of terroir plays just as important a part in crafting wines that express a sense of place. Who would know the land better than the people who have lived on it for generations? The understanding of the land's nuances, and how best to guide the finest grapes from juice to wine, which may have been passed down through numerous generations, are just as important as the physical makeup of the vineyard and its vines. The human touch plays an integral part within the terroir as the guardian, the shepherd that directs and ultimately transforms simple grapes into a complex beverage.

For many DRC or Domaine Leroy lovers, they appreciate this human signature, which may be even stronger than the terroir. In a blind tasting of Cortons,

it is not difficult to figure out which one was made by DRC or Leroy, for their signature in the wine is as obvious as the expression of the Corton vineyard they farm. DRC has transformed the Cortons previously made by Prince Florent de Merode into a majestic Grand Cru deserving of its status, while Madame Bize-Leroy has farmed her half of one hectare of Corton Renardes with such low yields that the wine has laser-like precision, detail, and persistence. Is it easier to identify these wines more as a Corton Grand Cru or as a wine from DRC or Leroy? The

answer depends on the taster and their experience with the two domaines and their experience with Corton; one could easily argue either way. I suggest that the human factor in terroir and the wine's expression is inextricable, and to try to separate them would be to dismantle a thing of beauty just for the sake of analysis, and that understanding the parts is not the same as appreciation of the whole.

All the winegrowers I admire from Burgundy, who are the growers in this book, have always expressed their desire to be faithful to the terroir and to express the land to the best of their ability. A Chambertin from Rousseau is completely different from that of Dugat-Py, Trapet, or Mortet, yet some similar traits of the terroir's character can be found: haunting depth, strong backbone, and profundity. All four growers will explain how their wine is their own faithful expression of a Chambertin, dubbed "the King of Wines." That all four wines are from the same small, east-facing, thirteen-hectare site, with brown chalky soil and excellent exposure to sunlight, also has much to do with their similar characteristics despite their individual differences.

RISING STARS

It is hard to keep up with the growing momentum within the shifting Burgundian landscape. Every time I travel to Burgundy I hear about newcomers, another new micro-négociant, or a younger generation challenging the status quo. In the past, outsiders were not embraced in this tightly knit region, where marriage among neighboring landowners was common to amass family holdings. Times have changed, and intrepid foreigners have rooted themselves here over the past thirty years to realize their "Burgundian Dream." Success stories abound, and many outsiders have achieved success in a short period of time, including Olivier Bernstein, Alex Gambal, Mark Haisma, Pascal Marchand, and Rotem and Mounir Saouma.

At the same time, the region is energized by a new generation of quality-oriented growers, elevating their family's good wines to great ones. Just taste the recent vintages made by Charles Van Canneyt at Domaine Hudelot-Noëllat, Mathilde Grivot at Domaine Grivot, Amélie Berthaut at Domaine Berthaut-Gerbet, or Charles Lachaux at Domaine Arnoux-Lachaux. New domaines that are less than twenty years old, with super-talented vignerons like Cécile Tremblay at Domaine Tremblay and Pierre-Yves Colin-Morey at his eponymous estate, are producing wines that are commanding jaw-dropping prices. Micro-négociants aiming for small quantities from only the best vineyards contribute to the dynamic atmosphere: Nicolas Potel in 2005 with Maison Roche de Bellene, and Benjamin Leroux since 2007. A noteworthy new winery, the Domaine du Cellier aux Moines, operating out of a renovated twelfth-century abbey and established only in 2004, is producing incredibly intense wines; its densely planted Clos Pascal has singularly put Givry on the fine wine map.

Below is a select list of exceptional producers not listed among the 100 that deserve special mention and are worth seeking out:

- Benjamin Leroux
- Domaine Alain Chavy
- Domaine Antoine Jobard
- Domaine Benoît Ente
- Domaine Bernard Moreau et Fils
- Domaine Berthaut-Gerbet
- Domaine d'Arlot
- Domaine du Cellier aux Moines
- Domaine George Noëllat
- Domaine Genot-Boulanger
- Domaine Glantenay
- Domaine Heitz-Lochardet
- Domaine Hubert Lamy
- Domaine Launay Horiot
- Domaine Marc Colin et Fils
- Domaine Michel Magnien
- Domaine Michelot
- Domaine Mongeard-Mugneret
- Domaine Paul Pillot
- Jean-Claude Boisset
- Lucien le Moine
- Olivier Bernstein
- Olivier Leflaive

Ultimately, the best wines are the ones that offer pleasure, in moments of quiet contemplation or at celebratory times with friends and family. Great Burgundy wines leave indelible impressions on the taste buds and in the mind, leaving you thirsty for more. With a glass in hand, I hope you enjoy the journey, taking delight in each glimpse into the spirit of the Côte d'Or.

NOTES

1. Robinson, J., *The Oxford Companion to Wine*, p. 117.
2. Bourgogne Wine Board (BIVB), www.bourgogne-wines.com.
3. Rigaux, J., *Burgundy Grands Crus*, p. 78.
4. Meadows, A., *The Pearl of the Côte: The Great Wines of Vosne-Romanée*, pp. 120-121.
5. Wilson, J., *Terroir: The Role of Geology, Climate, and Culture in the Making of French Wines*, p. 116.
6. Morris, J., *Inside Burgundy: The Vineyards, the Wine, and the People*, p. 21.
7. Platret, G. and Pascal, P., *Nine Centuries in the Heart of Burgundy: The Cellier aux Moines and Its Vineyards*, p. 12.
8. Ibid., p. 14.
9. Ibid., p. 24.
10. Ibid., p. 32.
11. Blake, R., *Côte d'Or: The Wines and Winemakers of the Heart of Burgundy*, p. 31.
12. Berlow, R.K., "The 'Disloyal' Grape: The Agrarian Crisis of Late Fourteenth-Century Burgundy," *Agricultural History*, vol. 56, no. 2, April 1982, p. 429.
13. OIV (The International Organisation of Vine and Wine) State of Vitiviniculture World Market, 2017.
14. Meadows, op. cit., p. 271.
15. Ibid., p. 21.
16. Pitiot, S. and Servant J.C., *The Wines of Burgundy*, p. 113.
17. Nanson, B., *The Finest Wines of Burgundy: A Guide to the Best Producers of the Côte d'Or and Their Wines*, p. 18.
18. Meloni, G. and Swinnen, J., "The Rise and Fall of the World's Largest Wine Exporter," *Journal of Wine Economics*, vol. 9, no. 1, 2014, p. 3.
19. Ibid., p. 3.
20. Parker, R., *Parker's Wine Buyer's Guide*, 7th edition, p. 299.
21. Kramer, M., *Making Sense of Burgundy*, pp. 39–45.

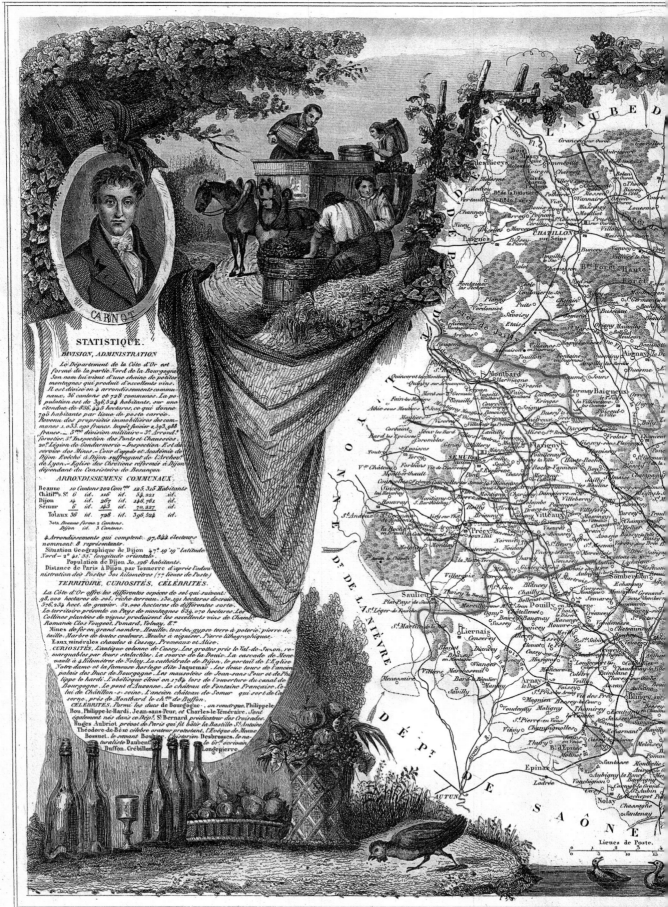

CARNOT

STATISTIQUE.

DIVISION, ADMINISTRATION

Le Département de la Côte d'Or est formé de la partie Nord de la Bourgogne. Son nom lui vient d'une chaîne de petites montagnes qui produit d'excellents vins.
Il est divisé en 4 arrondissements communaux, 36 cantons et 728 communes. La population est de 396,524 habitants, sur une étendue de 836,428 hectares, ce qui donne 798 habitants par lieue de poste carrée.
Revenu des propriétés immobilières des communes 1.033,090 francs. Impôt foncier 2,393,988 francs. 5me division militaire - 3e Arrond. forestier. 3e Inspection des Ponts et Chaussées. 20e Légion de Gendarmerie - Inspection l'Ecole de service des Mines - Cour d'appel et Académie de Dijon Evêché à Dijon suffragant de l'Archevt de Lyon. - Eglise des Chrétiens reformés à Dijon dépendant du Consistoire de Besançon.

ARRONDISSEMENS COMMUNAUX

Beaune	10 Cantons	202 Comnes	125,315 Habitants
Chatillon St	6 id.	116 id.	54,921 id.
Dijon	14 id.	267 id.	146,761 id.
Semur	6 id.	143 id.	70,227 id.
Totaux 36	id.	728 id.	396,524 id.

Nota Beaune forme 2 Cantons.
Dijon id. 3 Cantons.

4 Arrondissements qui comptent 97,844 électeurs nomment 8 représentants.
Situation Géographique de Dijon 47° 19'29" latitude Nord - 2° 41'55" longitude orientale.
Population de Dijon 30,126 habitants.
Distance de Paris à Dijon par Tonnerre d'après l'administration des Postes 301 kilomètres (77 lieues de Poste.)

TERRITOIRE, CURIOSITÉS, CÉLÉBRITÉS.

La Côte d'Or offre les différentes espèces de sol qui suivent. 98,000 hectares de sol, riche terreau. 130,191 hectares de craie. 576,254 hect. de gravier. 52,000 hectares de différente sorte.
Le territoire présente en Pays de montagnes 639,070 hectares. Les Collines plantées de vignes produisent les excellents vins de Chambé Romanée Clos Vougeot, Pomard, Volnay, &c.
Mines de fer en grand nombre. Houille, tourbe, gypse terre à poterie, pierre de taille. Marbre de toutes couleurs. Meules à aiguiser. Pierre lithographique. Eaux minérales chaudes à Cessay, Premeaux et Alise.
CURIOSITÉS. L'antique colonne de Cussy. Les grottes près du Val-de-Saxon, remarquables sur leurs stalactites. La cascade de la Douix. La cascade de Mone vault à 5 kilomètre de Notay. La cathédrale de Dijon, le portail de l'Eglise Notre dame et la fameuse horloge dite Jaquemar. Les deux tours de l'ancien palais des Ducs de Bourgogne. Les mausolées de Jean-sans-Peur et de Philippe le hardi. L'obélisque élevé en 1784 lors de l'ouverture du canal de Bourgogne. Le pont d'Auxonne. Le château de Fontaine Française. Celui de Chatillon-s-seine. L'ancien château de Semur qui sert de Caserne, près de Montbard le chau de Buffon.
CÉLÉBRITÉS. Parmi les ducs de Bourgogne, on remarque, Philippe-le-Bon, Philippe le-Hardi, Jean-sans-Peur, et Charles-le-Téméraire, sont également nés dans ce Dépt. St Bernard prédicateur des Croisades. Hugues Aubriot, prévôt de Paris qui fit bâtir la Bastille St Antoine. Théodore-de-Bèze célèbre orateur protestant, l'Evêque de Meaux Bossuet, le savant Bouhier, l'historien Desbrosses, le naturaliste Daubenton, le 6me écrivain Buffon, Crébillon, Piron, Longepierre.

Géographie et Statistique par Levasseur Ingr Géographe, rue de Malte, 24.

Illustré par A.M. Perrot attaché au Gén

Lemercier Impr Paris.

DÉPt DE LA

DÉPt DE L'AUBE

Lieues de Poste.

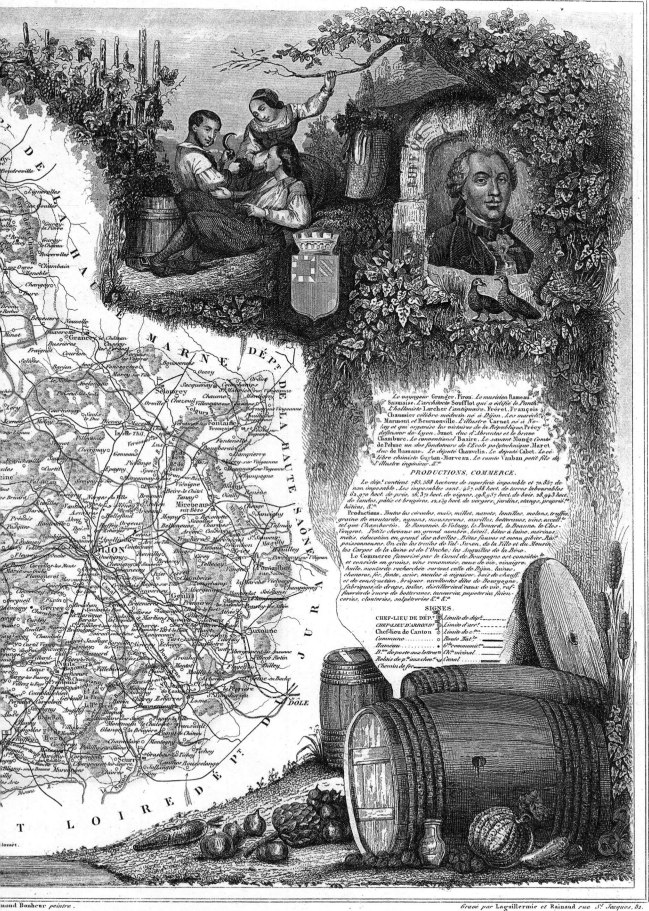

Le voyageur Granger. Piron. Le musicien Rameau Saumaise. L'architecte Soufflot qui a édifié le Panthon. L'helleniste Larcher l'antiquaire. Freret. François Chaussier celèbre médecin né à Dijon. Les maréchaux Marmont et Beurnonville. L'illustre Carnot né à Nolay et qui organise les victoires de la République. Précy défenseur de Lyon. Junot duc d'Abrantès et le brave Chambure. Le conventionnel Bazire. Le savant Monge comte de Péluse un des fondateurs de l'École polytechnique. Maret duc de Bassano. Le député Chauvelin. Le député Cabet. Le celèbre chimiste Guyton-Morveau. Le comte Vauban petit fils de l'illustre ingénieur &c.

PRODUCTIONS, COMMERCE.

Le dép.t contient 783,388 hectares de superficie imposable et 70,857 de non imposable. Les imposables sont : 457,688 hect. de terres labourables 63,970 hect. de prés, 26,371 hect. de vignes, 198,937 hect. de bois. 38,943 hect. de landes, pâtis et bruyères, 12,139 hect. de vergers, jardins, étangs, propriét.s bâties, &c.s. Productions. Toutes les céréales, maïs, millet, navets, lentilles, melons, truffes, graine de moutarde, oignons, mousserons, morilles, betteraves, vins, excell.ts tel que Chambertin. le Romanée, le Volnay, le Pomard, le Beaune, le Clos-Vougeot. Petits chevaux en grand nombre, bétail, bêtes à laine, mérinos métis, éducation en grand des abeilles. Bêtes fauves et menu gibier. Riv.s poissonneuses. On cite les truites de Val-Saxon, de la Ville et du Meusin les Carpes de la Seine et de l'Ouche; les Anguilles de la Bèze. Le Commerce favorisé par le Canal de Bourgogne est considér.e et consiste en grains, vins renommés, eaux de vie, vinaigre, huile, moutarde recherchée surtout celle de Dijon, laines, chanvres, fer, fonte, acier, meules à aiguiser, bois de chauff. et de construction, briques, excellentes dites de Bourgogne, fabriques de draps, toiles, distilleries d'eaux de vie, raffineries de sucre de betteraves, tanneries, papeteries faïenceries, clouteries, salpêtreries &c.s &c.s.

SIGNES

CHEF-LIEU DE DÉP.T	Limite de dép.t
CHEF-LIEU D'ARROND.T	Limit d'arr.t
Chef-lieu de Canton	Limite de c.on
Commune	Route Nat.le
Hameau	6.te communic.t
B.au de poste aux lettres	Ch.in vicinal
Relais de p.te aux chev.x	Canal
	Chemin de fer

amond Bonheur, peintre.

Gravé par Laguillermie et Rainaud rue St. Jacques. 82.

ÔTE D'OR.

Map of the Cote d'Or by French cartographer Victor Levasseur, 1852.

BUYING AND ENJOYING BURGUNDY

STARTING A CELLAR

Having a private wine cellar is the ultimate luxury, but one that is also practical and economical. When I am asked about smart wine buying, I always suggest buying young and buying early. Thus, investing in wine storage or a cellar, even if it is initially simply a 100-bottle wine fridge, can save you money in the long run. If you bought Domaine Fourrier's Clos Saint-Jacques 2010 when it was released in 2012, you would have paid no more than US$400 per bottle. If you want to enjoy this wine now, the average retail price is above US$700 in 2019. Even for Village-level wines like Chambolle-Musigny from Christophe Roumier, on release you might have paid around US$100, but in 2019 it retails for over US$300. Buying young and early especially makes sense for Burgundy, because quantities of top wines are so scarce that sourcing and obtaining allocations is much more difficult than for wines from other regions. Buying ahead may be the only chance to find the desired wines, when they are just released from the domaine,

at the best price. Besides, what can be better than having a cellar of wines to be enjoyed for different occasions and moods?

In the early 1990s, when I began buying cases for my own current and future pleasure, I wish someone had told me to be more methodical, because my selection was random rather than strategic. I would advise anyone who wants to start a cellar to first set a clear budget and to be realistic about how much of Burgundy wines it will buy. To acquire all 100 wines in this book would require a budget of around US$200,000, calculated at the end of 2018. This "dream cellar" of the very best wines chosen for special occasions does not reflect the large variety of Burgundy wines available for everyday drinking.

First, determine how much you want to enjoy in the short term and the amount you want to lay away for the future. My own cellar consists of the entire range of Burgundies from Bourgognes to Grands Crus. I enjoy young, vibrant Bourgogne from many producers in this book, including Bourgogne Blanc from Arnaud Ente, d'Auvenay, and Roulot, and Bourgogne Rouge from Maison Leroy, Denis Mortet, and Claude Dugat. I find myself buying about one-third to drink in the coming one to five years, and the majority for the future.

I like to follow wines as they age, and I love to open a wine to understand its evolving personality. A Village Burgundy red from a good producer I might open around five years old, and check on it every few years to see how it is changing; for a Premier Cru I would wait eight years, and Grand Cru ten to twelve years. White Village wines I start sampling at three to four years old, depending on the grower and the vineyard reputation; Premiers Crus I like to check at five years old, and Grands Crus at eight years old. The goal is to see whether the wines are opening up, knowing that the wines are probably still too young, but following the wine's evolution is part of the fun in understanding each wine's personality.

Once budget and clear objectives are set, the next step is identifying the best suppliers. For most people, it will be local wine retailers and merchants. It is worth asking for the specialist wine buyer for Burgundy, to discuss what styles you enjoy and are interested in exploring. Often retailers hold wine tastings that are complimentary, discounted, or the price deducted if wines are purchased. When buying Burgundy, I prefer to try a bottle before committing to a full or half case. To find out if the retailer is a Burgundy specialist, ask for their full list, inquire how many wines are direct domaine allocations, note the number of top growers and producers they work with, and always ask for the Burgundy specialist to discuss your purchase.

For those able to travel and bring back wines, it is worth spending time in villages in Burgundy that have retail caves filled with wines from small growers. Venture beyond Beaune and opt instead for the smaller village shops, such as those in Chassagne-Montrachet and Gevrey-Chambertin. (There is a list of favorite sources at the end of this book for discovering Burgundies not often exported.) Spend time with the manager and tell them what styles and producers you currently enjoy, and ask them to suggest a

few smaller domaines to try—then either taste the wine by the glass if possible or buy one bottle to see if it is indeed a style you enjoy.

Auction houses may sometimes be the only way to acquire rare Burgundies that are on strict allocation around the world. Buying at auction—besides being expensive, if you include the buyer's premium—entails risks, since standards vary by auction house, and strict provenance checks can be lacking. Rudy Kurniawan's fraud case tainted the reputation of some auction houses in the United States, but since then more stringent checks have been put in place and money-back guarantees continue to entice buyers. Another important consideration is to find out the details of the sale consignor and request the provenance of the wines. If this is not forthcoming, then buy at your own risk! The safest lots at auction are those consigned directly from the château or domaine. This is becoming more and more common, as producers realize the high margins they can make by offering wines to the end buyer without middlemen.

Currently the global auction market is dominated by "the big five"—Christie's, Sotheby's, Acker Merrall, Zachy's, and Hart Davis Hart—plus a handful of smaller companies such as Bonhams, Heritage, and Spectrum. Buying at auction should be approached carefully, taking time to review the lots, setting a budget, and creating a checklist:

1. Know the reputation of the consignor.
2. Read buying terms carefully and remember to include the buyer's premium in the total price.
3. Check the minimum price of each lot and understand its market value before determining how much you are willing to pay.

4. Attending the auction is often not necessary, and sometimes distracting, because frenzied bidding can mean spending more than you wanted, so fax your bids or appoint an auction house representative with your budget limit.

5. If the lots are rare or very expensive, ask for a viewing of the bottles to assess the levels and condition, and to ask questions.

Another option to consider when buying rare Burgundies is to work with a broker, often a lone consultant or a small company, which specializes in sourcing fine wines for private customers. This is a growing sector, and every major city has a dozen or more fine wine brokers, many of whom used to work for auction houses. This channel has its risks, and trust is key. Do a thorough background check to find out the reputation of the broker, and request a full provenance report on all wines.

This quote from Allen Meadows aptly summarizes buying fine Burgundy: "You may not get what you pay for, but you will almost certainly never get what you don't pay for."[1]

BUYING TIPS

My Top Ten Tips for savvy Burgundy buying:

1. Golden Rule: Follow producers and get to know their strengths. If you don't recognize any producers on a wine list, then choose top vintages and consider the reputation of the communes.

2. In the best vintages, buy one classification down for great value; a Premier Cru may have Grand Cru quality in top vintages from the best growers. In weaker or modest vintages, follow the Golden Rule.

3. For value buying, choose lesser-known appellations such as Marsannay, Savigny, Fixin, or Saint-Aubin from top growers, and choose good but not great vintages such as 2000, 2001, 2007, 2008, 2011, 2012, or 2014. Learn the differences between great red and great white vintages.

4. Top négociants such as those listed in this book offer good value across their range, due to their size and ability to share the cost of production among their entire range.

5. When buying unknown producers to assess their quality, buy its largest classified vineyard holding from a good vintage.

6. Buy from merchants who are the official importers and retailers for the domaine: Ask if they are brokers obtaining the wines from sources other than the domaines, or if they are given an allocation directly from the domaine. Choose the latter as often as possible.

7. Develop a relationship with your local Burgundy buyer or specialist wine merchant, ask for guidance, and taste as frequently as possible.

8. Always ask how the wines were transported and the storage conditions. Ideally, wines would have been

transported in refrigerated containers and delivery trucks, and stored in temperature-controlled warehouses.

9. Prices are generally, but not always, good indicators of quality, since the market rules in Burgundy, rather than critics' ratings; however, high price does not always indicate great wine, since growers sometimes live off their past reputation or the reputation of their vineyard, or the wines may simply be scarce, not necessarily great.

10. Buy magnums for laying down when possible, since they age better and longer than standard 750ml bottles.

THE LOGISTICS

Burgundy wines, especially older vintages, are highly fragile, and they do not like to travel. Make sure the retailer you are buying from is using refrigerated and temperature-controlled transportation and storage facilities. When starting a cellar, questions of space and logistics come into play: How many bottles can you store, and do you need to consider wine storage facilities? How easy is it to access your inventory, and how will you manage it?

The easiest first step is to start small, with a few wine fridges, but beyond a few hundred

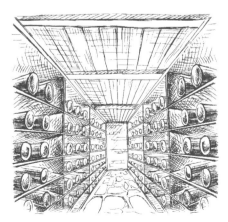

bottles you may need to convert a closet or room in your home, or rent a warehouse facility, or both. In most major cities, including Hong Kong, Tokyo, New York, or London, excellent storage facilities exist for private customers, as well as companies that specialize in creating home cellars.

I always prefer to buy Burgundy when it is young and therefore less fragile and sensitive to transportation and handling, and mature it in my own cellar, rather than take the risk of poor transportation or storage. When buying mature Burgundy, twenty years or older, it is essential to ask how it was transported and stored. Ideally, the wines did not travel during hot summer months, and customs did not keep it in warm conditions for days; overseas transportation should be in refrigerated containers; local transportation should be in refrigerated trucks below 18° C or 65° F. These important steps for ensuring the best conditions for Burgundy were not widely followed in the U.S. until the 1990s, and in Hong Kong only after 2008.

THE ESSENTIALS

Burgundy has just two key grape varieties: Pinot Noir and Chardonnay. Other varieties like Aligoté, Pinot Blanc, or Gamay may surface from time to time, but the most sought-after wines are crafted from these two varieties. Arguably, this monoculture with only two varieties helps us to experience terroir more precisely because the key variables are fixed. A small domaine will often produce ten to fifteen different wines, some over thirty, because they refuse to create blends and would rather make five different Premiers Crus with identifiable vineyards than blur the expressions that different terroirs can produce.

Burgundy is a great way to experience firsthand how a wine can precisely reflect the place where it is grown. Pinot Noir is one of the most transparent red grape varieties, due to its thin skin, delicate aromatic character, and lean body. It is notoriously finicky: Too much or too little sun, and the wine can be green and tart or flabby; poor weather, and the fragile skins will give way to all types of fungal disease, such as botrytis. Pinot Noir can handle only so much intervention before the wine starts to look too made-up, a caricature.

Size and quantity matters with Pinot Noir: High yield is its nemesis. Over-cropped Pinot Noir is insipid, pale, high in acidity, with a hollow palate and short finish. The grape loves limestone in its hundreds of variations, in light and dark colors interspersed with marl or clay; it especially thrives in the Côte de Nuits, Pinot Noir's heartland. The high content of its diverse limestone soils distinguishes the Côte de Nuits from its southern neighbor, the Côte de Beaune, where clay and marl dominate rather than limestone.

The Chardonnay grape is completely different from Pinot Noir. Where the latter is difficult and picky, Chardonnay is easy-going and hardy. Tolerating a wide range of climatic conditions and making good wine in tropical as well as very cool climates, Chardonnay is the ultimate chameleon. In Burgundy, styles vary widely—from

sleek, minerally, unoaked white wines from Chablis to rich, powerful barrel-matured wines built for aging from Corton-Charlemagne.

Chardonnay's popularity among growers is due to its adaptable, versatile personality, tolerance to different climates and site conditions, and extremely generous yield, unlike the stingy Pinot Noir, whose cone-shaped bunches offer small clusters of small berries. Although Chardonnay can be grown and made into decent wine almost anywhere in the world, great wine requires marginal and cool climates like Chablis and Côte de Beaune in Burgundy. For many of the top white Burgundy producers, making great wine from Chardonnay is first about taming its natural vigor and limiting its yield. Chardonnay with modest yield is a conduit that best allows the maximum expression of Chablis Les Clos, Montrachet, or Meursault-Perrières.

Even within such a small region, the diversity of styles is enormous, varying not just by commune and terroir but also by the numerous viticultural and winemaking choices that influence each wine's style and personality. Reducing yield and increasing microbial activity in the vineyard add to the complexity and depth in the wines for producers like Leflaive and Leroy, while old vines and minimal new oak create a minerally, pure style for Roulot and Ente. Coche-Dury prefers crushing the grapes before pressing and long barrel aging to produce its intense, powerful style.

Hundreds of winemaking decisions are involved in making white Burgundy, but some of the most crucial ones include: harvest date and parameters, sorting and selection, type and rate of press, fermentation vessel and temperature, lees quality and contact, maturation length and vessel, bottling parameters, and time. Every decision shapes and defines the wine, which is why a Meursault-Genevrières from one producer can be vastly different from another.

Making red wine from Pinot Noir requires a different set of considerations, because much of the character and quality is derived from the grape skins. In addition to the aforementioned touch points, a key factor is how best to use the skins, and even the stems, to extract the most flavor and increase complexity. For example, proponents of "cold soak" or "cold maceration"—keeping the grapes in a cold environment (5-15º C) for three to ten days before fermentation—say this step extracts greater color, aromatics, and flavors, while others believe it is not necessary.

The central question for all red Burgundy winemakers is how to best extract flavor, tannin, and acidity from the grapes and skins. Some believe that fermenting whole bunches is the answer, while others discard the stems and rely more on fermentation temperature and extraction methods. To destem or use whole bunches is an ongoing contentious and stylistic debate that has the older generation divided, but the younger generation is far less dogmatic; they simply shrug and say they use whole bunches when the wine needs it, and the usage varies by wine and by vintage.

Using whole bunches rather than destemming complicates the fermentation and extraction process. There are many risks to including whole bunches: If the vintage is cool and the stems are not fully ripe and brown, it can impart a green, bitter note to the wine. Stems generally reduce color, acidity, and alcohol level, so it takes experience to understand the final impact of the stems on the wine. The most successful growers with decades of experience, such as DRC, Dujac, and Leroy, understand exactly what the stems can add or remove, and manage the must

and extraction process to maximize the benefits while reducing the effects that can detract from quality. My own experience suggests that those who best employ the "whole bunch" method create complex, layered, and intriguing wines without any stemmy character. The less successful produce wines with a bitter, hard character, leaving a taste of stems on the palate.

In terms of barrel aging, the trend since 2010 has been to reduce the use of new oak for both white and red wines. This is welcome news overall, since new oak can dominate delicate flavors and contribute to a heavier style that lacks finesse. However, top-end producers who understand how new oak marries with the intensity of their old vines, low yields, and great concentration don't follow trends, such as DRC and Leroy, whose wines are all matured in 100 percent new oak.

ENJOYING BURGUNDY

Burgundy is not only finicky about where and how it is grown and vinted, it is also quite particular about temperature and glassware. As mentioned earlier, the storage conditions are extremely important to preserve Burgundy's complex bouquet and delicate flavors, and the same is true of serving conditions. To get the maximum pleasure from top red and white Burgundy wines, follow this checklist:

- Temperature is crucial, so serve top white Burgundy at 50-55º F (10-13º C) or even slightly warmer, up to 56-57º F for Grands Crus. For red Burgundy the recommended range is 60-62º F (15-17º C). Generally, higher quality wines benefit from the higher end of the temperature range, while simpler wines are better at the lower end of the range.

- Glassware makes a huge difference in maximizing Burgundy's aromatics—essential components of its quality and appreciation. For reds, look for large, bowl-shaped glassware with a narrow opening, which allows the wine to release its esters within the glass and channel them up toward the small rim so one can inhale all its layered aromas. For white wines, especially Grands Crus, a large bowl with narrow rim is also beneficial. Check the glassware before using: Ensure the bowl is clean and smell-free with no residual detergent or odor to taint the wine. Smaller glasses and smaller pours for white wines ensure that the wine temperature does not rise as quickly as it does in larger glasses.

- Decanting Burgundy is controversial; my advice is *not* to decant even young Burgundy except just prior to serving. I prefer decanting Burgundy inside the glass slowly, rather than risk over-decanting, which could strip some of the delicate aromatics of fine Burgundy. For mature Burgundy, I definitely would *not* recommend decanting it or even opening it too far in advance. Fragile wines oxidize more quickly and easily, and some of the wine's complex, delicate flavors may be lost before it even reaches the glass. However, I *do* suggest opening the bottles in advance, without decanting, so that just the surface of the opened wine bottle enjoys a slow oxygen exchange: For young wines, opening the bottle several hours before serving and keeping it at cellar temperature (60º F, or 15º C) works well; for mature and more fragile wines, reduce this time to well under an hour.

- Mature Burgundy, over thirty-five years old, should be handled carefully. It is best to stand the bottle up for twenty-four hours prior to opening, and using a twin-prong opener for the fragile corks, rather than the standard waiter's wine opener. I recommend the Durand or similar type of two-prong cork puller for collectible, older wines.

- Enjoying Burgundy wines with food does not have to be challenging or stressful. It is among the most versatile wines in the world, even with spicy, intense Asian dishes. Given its high acidity and low tannins, compared with wines from other regions in the world, it adapts well to various ethnic cuisines, especially those that are not heavy or rich. I consider Burgundy reds and whites at the generic Bourgogne and Village levels to be among the most food-friendly. For wines higher on the quality scale, food pairing becomes a bit more challenging: the food flavors should not overwhelm the delicate and complex wine flavors. For Grands Crus and top Premiers Crus, opt for regional Burgundian dishes or mild, delicately flavored ethnic cuisine, avoiding strong seasonings and spices.

ASSESSING QUALITY

The best wines of Burgundy are more delicate and detailed than wines from nearly anywhere else in the world. Therefore, I assess Burgundy's quality in a different way. For the best Burgundy white wines, in addition to the intensity of its flavors, its depth, balance, and length, I also look for delicacy, elegance, and finesse. The additional quality component that makes a white Burgundy great is the ability to balance firm acidity with purity and lightness, which makes the wine dance on the palate rather than make a forthright statement. For white Burgundy, quality lies as much in the subtle but persistent layers, the flavors that are woven into the fine acidity and crystalline clarity in the wine as much as in the length and intensity.

Diverse soil and mesoclimate conditions produce very different styles of white Burgundy. In Chablis, the best wines from this region are about minerals, slate, and crushed rocks, while in Puligny-Montrachet, gentle floral aromatics and fine acidity provide structure to the delicate flavors and slim frame. These characteristics are gathered through tasting and exploring the regions and paying close attention to their unique characters. The finest white Burgundy wines have elegance and finesse along with intensity and an impressive ability to age.

Red Burgundy wines are unique because of the combination of Pinot Noir grapes grown on ancient limestone soils in a cool climate. Like the whites, the red wines of Burgundy are about balance and elegance, but this thin-skinned grape can create wines that are as concentrated as thicker-skinned, fuller-bodied red wines and age equally long. It is not the color, body, or power that sets red Burgundy apart, but rather its glorious perfume, grace, silky texture, and purity.

Assessing quality in Burgundy reds requires a mind-set that focuses on finding balance and harmony in its components, with finesse as a core framework. Because the aromatics of red Burgundy are so important, it is essential to get exposure and training to recognize some key wine faults, such as a "corked," or musty smell from trichloroanisol (TCA), intense farmyard smells from brettanomyces, or sulfuric aromas like burnt matchstick or rotten egg. For me, half the pleasure of a great bottle of Burgundy at its peak is its heady, intoxicating bouquet—I almost don't need to taste the wine to get pleasure; it is wine perfume in a glass.

Grand Cru red Burgundies will be more concentrated and powerful than Village wines, because they have the structure to enable them to age for decades; their intensity and quality come as much from their firm acidity as from the quality of their tannins. Thus young red Burgundy can taste quite sharp and pointed in its youth, and with age adopt a silky texture with aromatics of the earth, undergrowth (known as "sous bois"), and fresh mushrooms. The floral and red fruit bouquet of youth makes a complete transformation with a few decades of bottle age, evolving into dried rose petals, leather, and truffles.

Great Burgundy must have balance, intensity, complexity, and length, like all great wines of the world; however, along with it, the wines should also be subtle, delicate, fine, graceful, and pure. These characters become recognizable with time, and there is no shortcut to assessing quality in Burgundy except to taste as often and as widely as possible.

NOTE

1. Meadows, A., *The Pearl of the Côte: The Great Wines of Vosne-Romanée*, p. 53.

THE 100 WINES

Listed in Alphabetical Order
by Domaine Name

Giorgio Morandi, *Still Life*, 1918.

CHEVALIER-MONTRACHET GRAND CRU LA CABOTTE, PULIGNY-MONTRACHET

Bouchard is the largest vineyard owner in the Côte d'Or, and some may argue the best négociant in Burgundy. Quietly, they have amassed 130 hectares of vineyards across all of the region's most prestigious communes, including 12 Grand Cru and 74 Premier Cru vineyards. Since 1995, when Champagne Henriot purchased the company, there has been enormous investment in the vineyard and the cellar. Bouchard increased its land holdings by one-third when it purchased a large estate in Meursault in 1996. There have been some changes at the management level, with the appointment of Christian Albouy at the helm as CEO in 2010, and the much younger winemaker Frédéric Weber taking over from the effervescent Philippe Prost. Quality has been increasing steadily and there is greater **precision** and detail in the wines than ever before.

At the top of its white wine portfolio stands Chevalier-Montrachet La Cabotte; it is not below its Montrachet, it stands beside it. The La Cabotte plot was historically part of the original walls of the Montrachet vineyard. Although Bouchard owns a total of 2.33 hectares of Chevalier-Montrachet, it chooses to vinify the 0.21-hectare La Cabotte vineyard separately to preserve its own unique identity. Most Chevalier-Montrachet lovers appreciate the more intensely mineral flavors of this vineyard when compared with the Montrachet, due to its cooler positioning higher on the slope and more white limestone in the soil. However, Bouchard's La Cabotte is more like a Montrachet, but with greater tension: In vintages like 2010, there is **penetrating** acidity and **energy** that lifts the layers of flavors that include yellow fruit, white flowers, and crushed stones. Vintages to seek out are the 2002, 2004, 2008, and 2010. There is not much vintage variation here, although very hot vintages are to be avoided. The more important factor is timing—La Cabotte has the structure and depth of a Montrachet and is best approached after 8 to 10 years in bottle.

IN THREE WORDS *Minerally, persistent, racy.*

BOUCHARD PÈRE & FILS

address	15 Rue de Château, 21200 Beaune, Burgundy, France www.bouchard-pereetfils.com Tel: + 33 3 80 24 80 24
contact	Frédéric Weber
farming philosophy	Sustainable viticulture.
in the cellar	Grapes for red wine are mostly destemmed, depending on the wine and vintage; new oak used sparingly for both reds and whites.
total vineyard area	130 hectares

total annual production	3,000,000 bottles

key vineyard holdings

Red

Bonnes-Mares Grand Cru	0.24 ha
Chambertin Grand Cru	0.15 ha
Clos de Vougeot Grand Cru	0.45 ha
Échezeaux Grand Cru	0.39 ha
Le Corton Grand Cru	3.20 ha
Beaune Premier Cru Teurons	2.60 ha
Beaune Premier Cru Clos de la Mousse Monopole	3.36 ha
Beaune Premier Cru Grèves Vigne de l'Enfant Jésus	3.91 ha
Beaune de Château Premier Cru	26.00 ha
Beaune Premier Cru Marconnets	2.30 ha
Gevrey-Chambertin Premier Cru Les Cazetiers	0.25 ha
Monthélie Premier Cru Les Duresses	1.72 ha
Monthélie Premier Cru Les Champs Fulliot	0.88 ha
Nuits-Saint-Georges Premier Cru Les Cailles	1.07 ha
Nuits-Saint-Georges Premier Cru Les Porrets	0.32 ha
Pommard Premier Cru Rugiens	0.41 ha
Pommard Premier Cru Pézerolles	0.31 ha
Savigny Premier Cru Les Lavières	3.90 ha
Volnay Premier Cru Taillepieds	0.38 ha
Volnay Premier Cru Clos des Chênes	0.85 ha
Volnay Premier Cru Frémiets Clos de la Rougeotte	0.44 ha
Volnay Premier Cru Caillerets Ancienne Cuvée Carnot	3.75 ha
Monthélie	5.93 ha

White

Montrachet Grand Cru	0.89 ha
Chevalier-Montrachet Grand Cru La Cabotte	0.21 ha
Chevalier-Montrachet Grand Cru	2.33 ha
Bâtard-Montrachet Grand Cru	0.08 ha
Corton-Charlemagne Grand Cru	3.98 ha
Beaune du Château Premier Cru	9.92 ha
Beaune Premier Cru Clos Saint-Landry Monopole	1.98 ha
Chassagne-Montrachet Premier Cru En Remilly	0.05 ha
Meursault Premier Cru Perrières	1.20 ha
Meursault Premier Cru Genevrières	2.65 ha
Meursault Premier Cru Charmes	0.28 ha
Meursault Premier Cru Les Gouttes d'Or	0.55 ha
Meursault Premier Cru Le Porusot	0.44 ha
Meursault Premier Cru Les Bouchères	0.38 ha
Meursault Les Clous	8.66 ha
Bouzeron Ancien Domaine Carnot	6.70 ha
Meursault	6.30 ha

CLOS DE TART

address	7 Route des Grands Crus, 21220 Morey-Saint-Denis, Burgundy, France www.clos-de-tart.com Tel: + 33 3 80 34 30 91
contact	Alessandro Noli
farming philosophy	Organic cultivation but without certification.
in the cellar	Mostly destemmed berries, with a proportion of whole bunch depending on vintage; matured about 18 months in 100% new Tronçais oak barrels.

total vineyard area	7.5 hectares	**total annual production**	25,000 bottles
key vineyard holdings	Clos de Tart Grand Cru	7.53 ha	

GRAND CRU MONOPOLE, MOREY-SAINT-DENIS

Clos de Tart is a rare *clos,* or walled vineyard, that is the largest Grand Cru monopole in Burgundy and one that has remained intact for nearly 900 years. The Cistercian nuns, named the Order of the Bernardines de Tart, bought the 7.5-hectare vineyard site in the 12th century. It remained under church ownership until the French Revolution, and it has had only three owners since then. In 2017, Groupe Artémis, the holding company of François Pinault's growing wine empire, purchased Clos de Tart for a rumored 200 million euros. The value of the estate has been escalating steadily, not just because of the growing demand for Burgundy, but largely due to the refinement and improvements made by the former manager of the domaine, the erudite Sylvain Pitiot, starting in 1996. Under Pitiot's careful direction, Clos de Tart's vineyard has been mapped out and divided into distinctive parcels and vinified separately to understand how each plot contributes to the blend. Pitiot retired in 2015, handing over the reins to the talented Jacques Devauges, who was recently replaced by Alessandro Noli in February 2019. In a vertical tasting that included all the important vintages of Clos de Tart going back to 1937, it was clear to me that this terroir has a *distinctive* voice: In great vintages like 1985, 1990, 1999, 2002, 2005 and 2015, the wine is majestic and *muscular* with great tension and depth. Even in the lighter vintages like 1988, 1996 or 2012, the wine's *earthy*, minerally, spicy core remains unchanged. Clos de Tart is on the riper, denser end of the spectrum, especially when compared with its neighbor, Clos des Lambrays. It is a wine that demands long cellaring and lots of patience. For the less patient, try its second wine, La Forge du Tart, made from younger vines; it offers a lighter, earlier-drinking version of the *grand vin.*

IN THREE WORDS *Concentrated, profound, majestic.*

"Burgundy makes you think of silly things, Bordeaux makes you talk of them, and Champagne makes you do them."

Jean-Anthelme Brillat-Savarin

DOMAINE ALAIN HUDELOT-NOËLLAT

address	5 Ancienne RN 74, 21220 Chambolle-Musigny, Burgundy, France www.domaine-hudelot-noëllat.com Tel: + 33 3 80 62 85 17
contact	Charles Van Canneyt
farming philosophy	Classic *lutte raisonnée* cultivation, with minimal intervention.
in the cellar	Small proportion of whole bunch, depending on the vintage and wine; aged 12–18 months in 50% new oak for the Grands Crus, 30% for Premiers Crus, and 20% for Village wines.

total vineyard area	10.5 hectares	**total annual production**	50,000 bottles

key vineyard holdings			
Red		Vosne-Romanée Premier Cru	
Clos de Vougeot Grand Cru	0.69 ha	Les Suchots	0.46 ha
Richebourg Grand Cru	0.29 ha	Vougeot Premier Cru	
Romanée-Saint-Vivant Grand Cru	0.48 ha	Les Petits Vougeots	0.54 ha
Chambolle-Musigny Premier Cru		Chambolle-Musigny	0.85 ha
Les Charmes	0.21 ha	Nuits-Saint-Georges	
Nuits-Saint-Georges Premier Cru		Les Bas de Combes	0.21 ha
Les Murgers	0.68 ha	Vosne-Romanée	0.78 ha
Vosne-Romanée Premier Cru			
Les Beaumonts	0.32 ha	*White*	
Vosne-Romanée Premier Cru		Meursault Clos des Écoles	0.50 ha
Les Malconsorts	0.14 ha		

ROMANÉE-SAINT-VIVANT GRAND CRU, VOSNE-ROMANÉE

For the past decade, ever since Charles van Canneyt arrived in Domaine Alain Hudelot-Noëllat to take over his grandfather's domaine in 2008, there has been a youthful energy and vigor in both the wines and the winery. While the style of Hudelot-Noëllat remains unchanged, there is noticeable refinement and precision in the wines. According to Canneyt, he hasn't changed much—still destemming most of the fruit, continuing the discrete use of new oak, *lutte raisonnée* farming in the vineyard, indigenous natural fermentation, and cellaring the wines for 18 months. Small refinements have been made, such as decreasing yield, more careful sorting, and using a small percentage of whole clusters for certain wines in vintages that can support the influence of stems in the wine.

It helps that he is charming, well-spoken, and handsome. With his blond hair and deep brown eyes, he looks as comfortable in front of a camera as he does walking through his vineyard. The domaine owns some of the most exalted vineyards, such as Richebourg and Romanée-Saint-Vivant. Very few producers make both, with the exception of Domaine de la Romanée-Conti and Domaine Leroy. Hudelot-Noëllat farms 10.5 hectares of vines, and its parcels include some of the oldest vines in Burgundy—the Romanée-Saint-Vivant vineyard is nearly 100 years old. One can debate whether its Richebourg or Romanée-Saint-Vivant should make this list. For me, the Romanée-Saint-Vivant has the **seductive** quality of intoxicating perfume added to its **alluring** depth and **persistence**. Quality has improved dramatically since the 2010 vintage, so I would recommend buying the younger vintages, such as the 2010, 2012 or 2015.

IN THREE WORDS *Sensual, intoxicating, regal.*

DOMAINE ANNE GROS

(FORMERLY DOMAINE FRANÇOIS GROS, ALSO DOMAINE ANNE & FRANÇOIS GROS)

address	11 Rue des Communes, 21700 Vosne-Romanée, Burgundy, France www.anne-gros.com Tel + 33 3 80 61 07 95
contact	Anne Gros
farming philosophy	Lutte raisonnée, with no insecticides or herbicides.
in the cellar	Destemmed whole berries, cold maceration with minimal racking; 16 months of barrel aging using 70% new oak for Grands Crus, 50% for Village wines, and 30% for regional wines.

total vineyard area	7 hectares	total annual production	30,000 bottles

key vineyard holdings			
Richebourg Grand Cru	0.60 ha	Vosne-Romanée Les Barreaux	0.39 ha
Clos de Vougeot Grand Cru	0.94 ha	Chambolle-Musigny La Combe d'Orveau	1.10 ha
Échezeaux Grand Cru	0.76 ha	Hautes-Côtes de Nuits (white and red)	1.73 ha

RICHEBOURG GRAND CRU, VOSNE-ROMANÉE

Anne Gros is one of the most respected winemakers in Burgundy, having taken over her father's domaine in 1988, when very few women were at the helm of top domaines. Like many working women, she juggled running the 7-hectare vineyard and raising three children. Although Domaine Anne Gros was established recently in 1995, Anne comes from a long lineage of distinguished vignerons with strong holdings in Vosne-Romanée. The Gros name often causes confusion, since about a dozen domaines with the name *Gros* exist. For example, Anne & François Gros was the name when Anne took over her father's property in 1988, and prior to that it was called François Gros. A.F. Gros, Domaine Gros Frère et Soeur, and Michel Gros

are different wineries, run by her cousins who inherited Domaine Jean Gros. All the hard work and investment that Anne has made in the winery and in the vineyard over the past few decades have paid off. Her wines are ***detailed***, attractive, and vibrant. The Richebourg is Anne's crown jewel, and here the delicate touch in her winemaking steers Richebourg away from sheer power and richness and directs it toward a more ***graceful***, elegant style. Vintages like the 2005 and 2010 are ***brilliant***, and even more modest vintages like the 2001 and 2012 are terrific. However, to enjoy now, opt for the vintages from the 1990s such as the 1999 and the 1996. Only 2,500 bottles are produced per year.

| IN THREE WORDS | ***Elegant, complex, vibrant.*** |

Pablo Picasso, *Pot, Wineglass and Book*, 1908.

DOMAINE ARLAUD

address	41 Rue d'Épernay, 21220 Morey-Saint-Denis, Burgundy, France www.domainearlaud.com Tel: + 33 3 80 34 32 65		
contact	Cyprien Arlaud		
farming philosophy	Organic since 2004 and certified biodynamic since 2014.		
in the cellar	Mostly destemmed, although a small portion can have whole bunch added; barrel aging for about a year with new oak use between 15% for Village level and up to 30% for some Grands Crus.		
total vineyard area	15 hectares	total annual production	70,000 bottles

key vineyard holdings	Bonnes-Mares Grand Cru 0.21 ha
	Charmes-Chambertin Grand Cru 1.14 ha
	Clos Saint-Denis Grand Cru 0.18 ha
	Clos de la Roche Grand Cru 0.44 ha
	Chambolle-Musigny Premier Cru
	  Les Châtelots 0.07 ha
	Chambolle-Musigny Premier Cru
	  Les Noirots 0.17 ha
	Chambolle-Musigny Premier Cru
	  Les Sentiers 0.23 ha
	Gevrey-Chambertin Premier Cru
	  Aux Combottes 0.45 ha
		Morey-Saint-Denis Premier Cru
		  Les Ruchots 0.71 ha
		Morey-Saint-Denis Premier Cru
		  Les Blanchards 0.27 ha
		Morey-Saint-Denis Premier Cru
		  Aux Cheseaux 0.71 ha
		Morey-Saint-Denis Premier Cru
		  Les Millandes 0.41 ha
		Chambolle-Musigny 0.96 ha
		Gevrey-Chambertin 1.04 ha
		Morey-Saint-Denis 0.96 ha
		Bourgogne 4.89 ha		

CLOS DE LA ROCHE GRAND CRU, MOREY-SAINT-DENIS

Although this family-run domaine was established in 1942, it was not until the third generation became involved and made significant changes in the vineyard and winery that the wines started to stand out, since 2005. The vineyard converted first to organic farming in the late 1990s, then eventually to biodynamics. The cellar was overhauled and moved to its current modern facilities in Morey-Saint-Denis. The charming Cyprien Arlaud took over the estate in 2013, and together with his younger brother, Romain, and sister, Bertille, they manage its 15-hectare holdings, including four Grand Cru and eight Premier Cru vineyards. Those familiar with Domaine Arlaud will have noticed a shift in style since 2005: There is

more **precision** and detail, and a lighter touch compared with the wines from the late 1990s, which were chunkier and richer. Biodynamics has also played a role in creating more **finesse** and elegance in the wines. While Clos Saint-Denis may be Arlaud's more famous and more sought-after wine, I find the Clos de la Roche just as good since 2010. Arlaud only owns 0.17 hectares of Clos Saint-Denis, while the 0.43-hectare plot of Clos de la Roche is more accessible, in terms of price, quantity, and style. Recent vintages like 2015 and 2016 show the intensity, stature, and **energy** that this vineyard can offer, and prices are still fairly reasonable. I also recommend its Bonnes-Mares as well as its Morey Premiers Crus, especially the Les Ruchots.

IN THREE WORDS *Seamless, nuanced, gracious.*

Domaine Armand Rousseau Père & Fils

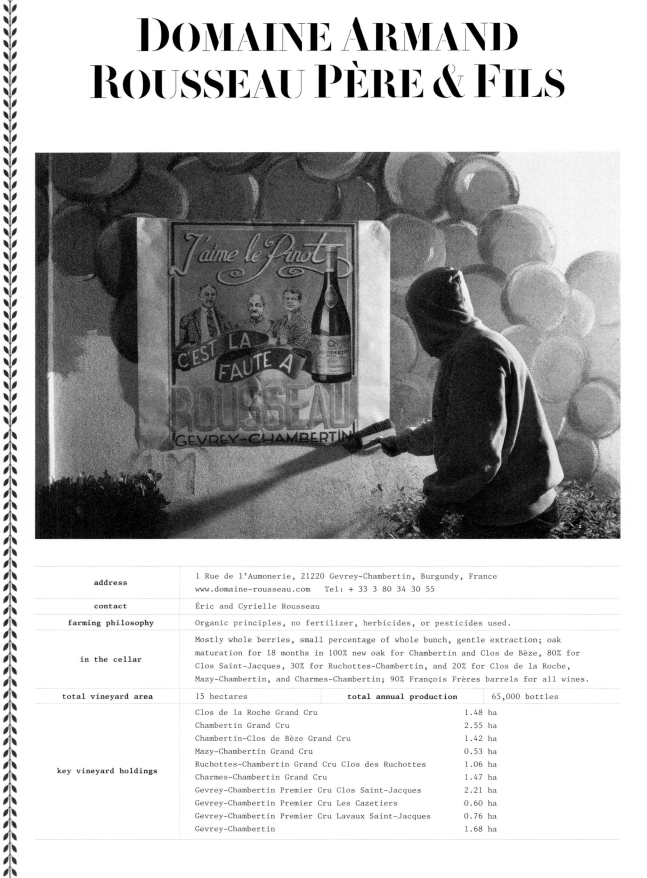

address	1 Rue de l'Aumonerie, 21220 Gevrey-Chambertin, Burgundy, France www.domaine-rousseau.com Tel: + 33 3 80 34 30 55
contact	Éric and Cyrielle Rousseau
farming philosophy	Organic principles, no fertilizer, herbicides, or pesticides used.
in the cellar	Mostly whole berries, small percentage of whole bunch, gentle extraction; oak maturation for 18 months in 100% new oak for Chambertin and Clos de Bèze, 80% for Clos Saint-Jacques, 30% for Ruchottes-Chambertin, and 20% for Clos de la Roche, Mazy-Chambertin, and Charmes-Chambertin; 90% François Frères barrels for all wines.

total vineyard area	15 hectares	total annual production	65,000 bottles

key vineyard holdings	Clos de la Roche Grand Cru	1.48 ha
	Chambertin Grand Cru	2.55 ha
	Chambertin-Clos de Bèze Grand Cru	1.42 ha
	Mazy-Chambertin Grand Cru	0.53 ha
	Ruchottes-Chambertin Grand Cru Clos des Ruchottes	1.06 ha
	Charmes-Chambertin Grand Cru	1.47 ha
	Gevrey-Chambertin Premier Cru Clos Saint-Jacques	2.21 ha
	Gevrey-Chambertin Premier Cru Les Cazetiers	0.60 ha
	Gevrey-Chambertin Premier Cru Lavaux Saint-Jacques	0.76 ha
	Gevrey-Chambertin	1.68 ha

The wines of Armand Rousseau are distinctively pure and effortlessly confident; there is no excess, and even in the most powerful vintages of Chambertin or Clos Saint-Jacques the wines have finesse and grace. This is a truly great domaine that continues to be family-run and is now in its fourth generation. It has undeniably great terroir, with six sizable Grand Cru vineyards totaling 8 hectares, and a 2.22-hectare Premier Cru vineyard, Clos Saint-Jacques, considered by many to be of Grand Cru status.

Éric Rousseau, the grandson of the founder, is in charge of the vineyard and winery, but he has been handing over the reins to his young, talented daughter Cyrielle. There are no secrets to their winemaking and nothing unusual—they have just honed their skills in coaxing the most out of their great vineyards in the gentlest, most respectful way. All the hard work is done in the vineyard, with plowing, limiting yield and vigor, shunning pesticides and herbicides, selecting the right clones, and opting for high density. When the grapes arrive at the winery, they are ripe but not overripe, and the wines are treated gently throughout the journey. The extraction and pressing is gentle, adhering to the philosophy of preserving everything that was captured in the vineyard.

The vineyards owned by Rousseau are enviable and set the gold standard for all the Grand Cru and Premier Cru vineyards it owns. The Rousseau Chambertin is the benchmark wine to which the two dozen other producers of Chambertin compare themselves. It also happens that it is the largest owner of Chambertin, with over 2 hectares. Its Chambertin–Clos de Bèze is another benchmark wine, all perfume and sensuality compared with the Chambertin, but equally complex and even more expressive. Its Gevrey-Chambertin Premier Cru Clos Saint-Jacques is of Grand Cru standard and is treated as such.

What I love about the wines from this domaine is the purity of the expressions and the signature silky texture. The wines have an honesty and clarity at their core, from the pale color and delicately layered aromatics to the finely etched flavor profile and silky tannins. There is no makeup, no heavy hand in the winemaking; just simple, honest, great wines from great terroirs.

CHAMBERTIN–CLOS DE BÈZE GRAND CRU, GEVREY–CHAMBERTIN

Among the nine Grands Crus of Gevrey-Chambertin, two stand out as being the best: Chambertin–Clos de Bèze and Chambertin. Clos de Bèze is a fairly large vineyard, with over 15 hectares, so there is variation among the wines produced by the 18 owners. Clos de Bèze is slightly steeper than Chambertin and there is a cooling effect of the Combe de Lavaux to its north. There are good producers here, and by far the largest is Pierre Damoy, with 5.3 hectares. Armand Rousseau's parcel is the second largest, at 1.4 hectares, and sets the standards for Clos de Bèze. The east-facing site located mid-slope offers sensual wines with more aromatic intensity and spices compared with the Chambertin. But it often depends on vintage and the time of tasting—in the 2015 and the 2017 vintages I loved the Clos de Bèze slightly more than the Chambertin when I tasted it in barrel, but in the 2014 I preferred the Chambertin. Typically in great vintages of Clos de Bèze, like the 1990, 1993, 2005, and 2010, the wines are *exuberant*, complex, and incredibly *sensuous*. Like all the wines from Rousseau, the tannins are fine-grained and silky, but this great vineyard offers depth and incredible intensity without being heavy. Older vintages such as the 1976 and 1978 are phenomenal, still *vigorous*, and reveal their capacity for long aging. It isn't just the great years where Clos de Bèze shines—there are hardly any weak vintages for this wine, especially since the 1990s. This is a first-rate domaine at the top of its form. | IN THREE WORDS | *Captivating, exhilarating, intricate.*

CHAMBERTIN GRAND CRU, GEVREY–CHAMBERTIN

Chambertin reigns supreme in Gevrey-Chambertin and is considered by some as the king of Grands Crus. As the largest owner, with over 2 hectares, Armand Rousseau looms large in this vineyard. Here, and at Clos Saint-Jacques, Rousseau leaves its indelible signature in defining the quality standards, and luckily for us, the standard is set very high. Rousseau's Chambertin is a blend of several parcels purchased at different periods from 1921 to 2009. The parcels are located in very different terroirs, with some being more powerful and dense while others are elegant and more aromatic. The blend of these parcels is what creates the symphony of flavors in Rousseau's Chambertin, which can be shy when tasted young. Unlike the Clos de Bèze, which is more expressive in its youth, Chambertin exudes refined power with fine tannins and a core minerality and taut **structure**. With time, the wine becomes even more complex, **nuanced**, and intense, growing in stature in the bottle. There are no disappointing vintages of Rousseau's Chambertin that I have come across, which is a testament to the wine's consistency and deservedly exalted reputation. Tasting Rousseau's Chambertin is to experience and glimpse greatness, and it is a humbling, **extraordinary** experience.

IN THREE WORDS   *Awe-inspiring, humbling, impressive.*

GEVREY-CHAMBERTIN PREMIER CRU CLOS SAINT-JACQUES, GEVREY-CHAMBERTIN

Armand Rousseau owns nearly a third of this Premier Cru clos, which many consider to be of Grand Cru quality. It is definitely the finest Premier Cru in Gevrey-Chambertin, and the market has priced it accordingly. With very high standards among the four other growers who own parcels in this 6.7-hectare vineyard, Clos Saint-Jacques enjoys a great reputation for reliability and high quality. The five parcels run vertically from the top of the slope to the bottom, where the soils are very different. Separate faults run transversely across the vineyard with different base rocks, creating complex soil combinations. The top of the slope is stony and has barely any soil, whereas the bottom has much more topsoil from runoffs and creates a chunkier style. The best part seems to lie mid-slope, identified as "En Saint-Jacques" by Rousseau and bottled separately "for fun" in 2013, just for the domaine's library collection.

In most years, Armand Rousseau as well as the other producers blend all the parcels, creating a tightly structured, complex wine with gorgeous *aromatic* intensity and persistent palate. The best vintages of Clos Saint-Jacques, such as the 1999, 2010, and 2015, are explosive—an enormously *concentrated* wine that still maintains poise and *grace*, with silky, firm tannins and racy acidity.

IN THREE WORDS **_Powerful, profound, poised._**

Piotr Konchalovsky, *The Artist's Guest
Aleksey Nikolayevich*, 1941.

DOMAINE ARNAUD ENTE

address

12 Rue de Mazeray, 21190 Meursault, Burgundy, France
Tel: + 33 3 80 21 66 12

contact

Arnaud Ente

farming philosophy

Certified organic.

in the cellar

Extremely low yields for concentration, and fairly early harvest to retain freshness; aged 1 year in both normal and 600-liter barrels, depending on the wine; minimal new oak use; no filtration.

total vineyard area

4.8 hectares

total annual production

15,000 bottles

key vineyard holdings

White

Puligny-Montrachet Premier Cru Les Referts	0.22 ha
Meursault Premier Cru Les Gouttes d'Or	0.22 ha
Meursault Clos des Ambres	0.72 ha
Meursault La Sève du Clos	0.32 ha
Meursault Les Petits Charrons	0.34 ha

Red

Volnay Premier Cru Santenots	0.48 ha

MEURSAULT LA SÈVE DU CLOS, MEURSAULT

Starting from the early 2000s, Arnaud Ente has been dubbed "Meursault's wunderkind" and a "rising star" by those who followed him since his time at Coche-Dury. The domaine was established just after he married Marie-Odile Thevenot in 1991, using vineyards rented from his father-in-law. His time at Coche-Dury initially influenced him to create an opulent, powerful style, but this started to change in the early 2000s, as he opted for earlier harvesting and more precision and freshness in his wines. Wines post-2007 are completely different from the powerful, heavier wines of the past. My visits to Ente always leave me energized and exuberant—the wines are minerally, precise, and so very fine that it lifts the spirits. Ente's two Bourgognes are a testament to his skill and ability to extract the most from even modest vineyards: The Aligoté planted in 1938 is always the best Bourgogne Aligoté that I taste in every vintage, while the Bourgogne Chardonnay is a layered, minerally powerhouse that can compete with top Village and even Premier Cru wines. I have been a huge fan and follower since my first visit to the domaine ten years ago, but the word has spread and the wines are no longer "good value"—prices have escalated to join the ranks of the most expensive white wines from Burgundy. Every wine in the portfolio is precise, *focused*, with amazing tension, but I have a soft spot for La Sève du Clos. The vines here are more than 100 years old and the yield is minuscule—in many years offering just one barrel. Maintaining it is becoming economically unfeasible, so Arnaud Ente waits year after year to see when he will have to make the tough decision to replant the vineyard. I am in love with this *piercing*, steely Meursault, *dancing* with crushed stones and oyster shells, and would be heartbroken if one day the vines are uprooted. IN THREE WORDS *Penetrating, lingering, multifaceted.*

> **"Visits to Ente always leave me energized and exuberant."**

DOMAINE ARNOUX-LACHAUX

(FORMERLY ROBERT ARNOUX)

address	3 Route Départementale 974, 21700 Vosne-Romanée, Burgundy, France Tel: + 33 3 80 61 08 41
contact	Pascal Lachaux
farming philosophy	Following mainly organic principles, but without certification.
in the cellar	Whole bunch and destemmed, moving more toward whole bunch; 5–6 days' cold maceration; new oak use is declining, though in the past it was usually 100% for all Grands Crus.

total vineyard area	13.5 hectares	**total annual production**	60,000 bottles

key vineyard holdings	Clos de Vougeot Grand Cru	0.45 ha	Vosne-Romanée Premier Cru	
	Échezeaux Grand Cru	0.90 ha	Les Reignots	0.15 ha
	Latricières-Chambertin Grand Cru	0.55 ha	Vosne-Romanée Premier Cru	
	Romanée-Saint-Vivant Grand Cru	0.35 ha	Les Suchots	0.43 ha
	Nuits-Saint-Georges Premier Cru		Chambolle-Musigny	1.83 ha
	Clos des Corvées Pagets	0.55 ha	Nuits-Saint-Georges	1.42 ha
	Nuits-Saint-Georges Premier Cru		Nuits-Saint-Georges Les Poisets	0.57 ha
	Les Procès	0.63 ha	Vosne-Romanée	1.53 ha
	Vosne-Romanée Premier Cru		Vosne-Romanée Hautes Maizières	0.60 ha
	Les Chaumes	0.74 ha	Bourgogne Pinot Fin	2.55 ha

VOSNE-ROMANÉE PREMIER CRU LES SUCHOTS, VOSNE-ROMANÉE

Robert Arnoux always had wonderful parcels across Côte de Nuits, but it was with the arrival of his son-in-law Pascal Lachaux in the mid-1980s, and then with Pascal's young son Charles taking over in 2012, that the wines made a big quality leap. Charles Lachaux is now experimenting with whole bunch, citing Lalou Bize-Leroy as his mentor, refining and redefining the domaine's style by making the wines more pristine, detailed, and less "modern." Tastings of recent vintages, such as the 2015, 2016, and 2017, reveal more purity and precision than in the past, though he still needs to refine the handling of stems; he is definitely heading in the right direction. The five wines from Vosne-Romanée, including three Premiers Crus and two Village wines, are wonderful examples of what this commune can produce at every level. Its small 0.4-hectare Vosne-Romanée Premier Cru vineyard Les Suchots, planted in the 1940s, is a standout among the group and is consistently *brilliant*, combining power with elegance. It often offers the depth of a Grand Cru, with polished tannins and great *persistence*. I am also a fan of Lachaux's Romanée-Saint-Vivant, which is intensely aromatic and sensual, and the 2016 Latricières-Chambertin is often a glorious wine, made with 100% whole bunch and less than 30% new oak, veering away from the decades-old formula of destemming and 100% new oak. Les Suchots in 2015 and 2016 are both superb and show *precision* and detail; these are two great recent vintages for Arnoux-Lachaux, and this Premier Cru vineyard produced Grand Cru–quality wines. This domaine is one to watch.

IN THREE WORDS *Detailed, polished, compelling.*

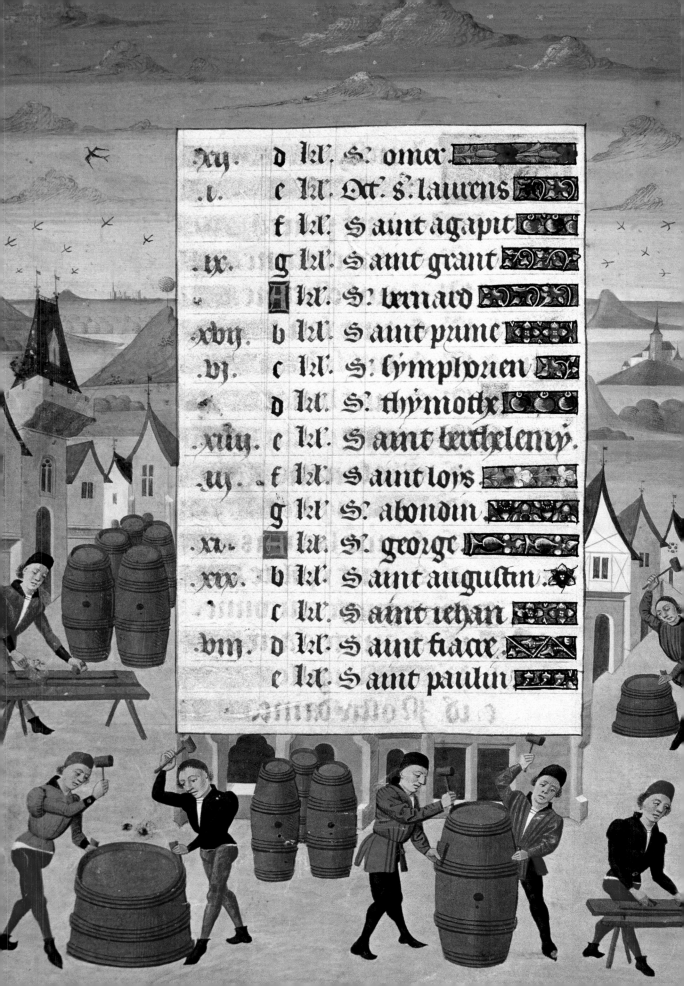

xij.	d	kl.	S. omer
.i.	e	kl.	Oct. s. laurens
	f	kl.	Saint agapit
.ix.	g	kl.	Saint grant
	H	kl.	S. bernard
xvij.	b	kl.	Saint prine
.vj.	c	kl.	S. symphorien
	d	kl.	S. thymothe
.xiiij.	e	kl.	Saint berthelemy
.iij.	f	kl.	Saint loys
	g	kl.	S. abondin
.xi.	H	kl.	S. george
.xix.	b	kl.	Saint augustin
	c	kl.	Saint iehan
vij.	d	kl.	Saint fiacre
	e	kl.	Saint paulin

DOMAINE BONNEAU DU MARTRAY

address	2 Rue de Frétille, 21420 Pernand-Vergelesses, Burgundy, France www.bonneaudumartray.com Tel: + 33 3 80 21 50 64
contact	Thibault Jacquet
farming philosophy	Biodynamic cultivation; average vine age nearly 50 years.
in the cellar	Whole bunches for white and destemming for red; slow, natural fermentation; matured 12 months in oak barrels, with about one-third in new wood and then a further 6 months in tank.

total vineyard area	11.1 hectares	**total annual production**	40,000 bottles
key vineyard holdings	Corton-Charlemagne Grand Cru 9.50 ha	Corton Grand Cru	1.59 ha

CORTON–CHARLEMAGNE GRAND CRU, ALOXE–CORTON AND PERNAND–VERGELESSES

When an 80% share of this historic domaine was sold in 2017 to American billionaire Stanley Kroenke, the owner of Napa Valley's Screaming Eagle, eyebrows raised in surprise. The French are notorious for their reluctance to part with what they consider to be cultural heritage sites. Bonneau du Martray is one such property, having been in the same aristocratic family for 200 years. The holdings represent one-eighth of the entire Corton-Charlemagne Grand Cru vineyard and is among the most beloved white wines of Burgundy. It is also the only Burgundy property that makes exclusively Grand Cru wines. The new team, led by Armand de Maigret, based in California, and the local manager, Thibault Jacquet, seem to be committed to continuing the tradition of excellence and the great work that former owner Jean-Charles le Bault de la Morinière has done over the past 22 years. This single contiguous plot in Charlemagne produces white wines of exceptional depth and ability to age. I enjoy its Corton-Charlemagne with at least 10 years of age, when it starts to develop honeysuckle notes and gain **profundity** and completeness. The wines age exquisitely, and those from 1989, 1990, and 1992 are drinking beautifully now. More recent vintages show greater **delicacy** and precision, but similar intensity and aging ability. I would recommend the 2005, 2010, 2014, 2015, 2016, and 2017 vintages, which are all **outstanding**. | IN THREE WORDS | *Aristocratic, brilliant, remarkable.*

August: Manufacture of wine barrels, illumination by Master Jean de Rolin, from The Hours of Adelaide of Savoy, Duchess of Burgundy, 1460-65.

DOMAINE BRUNO CLAIR

address	5 Rue du Vieux Collège, 21160 Marsannay-la-Côte, Burgundy, France www.bruno-clair.com Tel: + 33 3 80 52 28 95
contact	Bruno Clair
farming philosophy	Lutte raisonnée with organic principles, including plowing, no herbicides, and use of humus instead of artificial fertilizers; some parcels are farmed biodynamically.
in the cellar	Mostly destemmed; matured 15-22 months in oak, with minimal use of new barriques, up to 50% for top cuvées.

total vineyard area	23 hectares	**total annual production**	100,000 bottles

key vineyard holdings			
White		Savigny-Les-Beaune Premier Cru	
Corton-Charlemagne Grand Cru	0.34 ha	La Dominode	1.14 ha
Morey-Saint-Denis		Savigny-Les-Beaune Premier Cru	
En la Rue de Vergy	0.58 ha	Les Jarrons	0.57 ha
Marsannay	2.47 ha	Gevrey-Chambertin	0.71 ha
		Morey-Saint-Denis	
Red		En la Rue de Vergy	0.54 ha
Chambertin–Clos de Bèze Grand Cru	0.98 ha	Chambolle-Musigny Les Véroilles	1.60 ha
Bonnes-Mares Grand Cru	1.64 ha	Vosne-Romanée Les Champs Perdrix	0.93 ha
Gevrey-Chambertin Premier Cru		Pernand-Vergelesses	0.24 ha
Les Cazetiers	0.87 ha	Aloxe-Corton	0.31 ha
Gevrey-Chambertin Premier Cru		Marsannay Grasses Têtes	2.07 ha
Clos Saint-Jacques	1.00 ha	Marsannay Vaudenelles	1.27 ha
Gevrey-Chambertin Premier Cru		Marsannay Longeroies	1.38 ha
Clos du Fonteny	0.68 ha	Marsannay Charme aux Prêtres	0.77 ha
Gevrey-Chambertin Premier Cru		Marsannay Rouge and Rosé	2.54 ha
La Petite Chapelle	0.25 ha		

CHAMBERTIN—CLOS DE BÈZE GRAND CRU, GEVREY-CHAMBERTIN

Bruno Clair's holdings were formed from the remains of the previously famous Clair-Dau estate. Bruno's grandfather, Joseph Clair, founded Clair-Dau after World War I; the next generation disagreed about the estate's future, and the estate was dispersed, with some parts sold to Louis Jadot. Bruno Clair established the present domaine in 1979, and over the years was entrusted with the vineyard of his parents and siblings, then further expanded the holdings to choice vineyards across the Côte d'Or. Bruno Clair is best known for its range of affordable, well-made Marsannays, but it also produces excellent Grand Cru wines such as Corton-Charlemagne, Bonnes-Mares, and Chambertin—Clos de Bèze. Bruno Clair owns nearly a hectare of Clos de Bèze, a parcel that extends the entire slope from top to bottom. The wines from the best vintages, like 2002, 2005, 2010 and 2012, are taut, *refined*, and *gracious*; it is a wine that combines power with *finesse*. While Bruno Clair's Grands Crus are excellent, befitting their esteemed status, it is in the more humble appellations, like Savigny La Dominode and Marsannay Les Longeroies, that the dedication to quality shows itself. These wines soar above their appellations and help to place Bruno Clair firmly on the quality map. IN THREE WORDS *Precise, concentrated, impressive.*

> 66 **Bruno Clair's Grands Crus are excellent, befitting their esteemed status.** 99

DOMAINE CÉCILE TREMBLAY

2009

Echezeaux
"du dessus"

Grand Cru

NON
FILTRÉ

Domaine
Cécile Tremblay

ALC. 13% BY VOL. 750ML.

N° 90990

address	1 Rue de la Fontaine, 21700 Vosne Romanée, Burgundy, France www.domaine-ceciletremblay.fr Tel: + 33 3 45 83 60 08
contact	Cécile Tremblay
farming philosophy	Certified organic, moving toward biodynamics.
in the cellar	Combination of whole bunch and destemming, depending on the wine and vintage; gentle, long maceration, followed by 15-18 months in oak with 30-65% new.

total vineyard area	4 hectares	total annual production	15,000 bottles

key vineyard holdings	Échezeaux Grand Cru	0.18 ha	Nuits Saint Georges Premier Cru	
	Chapelle-Chambertin Grand Cru	0.58 ha	Les Murgers	0.17 ha
	Vosne-Romanée Premier Cru		Nuits-Saint-Georges Albuca	0.25 ha
	Les Beaumonts	0.15 ha	Morey-Saint-Denis Très Girard	0.40 ha
	Vosne-Romanée Premier Cru		Chambolle-Musigny	1.00 ha
	Rouges-du-Dessus	0.23 ha	Vosne-Romanée	0.60 ha
	Chambolle-Musigny Premier Cru		Bourgogne Côte d'Or	0.80 ha
	Les Feusselottes	0.45 ha		

ÉCHEZEAUX GRAND CRU, VOSNE-ROMANÉE

Despite the domaine being extremely young and quite small—established in 2003—the wines from Cécile Tremblay are on strict allocation and in high demand around the world. Tremblay's ancestral ties extend to the Confurons, Noëllats, and Jayers. The late, great Henri Jayer was a distant relation, the nephew of her great-grandfather, Édouard Jayer. In 2003, Cécile decided to take back the family vineyards, which were previously leased out. Within ten years she built a reputation for producing wines of amazing concentration and finesse. The vineyards she had taken over had potential but were not well looked after. Cécile's philosophy was to treat the vineyards like her own garden, adopting organic and biodynamic viticulture and striving to reveal their distinctiveness through ripe, healthy grapes. She transformed her "garden," and the wine-loving community took note. There are only 4 hectares total, including two Grands Crus, four Premiers Crus, and four Village wines. I love all her Vosne-Romanées, from the old-vine Village to the two Premier Cru wines; the Beaux Monts is exceptional, and in the best vintages easily reaches Grand Cru–level quality. However, it is the delicate, refined Échezeaux that is the most *emotional* wine in her portfolio. This small 0.18-hectare

vineyard is located in Échezeaux-Dessus, the upper mid-slope, considered to be one of the finest *climats* within the appellation. This wine does not have the forceful concentration of the Chapelle-Chambertin nor its taut nature; Échezeaux is consistently delicious, and in recent years always fabulous. In vintages like 2012, 2015, 2016, and 2017, the wines have exceptional *clarity* and elegance with persistent, *sumptuous* flavors that dance on the palate. This is a wine, and a domaine, to follow.

IN THREE WORDS *Suave, elegant, alluring.*

DOMAINE CLAUDE DUGAT

address	1 Place de la Cure, 21220 Gevrey-Chambertin, Burgundy, France Tel: + 33 3 80 34 36 18 Fax: + 33 3 80 58 50 64
contact	Claude Dugat
farming philosophy	Traditional cultivation, no herbicides.
in the cellar	Grapes are entirely destemmed; aged 12-18 months in a high percentage of new oak—60% for Village and 100% for Premiers and Grands Crus.

total vineyard area	6.5 hectares	**total annual production**	15,000 bottles

key vineyard holdings	Charmes-Chambertin Grand Cru	0.31 ha
	Griotte-Chambertin Grand Cru	0.16 ha
	Chapelle-Chambertin Grand Cru	0.10 ha
	Gevrey-Chambertin Premier Cru Lavaux Saint-Jacques	0.30 ha
	Gevrey-Chambertin Premier Cru (Craipillot, La Perrière)	0.30 ha
	Gevrey-Chambertin	3.80 ha
	Bourgogne	1.50 ha

CHAPELLE-CHAMBERTIN GRAND CRU, GEVREY-CHAMBERTIN

Claude Dugat, his wife, Marie-Thérèse, and their three children currently run the small 6.5-hectare vineyard that was established in 1955 by Claude's father, Maurice. The domaine has a cult-like following, especially strong in the United States, with collectors fighting for allocations for his three Grands Crus, two Premiers Crus, and his Village Gevrey-Chambertin, which is priced like other estates' Premiers Crus. The vines are fairly old, ranging from over 100 years at Chapelle-Chambertin to over 50 years for the Griotte-Chambertin. Even the 3.4-hectare Gevrey-Chambertin Village wine has an average vine age of 60 years. Claude Dugat looks for ripe but not overripe fruit, and keeps yields very low, around 18 hectoliters per hectare, which is half the average yield of other Grands Crus. Dugat's Chapelle-Chambertin is a small parcel, one-tenth of a hectare, producing just one to two barrels a year. In its youth it is often brooding and closed, and the immense **structure** is prominent. With at least 10 years of age, the wine unveils its power and **complexity**, offering **layers** of iron, game, spices, and earth. This wine requires patience, and rewards those who wait at least 15 years.

IN THREE WORDS *Focused, sumptuous, deep.*

> 66 **The domaine has a cult-like following, especially strong in the United States, with collectors fighting for allocations.** 99

GRIOTTE-CHAMBERTIN GRAND CRU, GEVREY-CHAMBERTIN

Griotte-Chambertin is the smallest Grand Cru appellation in Gevrey-Chambertin, totaling 2.7 hectares, and Dugat farms just 0.16 hectares, producing between one to two barrels a year. Griotte-Chambertin is a reliable Grand Cru, farmed by nine quality-conscious growers who each make compelling wine. The vineyard lies atop an old quarry and, as can be expected, there is a large amount of fragmented chalk in the soil. Claude Dugat's parcel was planted in 1957, and the wine is intensely *aromatic* and more *graceful* compared with the Chapelle-Chambertin. The structure is certainly there, but the dark fruits and floral characters lift the wine, and the flavors dance on the palate. In vintages like 2007, 2010, and 2012, the wines are remarkable, combining strength with *finesse*. Although this wine can be approached earlier than the Chapelle-Chambertin, it ages just as long. Those who wait at least 10 years before opening this wine will be well rewarded. IN THREE WORDS *Penetrating, harmonious, rare.*

FOLLOWING PAGES Treading grapes for winemaking, mosaic in the Roman Amphitheatre in Mérida, Badajoz province, Spain.

DOMAINE COCHE-DURY

address	25 Rue Charles Giraud, 21190 Meursault, Burgundy, France Tel: + 33 3 80 21 24 12 Fax: + 33 3 80 21 67 65
contact	Raphaël Coche
farming philosophy	Lutte raisonnée, minimal spraying; very low yields; massal selection.
in the cellar	Long, slow fermentation; frequent lees stirring; extended barrel maturation of 18-22 months; minimal new oak use except for top wines, up to 50%; reds are destemmed.
total vineyard area	10.4 hectares

total annual production	50,000 bottles

key vineyard holdings

White		Red	
Corton-Charlemagne Grand Cru	0.68 ha	Volnay Premier Cru	0.39 ha
Meursault-Genevrières Premier Cru	0.21 ha	Pommard Vaumuriens	0.34 ha
Meursault-Caillerets Premier Cru	0.18 ha	Auxey-Duresses	0.50 ha
Meursault Premier Cru Les Perrières	0.60 ha	Monthélie	0.28 ha
Puligny-Montrachet Les Enseignères	0.50 ha		
Meursault Les Chevalières	0.13 ha		
Meursault Les Rougeots	0.73 ha		
Meursault	3.00 ha		

The first sip of Coche-Dury Meursault is unforgettable: It stops you in your tracks, the surroundings fade away, and there is only that moment, sharp and vivid, just you and the wine. Jean-François has redefined Meursault, and he has opened my eyes to the realization that Meursault can possess immense power and depth yet be restrained and quietly intellectual.

Since Jean-François Coche-Dury took over from his father, starting in 1972, the wines have risen to cult status. Its wines are the single most sought after whites from Burgundy, and the

MISE EN BOUTEILLES A LA PROPRIÉTÉ

prices reflect this. During Jean-François's nearly 40 years managing the estate, he expanded its holdings, significantly reduced yields, replanted old vines individually with massal selection, and extended aging up to 22 months with limited new oak use.

Jean-François is a living legend who rarely gives interviews or markets his wine. The domaine has a policy of not allowing any journalists to taste its wines from barrel, so all of my experience, except for one vintage that I was allowed to taste in the cellar with a television crew, is with bottled wines. Coche-Dury doesn't need any press coverage or better communication—the wines speak for themselves loud and clear. Jean-François retired in 2010, handing over the reins to his son Raphaël, who is the fourth generation in the family to run the estate. Young and very serious, Raphaël is making incremental changes to the vineyard and winery, respecting the prodigious work his father has done before him. There is now a pneumatic press and more plowing and organic principles followed in the vineyard.

A visit to its modest cellars reveals no secrets and nothing unusual: The winery is clean,

the wines are carefully looked after while they undergo a slow, long fermentation, followed by a protracted aging process with minimal new oak. When questioned about the intensity and depth that his wines are capable of achieving, Raphaël just shrugs his shoulders and points to the vineyard. "Quality comes from there," he replies. Old vines certainly help; his Meursault Genevrières dates back to 1947, and some of his Village Meursault vines date back to 1930.

Coche-Dury fully deserves its crowned status as the king of white Burgundy, and it achieved this without many Grand Cru vineyards. This 10-hectare domaine redefines and elevates Meursault and also imparts some of that magic to its other wines, including Pommard, Monthélie, Auxey-Duresses, Puligny-Montrachet, and its majestic Corton-Charlemagne. Its Village Meursault is stunning, as is its Bourgogne Blanc, made from old vines dating back to 1930 and 1958; both are worth seeking out and allow a peek into the estate's style and quality. All Coche-Dury white wines are age-worthy and offer a once-in-a-lifetime experience—it is truly one of the greatest estates in the world.

CORTON–CHARLEMAGNE GRAND CRU, ALOXE–CORTON

Corton-Charlemagne is the single largest Grand Cru vineyard for white Burgundy, at 71 hectares, which includes the small area destined to be Charlemagne Grand Cru. Thus Corton-Charlemagne is bound to be diverse in expression as well as in quality. In comparison, Montrachet is tiny, only 8 hectares, and Bâtard-Montrachet 12 hectares. Coche-Dury's Corton-Charlemagne waves away the vineyard's mixed reputation by producing wines of immense depth and stature. The wines are powerful without being excessive or overripe. Flavors explode on the palate in succession, supported by *remarkable* acidity, firm structure, and depth. There are only a handful of producers who can achieve this level of brilliance, and Coche-Dury is one of them. When I tasted a 20-year-old Corton-Charlemagne in 2010, I wrote that the wine was still extremely youthful and would benefit from another 5 years in bottle. The wines have a life span similar to red wines, and thus benefit from patience and cellaring for a minimum of 10 to 12 years. The power in the wine doesn't just come from the *focused* flavors, it comes mainly from a *steely* minerality that forms the backbone of all Coche-Dury wines. The wine leaves you humble, at a loss for words; for what can be said in the presence of such beauty?

IN THREE WORDS *Magnificent, powerful, regal*

MEURSAULT PREMIER CRU LES PERRIÈRES, MEURSAULT

Coche-Dury *finesse* and precision is in every wine, and even vintage variations play a minor role in these **astonishing** wines. It is this level of consistency and spectacular quality that make its wines so coveted among wine lovers around the world. IN THREE WORDS *Striking, intense, lingering.*

Coche-Dury has three Meursault Premiers Crus, all minute holdings of between one-fifth and three-fifths of a hectare in size. Perrières is my favorite of the three, and it happens to be the largest parcel, so it is relatively more commercially available than the Genevrières and the Caillerets. It is Meursault Village and the Premiers Crus that placed on Coche-Dury the mantle of the greatest white wine producer, and these wines rarely disappoint, if you can find them. Caillerets is the lightest of the three Premiers Crus, and more approachable in its youth; Genevrières is aromatic and gorgeous, but with slightly less depth and *intensity* compared with the Perrières in many vintages. You can't go wrong with any of the three Meursaults, or even the Village-level Meursault, which is a blend of multiple vineyards. The signature

DOMAINE COMTE ARMAND

address	7 Rue de la Mairie, 21630 Pommard, Burgundy, France www.domaine-comte-armand.com Tel: +33 3 80 24 70 50
contact	Paul Zanetti
farming philosophy	Fully biodynamic since 2001.
in the cellar	Bunches are destemmed; short pre-fermentation cold maceration; 4-week extended maceration; aged 18-24 months in 30% new barrels.

total vineyard area	10 hectares	**total annual production**		45,000 bottles
key vineyard holdings	Pommard Premier Cru		Auxey-Duresses Rouge Premier Cru	1.08 ha
	Clos des Épeneaux Monopole	5.25 ha	Auxey-Duresses Rouge Largillas	0.49 ha
	Volnay Premier Cru Les Frémiets	0.39 ha	Volnay	1.18 ha

POMMARD PREMIER CRU CLOS DES ÉPENEAUX MONOPOLE, POMMARD

In Pommard there is a clear quality pyramid, and at the top sits Clos des Épeneaux. (Pommard has 28 Premiers Crus, having refused the Grand Cru designation when it was offered in 1936.) Just below Clos des Épeneaux are Les Petits Épenots and Les Grands Épenots. These two Premier Cru vineyards are over 10 hectares each, while Clos des Épeneaux is half that size, the sole monopole of Comte Armand, which has owned it for nearly 200 years. The wines were very good but did not reach their full potential until the talented Pascal Marchand arrived in 1985. He left after 14 years and was replaced by another hugely talented young winemaker, Benjamin Leroux, in 1999. After 15 vintages, Leroux passed the responsibility to Paul Zanetti. During Marchand's period the wines were meeting the vineyard's potential, but it was really Leroux who **elevated** and refined the style into a **sumptuous**, linear wine that can confidently claim its position at the top rank of Pommard's Premiers Crus. Unfortunately, with hail and other climatic challenges since 2010, the yields have been minuscule until the 2017 vintage. Despite these setbacks, quality has remained high, with none of the Pommard's grainy tannins and rugged edge. Vintages like 2002, 2005, 2010, and 2012 show what this Clos is capable of offering. The old vines, averaging around 55 years, create wines of authority, concentration, and **impressive** depth of flavor, suggesting it is best approached at least 10 years after bottling, like a Grand Cru.

IN THREE WORDS *Authoritative, refined, concentrated.*

Pommard

APPELLATION POMMARD 1ER CRU CONTRÔLÉE

CLOS DES EPENEAUX

MONOPOLE

Comte Armand

PROPRIETAIRE A POMMARD (CÔTE-D'OR)-FRANCE

DOMAINE COMTE GEORGES DE VOGÜÉ

Domaine Comte Georges de Vogüé is a historic domaine dating back to 1450, producing some of the most ethereal, complex, elegant wines in Burgundy. It has extensive holdings throughout Chambolle-Musigny, nearly 12.5 hectares, including some of the most sought-after Grand Cru vineyards, like Musigny and Bonnes-Mares. Chambolle-Musigny has a very high percentage of active limestone, which adds to the refined, floral, and delicate nature of its wines.

The current owners of Vogüé represent the twentieth generation—Comtesse Claire de Causans and Marie de Ladoucette have employed a talented trio to manage the domaine: François Millet in winemaking, Éric Bourgogne in the vineyard, and Jean-Luc Pépin running commercial activities. Although the domaine is not certified organic, the vineyards are farmed organically; no herbicides or fertilizers are used, and plowing is done by horse or tractor. Little new oak is used during the maturation process; approximately 15% for the Village Chambolle and 35% for the Grands Crus.

Tasting with François Millet is a thoughtful, spiritual exercise. He always offers the most visual, poetic descriptions about the vintage and of the different wines produced at Vogüé. For the 2011s, he describes them as easy-to-enjoy jellies with the spirit of the late afternoon sun. The 2012s, on the other hand, are hard candies with a sweet, syrupy core embodying "the joy of living." The 2015 is brunch on a summer day, sitting out in the sunshine on your porch. François describes the vintages like images in a *manga* graphic novel—visual, colorful, sharp scenes that capture the essence of a mood and place.

Vogüé's wines are without doubt the epitome of Chambolle-Musigny; they embody its delicate soul and elegant nature. All of Vogüé's wines have Chambolle's glorious perfume, filled with exotic wildflowers and sweet red berries; they also have the silkiest tannins and a complex delicacy, together with intensity and length that only a handful of properties are able to achieve.

Much of their success has to do with the impressive vineyards they cultivate—Vogüé is the largest holder of Musigny Grand Cru vineyards, with 7 hectares out of a total of ten. Their wines are so sought after, at even the Village level, that prices are often much above those of their neighbors. Parcels are divided into older and younger vines, with only the grapes from the older vines going into Musigny Grand Cru. Grapes from younger-vine Musigny goes into the Chambolle-Musigny Premier Cru, or "baby Musigny," which offers excellent value. Vogüé has long been the reference for both Musigny and Bonnes-Mares; these are wines that caress the palate and inspire the soul.

address	7 Rue Sainte-Barbe, 21220 Chambolle-Musigny, Burgundy, France Tel: +33 3 80 62 86 25
contact	Jean-Luc Pépin and François Millet
farming philosophy	Organic principles.
in the cellar	Grapes are destemmed; minimal use of new oak, about one-third for Grands Crus.

total vineyard area	12.44 hectares	**total annual production**	45,000 bottles

key vineyard holdings	*Red*		Chambolle-Musigny Premier Cru	
	Musigny Grand Cru	6.46 ha	Les Baudes	0.13 ha
	Bonnes-Mares Grand Cru	2.67 ha	Chambolle-Musigny	1.81 ha
	Chambolle-Musigny Premier Cru			
	Les Amoureuses	0.56 ha	*White*	
	Chambolle-Musigny Premier Cru		Musigny Blanc	0.65 ha
	Les Fuées	0.15 ha		

85

CHAMBOLLE-MUSIGNY PREMIER CRU
LES AMOUREUSES, CHAMBOLLE-MUSIGNY

Les Amoureuses is one of 24 Premiers Crus in Chambolle-Musigny but is priced and considered at the same level as a Grand Cru. Located northeast of Musigny, just down the slope, this 5.4-hectare vineyard benefits from having some wonderful growers. Robert Groffier and Joseph Drouhin, the two largest landowners, make beautiful renditions; Vogüé is the third-largest grower, with half a hectare, and makes the most ethereal, persistent, and some would argue the best example. Another excellent producer of Les Amoureuses is Roumier, whose wine offers a convincing challenge to Vogüé every year. This limestone-rich vineyard is similar in composition to Musigny, contributing to the wine's finesse, silky tannins, and *glorious* bouquet. If Musigny is a refined gentleman (though in some vintages it is clearly a woman), then Les Amoureuses is his elegant, sophisticated wife. It is never massive or big, rather the wine is slender, pure, and graceful. It is friendlier, more *approachable* than Musigny, and lighter in weight, with a *captivating* subtlety that pulls you in. The best examples from vintages such as 1998, 2010, 2012, and 2015 are enchanting, like a feather-light kiss from the person you love.

IN THREE WORDS *Luminous, bewitching, graceful.*

Engraving showing medieval peasants working during the harvest, 19th century.

MUSIGNY GRAND CRU CUVÉE VIEILLES VIGNES, CHAMBOLLE-MUSIGNY

While Grand Cru wines like Chambertin and Richebourg vie for positioning based on their size, muscularity, and concentration, Musigny confidently watches from the sidelines. Its essence is not about strength or power, it is about finesse, delicacy, and length. This 10.7-hectare Grand Cru has 17 owners, among them about half a dozen who make outstanding wines. Vogüé reigns supreme in this vineyard, with 60% ownership, including a tiny portion dedicated to Chardonnay to produce the extremely rare Musigny Blanc. It was a bottle of Vogüé 1978 Musigny that made me fall in love with Burgundy, and with this vineyard, more than 20 years ago. I was so lost for words describing this wine that I called it "sheer poetry in a bottle," "so beautiful and

so perfect that it is surreal," and as intoxicating as a woman's perfume. I admit there were some disappointments, as is inevitable with great Burgundy, but wines from the 1990s in great condition are *extraordinary* experiences. Some of the most *memorable* vintages have been 1993, 1999, 2002, and 2005; the 2015 vintage tasted in barrel is one of the best young Musigny I have ever tasted. However, Musigny is Musigny because of its *consistency*, and even in weaker vintages there is something to love and admire about this wine. Strength is combined with beauty, grace, delicacy, and refined, silky tannins. This is a wine that offers a spiritual experience.

IN THREE WORDS *Intoxicating, evocative, spiritual.*

DOMAINE D'AUVENAY

Lalou Bize-Leroy's two other properties, Domaine Leroy and Maison Leroy, are much more famous than this modest winery in Saint-Romain. Domaine d'Auvenay is a smaller, more intimate property that she inherited from her father upon his death, when its core holdings consisted of Meursault and Auxey-Duresses. After buying out her sister's shares in 1990, Lalou Bize-Leroy became sole owner and expanded the vineyard holdings to its current size. Domaine d'Auvenay is also her private home, a place filled with fond memories of her late husband, Marcel, who passed away in 2004, and wonderful times entertaining and hosting wine tastings in the past. Now, she prefers to entertain in Vosne-Romanée, in the cellars of Domaine Leroy.

Since she took over the property, Bize-Leroy converted the vineyards first to organic principles then to biodynamics. Just like at Domaine Leroy, yields are extremely low, and whole bunches are preferred to destemming for the reds. Here, the term *microvinification* applies to all the wines she produces. The total yield for most of her wines is just a few barrels, less than 600 bottles of each wine per year. The total production of d'Auvenay ranges between 300 to 400 12-bottle cases annually.

The white wines from d'Auvenay are breathtaking. Although she makes stunning reds such as Bonnes-Mares and Mazis-Chambertin, it is her racy, dazzling white wines that place this winery on the top of the list as Burgundy's premier white wine producer. In recent years,

the wines have become more precise and focused, less powerful and ripe than in the past, making them sinewy with great purity of flavors. Some may disagree and point to Coche-Dury, Ramonet, or Leflaive as contenders, but in my mind, no white wines have this level of minerality and complexity ensconced in a lithe body with incredible depth.

Lalou Bize-Leroy is a very private, controversial figure in Burgundy, and the wines of d'Auvenay more than from any of her other wineries offer a peek into her private life. She stands apart, clearly ahead of the pack, and like her wines, she is tenacious, focused, with an uncompromising commitment to quality.

address	Village Bas, 21190 Saint-Romain, Burgundy, France www.domaine-leroy.com Tel: + 33 3 80 21 21 10
contact	Lalou Bize-Leroy
farming philosophy	Organic and biodynamic since 1988.
in the cellar	Whole bunch for reds, with barrel maturation in new oak, mainly François Frères Tronçais barrels in temperature-controlled cellars.

total vineyard area	4.8 hectares	total annual production	4,000–6,000 bottles

key vineyard holdings	*White*
	Bâtard-Montrachet Grand Cru 0.30 ha
	Chavalier-Montrachet Grand Cru 0.16 ha
	Criots-Bâtard-Montrachet Grand Cru 0.06 ha
	Meursault Premier Cru
	  Les Gouttes d'Or 0.20 ha
	Puligny-Montrachet Premier Cru
	  Les Folatières 0.27 ha
	Puligny-Montrachet En la Richarde 0.24 ha
	Puligny-Montrachet Les Enseignères 0.63 ha
	Meursault Goutte d'Or 0.20 ha
		Meursault Chaume des Perrières 0.08 ha
		Meursault Les Narvaux 0.73 ha
		Meursault Pré de Manche 0.10 ha
		Auxey-Duresses Les Boutonniers 0.26 ha
		Auxey-Duresses Les Clous 0.31 ha
		Auxey-Duresses La Macabrée 0.63 ha
		Bourgogne Aligoté Sous Châtelet 0.32 ha
		
		Red
		Bonnes-Mares Grand Cru 0.26 ha
		Mazis-Chambertin Grand Cru 0.26 ha

CHEVALIER–MONTRACHET GRAND CRU, PULIGNY–MONTRACHET

This is a tiny parcel, even by Burgundian standards, less than one-fifth of a hectare, producing a mere 500-800 bottles a year. The wine is so rare that a decades-long Leroy collector told me he has never tasted the Chevalier-Montrachet. This small Grand Cru vineyard was added to the domaine in 1992, just a few years after the addition of Puligny-Montrachet Les Folatières and the Criots-Bâtard-Montrachet. The red Grands Crus were added to d'Auvenay's portfolio a few years later. While the even rarer Criots-Bâtard-Montrachet may be the dream wine, it is with Chevalier-Montrachet that Lalou Bize-Leroy shows herself most aptly: impressive presence, tensile strength, precision, elegance, and poise from start to finish. The wines are *magical*, and starting with the 2000 vintage the wines are consistently sublime. Recent standouts include 2001, 2004, 2010, 2011, and 2012. The wine that confirmed my opinion of d'Auvenay being the greatest producer of white Burgundy was the 2010 vintage, which went beyond my expectations: This wine can bring you to tears with its sheer beauty and *haunting*, persistent minerality. While her other brilliant minute-quantity Grands Crus such as Bâtard-Montrachet and Criots-Bâtard-Montrachet evoke awe,

Chevalier-Montrachet evokes raw *emotion*. For a more affordable glimpse into d'Auvenay's white wine universe, try the humble Auxey-Duresses Blanc or the crisp, herbal Bourgogne Aligoté.

IN THREE WORDS *Sublime, eloquent, poised.*

MAZIS–CHAMBERTIN GRAND CRU, GEVREY–CHAMBERTIN

A quarter-hectare of the Mazis-Chambertin vineyard was purchased by Lalou Bize-Leroy in 1994 from the Collignon family, from whom she had been buying fruit for many years. With Bize-Leroy's commitment to very low yields, only several hundred bottles are available for the entire world per year. I have been fortunate to taste the Mazis-Chambertin alongside Bonnes-Mares in multiple vintages, and most of the time I prefer the Mazis. In vintages like 1999, the wine is finely etched, still formidable and hardly showing its age. Even at nearly 20 years old, I feel it would benefit from several more years of cellaring. What distinguishes the d'Auvenay Mazis-Chambertin from the Maison Leroy rendition is the finer structure and greater detail in its expression. Domaine d'Auvenay creates magic with its white wines, and the same delicate, linear touch can be found in the reds. The *tension* and purity, rather than strength or power, is unrivaled in the Domaine d'Auvenay Mazis-Chambertin. But these are not delicate nor are they light; this is a wine built for the long haul, one that requires patience and time. Great vintages like 2005 and 2010 are best kept until they turn 25 or 30 years old. Even the earliest vintages from the 1990s are youthful and tightly wound. More approachable vintages like 2001 show a glimpse of the wine's greatness—a palate filled with **exotic** spices and dark berries wrapped around a **sinewy**, taut body.

IN THREE WORDS **Formidable, precise, linear.**

MEURSAULT LES NARVAUX, MEURSAULT

This is no ordinary Village Meursault, and the market has anointed it superstar status and priced it accordingly: At US$1,500 per bottle for the latest vintage, prices are higher than most Grand Cru wines from other domaines. Ignore the Village classification and the mediocre ratings for d'Auvenay's Meursault Narvaux found online. Enough buyers know the inherent quality of these wines and are happy to pay up—a great example

of how the market, more than the prestige of the vineyard, the vintage, or the critics, rules Burgundy. This wine epitomizes the ability of Domaine d'Auvenay to craft astonishing wines from even humble sites and firmly places it at the top of the ranks. The vines are over 60 years old, and the yields are kept low to increase concentration, but even with this formula no one has been able to craft Village Meursault into an inspiring wine filled with energy and **vibrancy**—at once refined, voluminous, and **sizzling** with minerality and acidity. Vintages like the great 2010 tasted blind could certainly pass for a Grand Cru—there is enough depth, intensity, and length for the wine to be in the same league. The best aspect of Meursault Narvaux is that at every stage of its life one can enjoy a different facet of its beauty: In the first decade the wine is floral, minerally, and focused; in the next decade the wine is more nutty, buttery, and gains depth; in the third decade the wine is **ethereal**, silky, and still intense, with the perfume of aged Sauternes and a palate of dried jasmine flowers and honeysuckle.

IN THREE WORDS **Inspiring, dazzling, impressive.**

DOMAINE D'EUGÉNIE

(FORMERLY RENÉ ENGEL)

address	14 Rue de la Goillotte, 21700 Vosne-Romanée, Burgundy, France domaine-eugenie.com Tel: + 33 3 80 61 10 54
contact	Frédéric Engerer
farming philosophy	Organic and biodynamic viticulture.
in the cellar	Combination of whole bunch and destemming depending on vintage and wine; cold maceration; aged 15-18 months for Grands Crus in 75% new oak, 15 months for Premiers Crus in 40% new oak, and 12 months for Village wines in 30% new oak.

total vineyard area	5.09 hectares	**total annual production**	20,000 bottles

key vineyard holdings	*Red*		*White*	
	Grands Échezeaux Grand Cru	0.50 ha	Montrachet Grand Cru	0.04 ha
	Clos de Vougeot Grand Cru	1.36 ha	Bâtard-Montrachet Grand Cru	0.04 ha
	Échezeaux Grand Cru	0.55 ha	Meursault Premier Cru Les Porusots	0.08 ha
	Vosne-Romanée Premier Cru		Chassagne-Montrachet Les Perclos	0.24 ha
	Les Brûlées	1.16 ha		
	Vosne-Romanée Clos d'Eugénie	0.57 ha		
	Vosne-Romanée	2.36 ha		

GRANDS ÉCHEZEAUX GRAND CRU, VOSNE–ROMANÉE

This is an old estate disguised as a young one: Domaine d'Eugénie was established in 2006 after the Artémis group purchased the estate of Domaine René Engel, with land holdings that belonged to the family dating back before World War I. René was an influential figure who was a professor at the University of Dijon and co-founded the Confrérie des Chevaliers du Tastevin, together with Camille Rodier and Jacques Prieur. When René's grandson Philippe Engel, who had resurrected the reputation and quality of the wines from 1988 to 2006, suddenly died of a heart attack, the estate was sold to Artémis, a company founded by François Pinault, which owns numerous prestigious wine estates, including Château Latour and Clos de Tart. Since the inaugural 2006 vintage, Frédéric Engerer manages the domaine while Michel Mallard makes the wines, refining and modernizing the Engel style. Organic and biodynamic viticulture is now practiced, and a new cellar was built in 2009. There are only six wines, including three Grands Crus, made in this small estate. Depending on the year, my favorite wine is either the Clos de Vougeot or the Grands Échezeaux. This is testament to its wonderful 1.3-hectare Clos de Vougeot parcel, made up of ancient vines offering consistently high-quality wines. For other estates, this Grand Cru vineyard normally ranks much lower in quality than the Grands Échezeaux, but at d'Eugénie the wines are sumptuous, deep, and incredibly complex. As good as the Clos de Vougeot can be, in most years I prefer the Grands Échezeaux, with its fine-grained tannins, intense minerality, and **gorgeous** bouquet. There is an added **dimension** of flavors and depth to this wine that doesn't exist in the Clos de Vougeot, a nobility and **stature** that shows itself in the finish. I am a huge fan of the 2010, 2012, and 2016 vintages: They are worth seeking out and laying down for a minimum of 15 years.

IN THREE WORDS *Noble, refined, complex.*

VOLNAY PREMIER CRU EN CAILLERETS CLOS DES 60 OUVRÉES, VOLNAY

Pousse d'Or is an ancient estate dating back to the Dukes of Burgundy. It was part of the vast Duvault-Blochet estate in the 19th century, which included Clos de Tart and Romanée-Conti vineyards. The estate went through many private hands, with inconsistent quality, until Gérard Potel managed it from 1964 to his sudden death in 1997. Its modern history begins with businessman Patrick Landanger, who purchased the estate in 1997. The vineyard and cellar have been totally revitalized, and Patrick's son Benoît has taken over the estate's management since 2018. The holdings have expanded to 17 hectares and now include five Grands Crus and 12 Premier Cru vineyards, most farmed biodynamically. While there were a few dips in the beginning, when Landanger took over the estate with no background in agriculture or winemaking, the winery is now back on track. At the heart of the estate's history and portfolio are the magnificent Volnay Premier Cru parcels, of which they own four, including three monopoles. Starting with the 2002 vintage, the wines have become finer, with greater detail and purity; the 2005 is another star vintage. Since the 2008 vintage, the winery has consistently been producing elegant, *ethereal* Volnays, among which, for me, the Clos des 60 Ouvrées, with vines dating back to the 1950s, is the pinnacle: It combines dazzling, *delicate* aromatics, ballerina-like lightness, silky-fine tannins, and a minerally, intense core along with a *lingering* finish. The terroir is magnificent, a 2.4-hectare clos in stony limestone soil located within Les Caillerets, considered by many to be the finest Premier Cru in Volnay. This domaine is a rising star, especially with Benoît now at the helm, and its investment and dedication to quality will likely pay off in the coming decade.

IN THREE WORDS *Elegant, graceful, sophisticated.*

DOMAINE DE LA POUSSE D'OR

© La Pousse d'Or

address	8 Rue de la Chapelle, 21190 Volnay, Burgundy, France https://lapoussedor.fr Tel: + 33 3 80 21 61 33
contact	Benoît Landanger
farming philosophy	Biodynamic viticulture.
in the cellar	Destemming; cold maceration; gravity flow; matured up to 18 months in one-third new oak; whites matured up to 18 months in larger 350-liter barrels.

total vineyard area	17 hectares	**total annual production**	90,000 bottles

key vineyard holdings			
Reds		Volnay Premier Cru En Caillerets	2.24 ha
Clos de la Roche Grand Cru	0.34 ha	Volnay Premier Cru En Caillerets	
Bonnes-Mares Grand Cru	0.17 ha	Clos des 60 Ouvrées Monopole	2.39 ha
Corton Grand Cru Clos du Roi	1.45 ha	Volnay Premier Cru	
Corton-Bressandes Grand Cru	0.48 ha	Clos de la Pousse d'Or Monopole	2.13 ha
Chambolle-Musigny Premier Cru		Volnay Premier Cru	
Les Amoureuses	0.20 ha	Clos d'Audignac Monopole	0.80 ha
Chambolle-Musigny Premier Cru		Pommard Premier Cru Les Jarolières	1.44 ha
Les Charmes	0.19 ha	Santenay Premier Cru Clos Tavannes	2.09 ha
Chambolle-Musigny Premier Cru			
Les Feusselottes	0.42 ha	*White*	
Chambolle-Musigny Premier Cru		Chevalier-Montrachet Grand Cru	0.20 ha
Les Groseilles	0.36 ha	Puligny-Montrachet Premier Cru	
Chambolle-Musigny Premier Cru	0.32 ha	Clos du Cailleret	0.73 ha
Chambolle-Musigny	1.49 ha		

DOMAINE DE LA ROMANÉE-CONTI

Domaine de la Romanée-Conti has no equal, and one can say the same for the person at its helm, Aubert de Villaine. For more than four decades, since 1974, Aubert de Villaine has worked tirelessly toward one goal: to continually strive for excellence and quality. One prominent Burgundian winegrower said to me, "Aubert is not just a leader for us, he is like a god."

Every time I meet Aubert de Villaine, he reminds me that he is "just" a custodian—it happens to be that the vineyards he looks after are some of greatest vineyards of Burgundy. All the steps he has taken over the past several decades—to introduce organic farming in 1985 then biodynamics, strict pruning, and very low yields—are to allow the terroir to speak through the wine. He says his role is minor and fleeting and is quick to add that credit must also be given to his great team, including his nephew Bertrand de Villaine and young cellar master Alexandre Bernier, who took over from Bernard Noblet. The co-director of this leading domaine is Perrine Fenal, the daughter of Lalou Bize-Leroy, appointed after the death of Henri-Frédéric Roch in 2018.

For connoisseurs, Domaine de la Romanée-Conti, also known as DRC, is the pinnacle of Burgundy. What other domaine manages over 27 hectares of Grand Cru wines, in the heart of Vosne-Romanée, in the region's most coveted vineyards? From the floral, silky Romanée-Saint-Vivant to the powerful and charismatic La Tâche,

address	1 Place de l'Église, 21700 Vosne-Romanée, Burgundy, France www.romanee-conti.com Tel +33 3 80 62 48 80
contact	Aubert de Villaine, Bertrand de Villaine, Perrine Fenal
farming philosophy	Biodynamic cultivation, with densely planted vines that average 40-50 years old.
in the cellar	Whole bunch use varies by vintage, from 70% to 100%; natural pre-maceration, length of time depending on vintage; reds aged 18 months in 100% new French oak.
total vineyard area	27.8 hectares, including *fermage*, or rented vineyards
total annual production	75,000-85,000 bottles

	Romanée-Conti Grand Cru	1.81 ha	Échezeaux Grand Cru	4.67 ha
	La Tâche Grand Cru	6.06 ha	Corton Grand Cru Clos du Roi	0.57 ha
key vineyard holdings	Richebourg Grand Cru	3.51 ha	Corton Bressandes Grand Cru	1.19 ha
	Romanée-Saint-Vivant Grand Cru	5.29 ha	Corton Renardes Grand Cru	0.51 ha
	Grands Échezeaux Grand Cru	3.53 ha	Le Montrachet Grand Cru	0.68 ha

DRC has within its holdings eight unique, highly desirable wines. All eight easily qualify to be included in this list of 100, but only six were chosen due to space constraints.

DRC is a discreet domaine, and even its new winery refurbished in 2011, the former cellar of the Saint-Vivant monks, is modern and understated. DRC is the single most celebrated, most collectible, and most coveted domaine in Burgundy. However, success has its price, and in 2010 there was a foiled threat to poison the vineyards, and in 2012 it was revealed that counterfeiter Rudy "Dr. Conti" Kurniawan, arrested by the FBI, had created numerous counterfeit DRC wines that had been circulating in the market during the previous ten years. Now DRC has one of the most sophisticated traceability systems, in which each bottle since the 2010 vintage can be traced through its distribution chain.

Those fortunate enough to have tasted the range of DRC wines often argue that the signature of the domaine is as strong as the signature of the vineyard. DRC wines, even the delicate and refined Romanée-Saint-Vivant, are more structured and almost muscular compared with the same wine from different vignerons. This core intensity and energy in all the DRC wines ensures their ability to age for as long as top red Bordeaux wines. This incomparable domaine sets the standards and raises the bar for quality higher and higher every year, and to be able to experience their wines at their peak is a once-in-a-lifetime opportunity.

GRANDS ÉCHEZEAUX GRAND CRU, VOSNE–ROMANÉE

DRC is the largest owner of Grands Échezeaux, farming 3.5 hectares. It is also the third-largest vineyard in DRC's portfolio, and yet only around 15,000 bottles are produced per year. It is one-quarter the size of Échezeaux Grand Cru, and a distinct step up in quality in comparison. In tight vintages like 2014, its excellent Comblanchien limestone and stony soils show their superiority by offering greater depth and generosity. Often, young Grands Échezeaux can be closed, wound up tight and hardly expressive. However, at around 20 years old, the wine begins to unravel and show its **magnificent** colors. The 1999, tasted numerous times over the past five years, is now at its peak and showing beautifully. The words I used to describe it were *magical, intense,* and *sheer delight.* Another **glorious** vintage to enjoy now is the 1993, which is **complex**, serious, and long. The 1990 is another beauty that is at its peak. On the other hand, great vintages like 2005 and 2002 deserve patience and are best approached in 2022 or later.

IN THREE WORDS *Serious, deep, magical.*

LA TÂCHE GRAND CRU MONOPOLE, VOSNE–ROMANÉE

If Romanée-Conti is the king in Domaine de la Romanée-Conti's portfolio, then La Tâche is the eldest son and heir apparent. Part of what makes La Tâche one of the most desirable wines from Burgundy is that it is more widely available compared with the minuscule amounts of Romanée-Conti produced, and it is always more expressive. This is one of DRC's two monopoles, and by far the larger of the two—while Romanée-Conti is 1.81 hectares, La Tâche is 6.06 hectares. If Romanée-Conti expresses the serious, cerebral, spiritual aspect of great Burgundy, then La Tâche expresses its joie de vivre. When tasted side by side from the same vintage, La Tâche is clearly more forceful, more vigorous, and well defined; it is also earlier maturing and much easier to enjoy young. At its heart, La Tâche is as powerful as it is *expressive* and as profound as it is *colorful*. I have tasted over 25 different vintages of La Tâche, and one key theme emerges: a high level of consistency and power. While my ratings and notes for other wines in DRC's portfolio can change widely by vintage, tasting date, or tasting conditions, La Tâche is consistently impressive, even in its youth. The variation between 2012 or 2013, for example, is merely one of style, since overall quality is still extremely high. Even

vintages like 1988 and 1989, considered good but not great years, were excellent for La Tâche. The 1990 is *sublime* and one of my favorite wines of all time. The best vintages to enjoy now are from the mid-to-late 1980s. While great vintages like 1978 and 1971 can be superb, there is much greater consistency now than there was 40 years ago. It is in the lesser vintages of La Tâche that one can taste the class and breeding that sets this vineyard and wine apart. IN THREE WORDS *Powerful, profound, glorious.*

MONTRACHET GRAND CRU, CHASSAGNE–MONTRACHET

This is the rarest wine in DRC's portfolio and its only commercial white wine, with around 2,000 bottles produced per year. Its other white, Bâtard-Montrachet, is made in such tiny quantities that it is only available at the domaine. Bâtard-Montrachet, with its sheer power and intensity, is like no other white wine I have ever come across in Burgundy; Montrachet, on the other hand, is much more refined, majestic, and subtle, yet no less intense. Many consider Montrachet the greatest dry white wine in the world, and I would have to agree. This narrow 8-hectare strip lies mid-slope, with Chevalier-Montrachet just above it and Bâtard-Montrachet

RICHEBOURG GRAND CRU, VOSNE–ROMANÉE

DRC is the largest owner of Richebourg, farming 44% of this 8-hectare Grand Cru site. There is an interesting debate surrounding this Grand Cru vineyard and the late addition of the 3-hectare Les Verroilles portion of it. Highly regarded author and physician Dr. Jules Lavalle wrote a seminal book about the great wines and the top vineyard sites of Burgundy, and he describes the Verroilles portion as being inferior to the core Richebourg vineyard. While the debate about the quality from the different sites continues, DRC blends the 2.5-hectare site from Les Richebourgs with the nearly 1-hectare site in Les Verroilles. This exceptional Grand Cru vineyard has 11 quality-conscious owners, with DRC's rendition leading the pack. Richebourg in its youth is **powerful** and muscular, and in ripe vintages like 2009 and 2003 it is lush and velvety. DRC's low yields, uncompromising vineyard work, and meticulous handling in the cellar mean its Richebourg is even more sumptuous and concentrated than other producers' versions. With time its black fruits turn into **seductive** decadence, its mineral character turns into seamless backbone, and its rich tannins into an **elegant** spine supporting its long life. The 1990 and 1996 are both mature and drinking beautifully now, while the 1995

below it. The quality of wine from this vineyard sliver was known for over 1,000 years, and in the hands of a great domaine like DRC, the terroir's resplendent characters are captured in a golden nectar that defies time. Young Montrachet like the 2008 offers a **heady** perfume of hazelnuts, jasmine flowers, and minerals, while one with a few decades, such as the 1999 or 1985, can be equally **enticing**, with butterscotch and toasted almonds. What is unusual is that this white wine ages like a red, gaining in **complexity** and depth with time. Vintages like the gorgeous 1966 or the ethereal 1978 show the wine's magnificence, revealing itself in stages with each passing decade. | IN THREE WORDS | *Transcendental, inimitable, regal.*

and 1999 vintages in comparison are still tightly wound and ungiving. Older vintages like the 1985 are still powerful and at their peak, and as long as storage conditions are good these great vintages should last 40 years easily. However, it is not just the best vintages that are gorgeous; less-heralded vintages like the 1969, 1966, or 1952 can be wonderful too—that is DRC Richebourg.

IN THREE WORDS *Sumptuous, opulent, muscular.*

ROMANÉE-CONTI GRAND CRU MONOPOLE, VOSNE-ROMANÉE

Romanée-Conti is a 1.81-hectare monopole, solely owned by DRC, and is treated with a reverence reserved for monarchs. It is clearly the king in DRC's portfolio, and for many, the king of red Burgundy. Romanée-Conti is the most intense Grand Cru, yet it is also reserved and thoughtful; the wine exudes breeding and class, possessing an inner quiet power that is majestic and at times breathtaking. Some wine lovers have been disappointed from their experience with

Romanée-Conti. This is often a combination of very high expectations (given its reputation, rarity, insane prices) and poor timing. Among all of DRC's Grands Crus, one needs to be the most patient with Romanée-Conti. My advice is to wait at least 15 years after the vintage, usually 20 is best, serve it at the correct temperature (15-18° C), and give it time—let it reveal itself in the glass slowly, preferably over a long, leisurely meal. At its youth, one senses the intensity of "somethingness," the power of the lingering finish, but the flavors are muted. At its peak, the wine is phenomenal, *majestic*, awe-inspiring, and its "somewhereness" shines. The 1996 or the 1999, for example, offers layer upon layer of intense black truffles interlaced with roasted herbs and a hint of cloves—the flavors changing and evolving with every sip. This wine is incredibly complex, youthful, and *vigorous* at nearly 20 years old. Older vintages like the 1971, 1966, and 1961 are still at their peak, *alluring* and alive, offering up a symphony of dark spices, savory herbs, forest floor, and black truffle notes. If you are not religious, this wine in the right vintage at its peak may change your mind; unfortunately, only 500 cases (12 bottles per case) are produced per year.

IN THREE WORDS *Magnificent, aristocratic, extraordinary.*

ROMANÉE-SAINT-VIVANT GRAND CRU, VOSNE-ROMANÉE

Romanée-Saint-Vivant is another Grand Cru vineyard where DRC dominates, owning 56% of the total. The ten key producers of this vineyard are all of the highest caliber, so buying a Romanée-Saint-Vivant is relatively risk-free. With its intoxicating perfume and finesse, it is hard not to fall in love with the wines. But up to the mid-1990s, DRC's Romanée-Saint-Vivant did not enjoy the highest reputation. My experience with the older vintages has been erratic—some were clearly disappointing, like the 1983 or 1986, and others like the 1985 and 1990 are beautifully ***delicate*** and elegant. Part of the reason may be due to the late acquisition of the vineyard compared with the other vineyards in DRC's portfolio (except for the much more recent Corton Grand Cru). DRC did not start making Romanée-Saint-Vivant until 1966, and it did not own the vineyard until 1988. I always loved the wine's ***seductive*** nose and its ***intoxicating*** lacy character, but in the past 20 years, the intensity and length of this wine has made me wonder if this vineyard is not better than even the Richebourg. In vintages like 2005 and 2010 one feels a tensile-like strength with an incredible finish that stands behind the delicacy and perfume. This is a wine of incredible finesse and elegance.

| IN THREE WORDS | ***Perfumed, exquisite, captivating.*** |

Poster for Les Vins de Bourgogne de Henri De Bahèzre, Nuits-St.-Georges, Côte d'Or, 1920.

DOMAINE DE LA VOUGERAIE

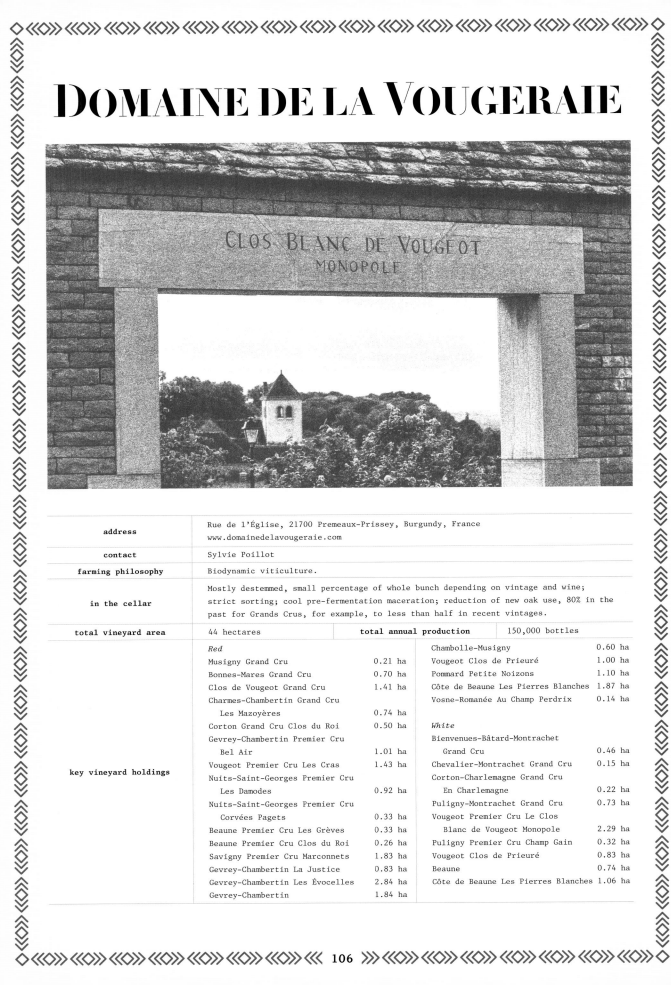

address	Rue de l'Église, 21700 Premeaux-Prissey, Burgundy, France www.domainedelavougeraie.com
contact	Sylvie Poillot
farming philosophy	Biodynamic viticulture.
in the cellar	Mostly destemmed, small percentage of whole bunch depending on vintage and wine; strict sorting; cool pre-fermentation maceration; reduction of new oak use, 80% in the past for Grands Crus, for example, to less than half in recent vintages.
total vineyard area	44 hectares

total annual production	150,000 bottles

key vineyard holdings

Red

Musigny Grand Cru	0.21 ha
Bonnes-Mares Grand Cru	0.70 ha
Clos de Vougeot Grand Cru	1.41 ha
Charmes-Chambertin Grand Cru Les Mazoyères	0.74 ha
Corton Grand Cru Clos du Roi	0.50 ha
Gevrey-Chambertin Premier Cru Bel Air	1.01 ha
Vougeot Premier Cru Les Cras	1.43 ha
Nuits-Saint-Georges Premier Cru Les Damodes	0.92 ha
Nuits-Saint-Georges Premier Cru Corvées Pagets	0.33 ha
Beaune Premier Cru Les Grèves	0.33 ha
Beaune Premier Cru Clos du Roi	0.26 ha
Savigny Premier Cru Marconnets	1.83 ha
Gevrey-Chambertin La Justice	0.83 ha
Gevrey-Chambertin Les Évocelles	2.84 ha
Gevrey-Chambertin	1.84 ha
Chambolle-Musigny	0.60 ha
Vougeot Clos de Prieuré	1.00 ha
Pommard Petite Noizons	1.10 ha
Côte de Beaune Les Pierres Blanches	1.87 ha
Vosne-Romanée Au Champ Perdrix	0.14 ha

White

Bienvenues-Bâtard-Montrachet Grand Cru	0.46 ha
Chevalier-Montrachet Grand Cru	0.15 ha
Corton-Charlemagne Grand Cru En Charlemagne	0.22 ha
Puligny-Montrachet Grand Cru	0.73 ha
Vougeot Premier Cru Le Clos Blanc de Vougeot Monopole	2.29 ha
Puligny Premier Cru Champ Gain	0.32 ha
Vougeot Clos de Prieuré	0.83 ha
Beaune	0.74 ha
Côte de Beaune Les Pierres Blanches	1.06 ha

VOUGEOT PREMIER CRU LE CLOS BLANC DE VOUGEOT MONOPOLE, VOUGEOT

This is a young estate created in 1999 by Jean-Claude Boisset to bring together the family's sizable 44-hectare holdings under one label. In the beginning, Pascal Marchand, who favored intense, fairly extracted wines, was in charge for six years. After his departure, Pierre Vincent did a marvelous job of defining the domaine's elegant, pure style, helped, no doubt, by biodynamic farming in the vineyard. Vincent left in 2016 and is now at Domaine Leflaive, but the style of Vougeraie remains unchanged. Some may accuse the top wines of going too far toward the light end of the spectrum, thereby crafting Musigny and Bonnes-Mares that are pale and ethereal, with a delicate touch. However, I support those that lean more toward the lighter end of the spectrum rather than its opposite. The entire portfolio from the Grand Cru vineyards, like Clos de Vougeot and Charmes-Chambertin, to its fruity, delicious Chambolle-Musigny is crafted with clarity, freshness, and a wonderful lightness. Among the numerous wines produced at this estate, I am a huge fan of its *gorgeous*, multifaceted Clos Blanc de Vougeot. It is a 2.3-hectare monopole on high limestone—content soil that was first planted with white wine nearly 1,000 years ago by the monks. Keeping with the centuries-old tradition of the wine being a blend of white varieties, this wine includes a small percentage of Pinot Blanc and Pinot Gris, the latter adding a *wonderful* savory spicy character to the wine. The wine ages gracefully, and vintages like 2008 were built to age as long as its Premier Cru reds. I am still enjoying this vintage now and keeping my 2014 and 2016 for the future. This is a special wine for many reasons: It is among the top five best white wines made in the Côte de Nuits; it is extremely rare, since very little Vougeot white wines are made and even less at the Premier Cru level; it is a monopole made by a single producer, so it is a *unique* expression. In sum, a white wine worthy of your cellar. IN THREE WORDS *Bewitching, harmonious, graceful.*

DOMAINE DE MONTILLE

address	Rue de But, 21190 Puligny-Montrachet, Burgundy, France www.demontille.com Tel: + 33 3 80 21 39 14
contact	Étienne de Montille
farming philosophy	Organic since 1995, biodynamic since 2005, officially certified in 2012.
in the cellar	Whole bunch use varies by vintage and by wine from none to 100%, with higher percentage usually for top wines; aged 16 months with minimal new oak, up to one-third for Premiers Crus and up to half for Grands Crus; all wines bottled with Diam technical cork closures.

total vineyard area	37 hectares (owned and farmed)	**total annual production**	180,000 bottles

key vineyard holdings			
Reds		Volnay Premier Cru Les Mitans	0.73 ha
Clos de Vougeot Grand Cru	0.29 ha	Volnay Premier Cru En Carelle	0.20 ha
Corton Clos du Roi Grand Cru	0.84 ha	Volnay Premier Cru Les Brouillards	0.37 ha
Vosne-Romanée Premier Cru		Beaune Premier Cru Les Grèves	1.26 ha
Les Malconsorts	0.89 ha	Beaune Premier Cru Les Perrières	0.64 ha
Vosne-Romanée Premier Cru		Beaune Premier Cru Les Sizies	1.62 ha
Les Malconsorts Cuvée Christiane	0.48 ha	Nuits-Saint-Georges Saint-Julien	0.58 ha
Nuits-Saint-Georges Premier Cru		Bourgogne Rouge	1.01 ha
Aux Thorey	0.73 ha		
Pommard Premier Cru Les Rugiens	1.02 ha	*White*	
Pommard Premier Cru Les Pézerolles	1.09 ha	Corton-Charlemagne Grand Cru	1.04 ha
Pommard Premier Cru		Puligny-Montrachet Premier Cru	
Les Grands Épenots	0.23 ha	Les Caillerets	0.85 ha
Volnay Premier Cru Les Taillepieds	1.51 ha	Beaune Premier Cru Les Aigrots	0.44 ha
Volnay Premier Cru Les Champans	0.96 ha	Meursault Les Narvaux	0.24 ha

VOSNE–ROMANÉE PREMIER CRU LES MALCONSORTS CUVÉE CHRISTIANE, VOSNE–ROMANÉE

Étienne de Montille explains to me that the domaine's recent expansion is simply reclaiming what once belonged to the family over a century ago. When Étienne de Montille joined his late father Hubert in 1983, eventually taking over in 1995, its initial holdings consisted of three hectares in Volnay and Pommard. Over many generations, his family once owned, but were forced to sell off, great vineyards like Musigny and Bonnes-Mares. Étienne has now expanded the estate to farm 37 hectares and established a successful négociant business, Maison de Montille. Étienne is a modern Renaissance man, a globe-trotter who is equally comfortable in the kitchen cooking, talking about wine with collectors in Hong Kong, or tending his vineyards in Burgundy, California, or Hokkaido. He is an extremely intelligent, thoughtful man who did not quite give up his former legal profession, specializing in mergers and acquisitions: He has initiated complex banking deals to expand his family estate. In 2005 he acquired the Thomas-Moillard estate with the Seysses family (Domaine Dujac), and in 2012 he acquired Château de Puligny-Montrachet.

The 2005 purchase included the **coveted** Malconsorts vineyard, just beside La Tâche and widely regarded as Grand Cru–level terroir in the best vintages. Cuvée Christiane comes from a half-hectare parcel that is practically inside the La Tâche vineyard. Named after Étienne's mother, this special parcel has more weight, **structure**, and **minerality** compared with Les Malconsorts. It is less fruity, less approachable, with more grip and power than the non-cuvée bottling. Recently I tried the 2009, and this ripe vintage was clearly too young to drink now. Treat Cuvée Christiane like a Grand Cru and put it away for at least 15 years. Best recent vintages to lay down include 2009, 2015, and 2016.

IN THREE WORDS · *Stately, lingering, beautiful.*

DOMAINE DENIS BACHELET

address	
3 Rue de la Petite Issue, 21220 Gevrey-Chambertin, Burgundy, France Tel: + 33 3 80 51 89 09	
contact	
Denis Bachelet	
farming philosophy	
Lutte raisonnée, no pesticides or herbicides.	
in the cellar	
Grapes destemmed; 1-week cold maceration; matured 18 months in 40% new oak for Villages, 50% for Premier Cru and Grand Cru wines.	
total vineyard area	
4 hectares	
total annual production	
20,000 bottles	
key vineyard holdings	

Charmes-Chambertin Grand Cru	0.43 ha
Gevrey-Chambertin Premier Cru Les Corbeaux	0.42 ha
Gevrey-Chambertin Les Évocelles	0.17 ha
Gevrey-Chambertin	1.42 ha
Côte de Nuits-Villages	1.04 ha
Bougogne Rouge	0.61 ha

CHARMES-CHAMBERTIN GRAND CRU VIEILLES VIGNES, GEVREY-CHAMBERTIN

This small, discrete domaine has a cultish following ever since the 1980s, when word got out about Denis Bachelet's skill as a vigneron. The wines he made in 1981, a challenging vintage, were outstanding, according to Jasper Morris. Winemaking skipped a generation in the Bachelet family: His grandparents had tiny holdings in Gevrey-Chambertin, but his father chose to settle in Belgium with his wife and was not interested in viticulture or winemaking. Denis decided early to be a vigneron and studied winemaking, eventually taking over the estate in the early 1980s. There were initially just 1.8 hectares, and over the years he grew this minuscule parcel into a small one. Now with his son Nicolas, who joined him in 2008, Denis is looking to expand. Denis is a humble, soft-spoken man and he smiles and gives direct answers about his grape-growing philosophy, which appears to be quite simple: Keep old vines and replace them one at a time, reject chemical use in the vineyard, destem all grapes, and do as little as possible in the cellar, including minimal new oak, to allow the wines to express themselves. That's it. It appears simple enough, but keeping alive vines that are more than 100 years old, such as the vineyards at both his Grand Cru and Village-level parcels, is backbreaking work that results in very low yields. Bachelet's Gevrey Village red, made from old vines, is frequently my top Village wine, with much more depth and complexity than one would expect at Village level; it often exceeds my expectations. Its finest wine, Charmes-Chambertin, is less than half a hectare and difficult to source. This large, diverse Grand Cru AOC does not have the best reputation, but Bachelet's two plots are in the prime Aux Charmes area (not Mazoyères), with vines planted in 1907 and 1917. His neighbors include Claude Dugat and Dugat-Py for the larger plot, and Joseph Roty for the smaller plot. The wines are *sumptuous*, elegant, and complex in their youth, and with a decade or more of bottle age they acquire *dazzling* aromatics and possess intense, refined flavors with an incredible finish. In recent years, since 2005, I have not tasted a weak vintage—even the light 2007 and 2011 vintages were *stunning*. This is a wine to experience at least once in a lifetime.

IN THREE WORDS *Gorgeous, refined, elegant.*

DOMAINE DENIS MORTET

address	5 Rue de Lavaux, 21220 Gevrey-Chambertin, Burgundy, France www.domaine-denis-mortet.com Tel: + 33 3 80 34 10 05		
contact	Arnaud Mortet		
farming philosophy	Lutte raisonnée, following organic principles.		
in the cellar	Grapes mostly destemmed; aged 18 months in François Frères barrels, mostly new for the Premiers Crus and Grands Crus.		
total vineyard area	12 hectares	**total annual production**	60,000 bottles

key vineyard holdings	Chambertin Grand Cru	0.15 ha	Gevrey-Chambertin Premier Cru
	Bonnes-Mares Grand Cru	0.35 ha	Champonnet 0.30 ha
	Mazis-Chambertin Grand Cru	0.20 ha	Gevrey-Chambertin Premier Cru
	Échezeaux Grand Cru	0.22 ha	Les Beaux Bruns 0.22 ha
	Clos de Vougeot Grand Cru	0.31 ha	Gevrey-Chambertin Premier Cru 0.25 ha
	Gevrey-Chambertin Premier Cru		Gevrey-Chambertin Mes Cinq Terroirs 5.56 ha
	Les Champeaux	0.41 ha	Fixin Champs Pennebaut 0.75 ha
	Gevrey-Chambertin Premier Cru		Marsannay Les Longeroies 1.12 ha
	Lavaux Saint-Jacques	1.16 ha	Bourgogne Pinot Noir 1.00 ha

Fifteen years ago, when I asked a highly regarded Burgundy grower, "Who is the next Henri Jayer?" his reply was, "Denis Mortet." It started out as a modest estate when Denis Mortet founded it in 1993, a vintage he launched to critical acclaim. He was building upon his father's legacy, for Charles Mortet had set up his own estate in 1956 with just 1 hectare of vines. In 1993, the property farmed 4.5 hectares, but Denis had bigger ambitions, and he lost no time acquiring vineyards from Gevrey-Chambertin and Chambertin Grand Cru to Marsannay. Currently the estate comprises 12 hectares and is run by Denis's wife, Laurence, and his son Arnaud.

Tragically, Denis took his own life in 2006, and since then Arnaud has been tasked to carry on his father's work and vision. Since acquiring his father's estate, split between himself and his brother Thierry, Denis shunned pesticides and herbicides and worked toward organic viticulture. He worked with Jacky Rigaux, researcher at the University of Bourgogne, to better understand the differences in his Gevrey-Chambertin parcels. He worked tirelessly in the vineyard trying to understand his land; he increased planting density and observed low yields. Arnaud continues to refine the work his father started in the vineyard, adhering to organic principles and taking it one step further by focusing on precision and detail in the wines.

Denis Mortet wines enjoyed a cult-like status in the 1990s among critics as well as a strong group of collectors who loved his dense, opulent, and oaky wines. Arnaud is stepping away from that style, opting instead to have a lighter touch, with less density and heaviness and much less overt oak influence. In the winery, the pump-over method (remontage) is favored over punch-down (pigéage) during extraction, and a shorter oak aging period to retain freshness. Since 2011, new oak has been reduced significantly. The results are impressive, and I am a big fan of the new direction the estate is taking. Since the 2008 vintage, the wines have become lighter, more precise, with wonderful minerality.

Denis Mortet would be very proud of his family, especially his son, who carries the torch and has continued to strive toward excellence. Today, Mortet's wines are considered the finest from Gevrey-Chambertin and among the most sought after. Its Bourgogne Rouge offers great value and is perennially one of my favorites—pretty, balanced, and delicious. Village Gevrey-Chambertin from its 5-hectare parcel is consistently good. It is with its Premiers Crus that Mortet distinguishes itself: Lavaux Saint-Jacques and Les Champeaux are both excellent examples of their respective vineyards, combining finesse and intensity.

Its Grands Crus are well deserving of their huge success. Mortet's Clos de Vougeot is one of the most elegant Vougeots produced, with refined tannins and wonderful depth. Bonnes-Mares is spicy and intense, with finely woven tannins, while the Chambertin, acquired in 1999, is the pièce de résistance. For me, this is the best wine in Mortet's portfolio and one of the best Chambertins produced. Arnaud is thriving in his new role and taking his family domaine to another level of excellence.

CHAMBERTIN GRAND CRU, GEVREY-CHAMBERTIN

Chambertin, despite its exalted reputation, can be a gamble for a buyer, since it is a fairly large Grand Cru, with nearly 13 hectares divided among 25 owners. There are at least a dozen great producers of Chambertin, including Dugat-Py, Dujac, Leroy, Ponsot, Rousseau, andTrapet. Mortet is certainly part of this company, and its Chambertin stands out for its precision and intensity. It is closer in style to Rousseau than Ponsot, and has the concentration of Dugat-Py but without its density. Sadly, there is just 0.15 hectare producing a few barrels, and in mean years like 2016, only one barrel was made. Despite its scarcity, it is well worth seeking out, for the wines are striking. Since 2008 there is more precision, and recent vintages such as 2010 and 2016 are *magnificent*. There is incredible *clarity* in the wines, which are sizzling with tension and minerality, and the 2016 is so beautiful it defies words and the 2017 is not far behind. It helps that the vines are over 60 years old, but applause goes to the family, who are able to coax such *soulful* music from this tiny, magical Grand Cru parcel.

IN THREE WORDS *Majestic, compelling, exceptional.*

GEVREY-CHAMBERTIN PREMIER CRU LES CHAMPEAUX, GEVREY-CHAMBERTIN

For the past ten years, this has consistently been my favorite among Mortet's Gevrey-Chambertin Premiers Crus. Navigating Gevrey-Chambertin's 26 Premiers Crus can be challenging. Les Champeaux is the northernmost Premier Cru, above Cazetières, on an east-facing exposition. This sizable vineyard is 6.7 hectares and around ten producers make wine from it. As with most Burgundian vineyards of this size, the interpretation of this site varies widely, ranging from fruity and fresh to dark and opulent. Mortet's Champeaux in the 1990s leaned toward the latter, but recent versions offer *silkier* texture and notes of crushed stone along with red fruits and firm structure. The twin vintages of 2015 and 2016 are wonderful examples of the *precision* and *elegance* this vineyard is now able to achieve under Araund Mortet's care.

IN THREE WORDS *Intense, inspiring, sensual.*

Diego Rivera, *Still Life*, 1913.

DOMAINE DES COMTES LAFON

address	5 Rue Pierre Joigneaux, 21190 Meursault, Burgundy, France www.comtes-lafon.fr Tel: + 33 3 80 21 22 17 Fax: + 33 3 80 21 61 64
contact	Dominique Lafon
farming philosophy	Biodynamic since 1998.
in the cellar	Long, protracted fermentation with minimal lees stirring; oak maturation for 16–18 months, no new oak for Villages, up to 70% for Charmes and Perrières, and 100% for Le Montrachet; Diam technological corks used for all white wines starting with the 2013 vintage; red grapes 100% destemmed, keeping berries whole, aged 18 months in 30% new oak.
total vineyard area	16.3 hectares
total annual production	85,000 bottles (excluding Mâcon and négociant bottlings)

key vineyard holdings				
White		Meursault	2.52 ha	
Le Montrachet Grand Cru	0.33 ha	Monthélie Blanc	0.15 ha	
Meursault Premier Cru Perrières	0.91 ha			
Meursault Premier Cru Genevrières	0.55 ha	*Red*		
Meursault Premier Cru Charmes	1.90 ha	Volnay Premier Cru		
Meursault Premier Cru Bouchères	0.30 ha	Les Santenots-du-Milieu	3.78 ha	
Meursault Premier Cru Porusots	0.96 ha	Volnay Premier Cru Clos des Chênes	0.38 ha	
Meursault Premier Cru Goutte d'Or	0.39 ha	Volnay Premier Cru Clos Champans	0.52 ha	
Meursault Clos de La Barre	2.12 ha	Monthélie Premier Cru Les Duresses	1.07 ha	
Meursault Désirée	0.43 ha			

Comtes Lafon has long been considered one of the finest estates in Meursault. This is partly due to its ideal parcels of top Meursault Premier Cru vineyards, partly to its historic reputation, and partly because of its exemplary wines. By the time Dominique Lafon took charge of the estate in 1985, his father, René, had done much of the work needed to put the estate into good order: Vineyards were replaced, wines were domaine bottled, and leased vineyards and share-cropping arrangements were returned to the estate. Dominique has continued to refine and upgrade the estate, and one of the most significant changes has been in the vineyard.

Dominique began by eliminating chemical treatments such as herbicides, insecticides, and fertilizers when he arrived. The estate became organic in 1992, and trials with biodynamic cultivation convinced him to convert; by 1998 all the vineyards were farmed biodynamically. There were stylistic changes too. My first encounter with Lafon's Meursaults was in the mid-1990s, when his wines were becoming hugely popular for their intense, buttery, extracted style. For many years, his wines, with their creamy richness, were benchmarks for powerful Meursaults. Although big, ripe Meursaults were not my preferred wines to drink, I could not deny their concentration and formidable style.

Ever since the conversion to biodynamics and the concerns over premature oxidation (or "premox," see page 24), Dominique has fine-tuned his winemaking and the style of the wines. Collectors reported Lafon's wines to be one of the worst affected with premox in the mid-1990s vintages; my personal experience supports this claim. This must have set off alarm bells, and Dominique made refinements to tackle the problem: less reductive handling at press, and allowing some of the juice to brown; lees stirring (*bâtonnage*) was reduced, with barrel rolling preferred; careful sulfur management to help stave off oxidation; corks with silicone coating (proven to reduce sulfur levels) eliminated. Other winemaking traditions have remained unchanged—long, protracted fermentation and malolactic fermentation, contact with fine lees during its 18 months of barrel maturation—all contributing to the wine's supple texture and incredible depth.

Lafon's Meursaults continue to have intensity and concentration, but they are much finer, less opulent, and better balanced now than in the past. Its red wines, which make up one-third of its production, are often overlooked. The Volnays are glorious expressions of the commune—intensely perfumed, pure and delicate, with fine-grained tannins. In recent years, its Premier Cru Volnay Santenots-du-Milieu is always among my top five favorite Volnays. Dominique's range of Mâcon whites are great value—he is crafting some of the most elegant, precise, delicious Mâcons at reasonable prices.

MEURSAULT PREMIER CRU LES PERRIÈRES, MEURSAULT

This is a stunning wine that I have fallen in love with since its 2005 vintage. Lafon's Perrières was always *gorgeous*, with great intensity and mineral concentration, but since 2005 it has achieved a level of *finesse* that was not there in the 1990s. The 2005 is purity plus intensity in a bottle; 2008 is outstanding and just starting to open up; the 2010, 2014, and 2015 are beauties in the making—well defined, with wonderful *clarity* and incredible length. These wines are so complete and fine that I think they are equivalent to Grand Cru wines. Since 2005, the estate has not missed a beat, with no weak vintages, and skillful handling of warm vintages like 2009. Lafon is picking early to retain freshness, tension, and vibrancy while losing none of the intensity and concentration. The estate is performing like a lovingly cared-for Stradivarius in the hands of a talented musician, producing hauntingly beautiful music for the soul. IN THREE WORDS *Dazzling, delicate, distinctive.*

MONTRACHET GRAND CRU, CHASSAGNE–MONTRACHET

Lafon's Montrachet has been part of the estate for 100 years, since 1918. In the past, the vineyard was farmed by the Morey family, until it was returned to Comtes Lafon in 1991. Lafon's parcel is located in the far southern corner of this 8-hectare Grand Cru vineyard, adjacent to DRC's parcel. Being on the Chassagne side (compared with the other half of the vineyard, which is in Puligny-Montrachet), the wines have immense weight and intensity. Chassagne-Montrachets have a reputation for being more muscular, powerful, and minerally, and Lafon's Montrachet is a great example. However, with biodynamic cultivation and a lighter touch in the cellar, the wine has become a bit more taut and *layered*, allowing some of its feminine facets and nuances to surface. If Meursault-Perrières offers chamber music, then Montrachet is a full orchestra offering a *symphony* of flavors that makes it a *memorable* experience worth seeking.

IN THREE WORDS *Formidable, multifaceted, persistent.*

66 **The estate is performing like a lovingly cared-for Stradivarius in the hands of a talented musician, producing hauntingly beautiful music for the soul.** 99

Pablo Picasso, *Still Life by Lamplight*, 5th state, 1962.

DOMAINE DES LAMBRAYS

address	31 Rue Basse, 21220 Morey-Saint-Denis, Burgundy, France www.lambrays.com Tel: +33 3 80 51 84 33
contact	Jacques Devauges
farming philosophy	Organic principles, horse plowing, no chemical spraying.
in the cellar	Mostly whole bunch; barrel-matured 18 months with minimal new oak, usually no more than 50%.
total vineyard area	11 hectares total; 8.6 hectares Clos des Lambrays
total annual production	50,000 bottles, including 35,000 bottles Clos des Lambrays

key vineyard holdings	*Red*		*White*	
	Clos des Lambrays Grand Cru	8.66 ha	Puligny-Montrachet Premier Cru	
	Morey-Saint-Denis Premier Cru	0.64 ha	Clos du Cailleret	0.37 ha
	Morey-Saint-Denis	1.71 ha	Puligny-Montrachet Premier Cru	
			Les Folatières	0.29 ha

CLOS DES LAMBRAYS GRAND CRU, MOREY-SAINT-DENIS

This is one of the youngest Grand Cru vineyards in Burgundy, having achieved this status only in 1981. This 8.6-hectare vineyard is a good example of how a great vineyard is unrecognizable when it is neglected. Prior to 1979 and the acquisition of the vineyard by the Saier brothers, the vineyard was so severely neglected that Thierry Brouin calls it a "ruin" when he arrived. Brouin, a young oenology graduate at the time, was hired by the brothers to reinvigorate the estate, and its application to upgrade the Premier Cru *clos* to Grand Cru was approved by INAO. This was not based on the wine's quality then but on the potential of the clos, given its long history and its ideal location, adjacent to and at the same level on the slope as Clos de Tart. Thierry Brouin reconstructed the domaine's buildings, upgraded the cellars, and replanted the vineyard; after 38 years with the estate, he retired and handed over the management to Boris Champy in 2018. The retirement took place three years after luxury conglomerate LVMH purchased the domaine for a reported 100 million euros. In February 2019, Jacques Devauges, previously of Clos de Tart, took over the estate. He may be new to the role, but there is no doubt he will work toward preserving Clos des Lambrays' identity and style as one of Burgundy's most refined and **delicate** Grand Cru wines. The 2016 and 2017 vintages are testament to the continuation of respecting the wine's identity and elegant style: These are wines of finesse and lacy detail, refreshingly lighter than its neighbor Clos de Tart. In great vintages since the domaine's renaissance, such as 1999, 2010, 2012, 2015, and 2017, the wines are exquisitely detailed, **silky** textured, with great **aromatic** complexity and an impressive finish.

IN THREE WORDS   ***Exquisite, detailed, refined.***

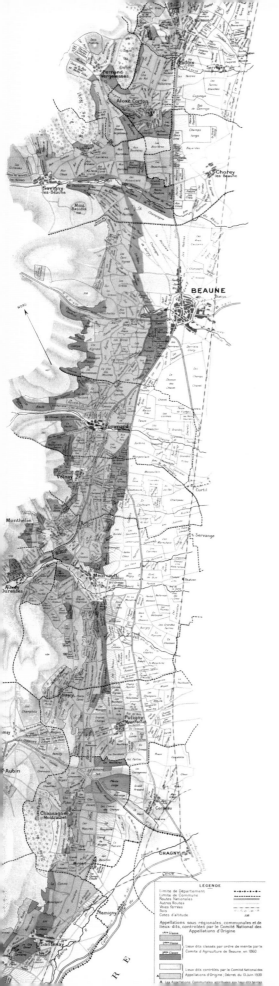

DOMAINE DU COMTE LIGER-BELAIR

address

Château de Vosne-Romanée, 21700 Vosne-Romanée, Burgundy, France   www.liger-belair.fr   Tel: + 33 3 80 62 13 70

contact

Louis-Michel Liger-Belair

farming philosophy

Certified biodynamic.

in the cellar

Bunches are destemmed, 1 week cold maceration; aged 16 months in mostly new oak.

total vineyard area

9 hectares

total annual production

42,000 bottles

key vineyard holdings

La Romanée Grand Cru Monopole	0.85 ha
Échezeaux Grand Cru	0.62 ha
Vosne-Romanée Premier Cru Aux Reignots	0.73 ha
Vosne-Romanée Premier Cru Les Suchots	0.22 ha
Vosne-Romanée Premier Cru Petits Monts	0.13 ha
Vosne-Romanée Premier Cru Chaumes	0.12 ha
Vosne-Romanée Premier Cru Aux Brûlées	0.12 ha
Nuits-Saint-Georges Premier Cru Aux Cras	0.38 ha
Nuits Saint Georges Premier Cru Clos des Grandes Vignes Monopole	2.19 ha
Vosne-Romanée Clos du Château Monopole	0.83 ha
Vosne-Romanée La Colombière	0.78 ha
Vosne-Romanée	0.63 ha
Nuits-Saint-Georges Aux Lavières	0.14 ha

Map of the wines of the Burgundy region, illustration from *Atlas de la France Vinicole*, by Louis Larmat, 1942.

LA ROMANÉE GRAND CRU MONOPOLE, VOSNE-ROMANÉE

This is a young domaine with a long family history linked to the greatest terroirs of Burgundy. Toward the end of the 19th century, the Liger-Belair family owned 60 hectares, including some of the greatest Grand Cru and Premier Cru vineyards throughout the Côte d'Or. Grand Cru vineyards included Chambertin, Richebourg, Clos de Vougeot, La Tâche, La Grande Rue, and La Romanée; the latter is the smallest appellation and smallest Grand Cru in France, consisting of only 0.8 hectares lying mid-slope just above Romanée-Conti. Due to family squabbles, most of the vineyards were sold at auction in 1933; the small parcel of La Romanée and a few of the Premiers Crus were kept in the family. Louis-Michel Liger-Belair, the seventh generation of the family, decided to reclaim the family vineyards starting in 2000. He quickly converted the vineyards to organic then eventually to biodynamic by 2008. In 2015, on the 200th anniversary of the

> **A spectacular vertical tasting back to 1911 of La Romanée, the family's crown jewel, showed the breeding of this vineyard.**

Liger-Belair family in Burgundy, Louis-Michel organized a vertical tasting of La Romanée, the family's crown jewel, going back to 1911. The spectacular tasting showed the breeding of this vineyard and its ability to age. My favorite older vintages included the ethereal and exquisite 1911 and 1966. Among the younger vintages, 1989, 1990, and the 2002 stood out as *exemplary* wines of *nobility* and class. Since 2002, when Liger-Belair reclaimed the vineyard, La Romanée has joined the ranks of the most collectible and coveted Grands Crus from Vosne-Romanée. Louis-Michel is well on his way to placing his family domaine, including this tiny parcel, in its rightful place at the top of the Burgundy pyramid. Its *pedigree* and quality are hard to deny; among the recent vintages, the 2005, 2009, 2010, 2012, and 2015 are extraordinary.

IN THREE WORDS *Regal, voluptuous, extraordinary.*

VOSNE-ROMANÉE PREMIER CRU AUX REIGNOTS, VOSNE-ROMANÉE

Although established only in 2000, the wines of Comte Liger-Belair quickly achieved cult status. It is not a surprise, given the winning combination of great vineyards belonging to the family for over a hundred years and thoughtful, intelligent vineyard and cellar management by the talented Louis-Michel Liger-Belair. With a global market perspective, Louis-Michel and his charming wife, Constance, who works alongside him, make the rounds to get their wine on the world's fine wine map, from New York to London to Hong Kong. In less than two decades, the domaine established a reputation for its **sumptuous**, concentrated, and **velvety** wines. Even though

it started out with only a few hectares of vines, by 2002 the portfolio had grown to include La Romanée Grand Cru and the Vosne-Romanée Premiers Crus Aux Reignots and Les Chaumes. By 2012, this expanded to around 10 hectares total either owned or farmed by the family, including Échezeaux Grand Cru and Premier Cru vineyards in Nuits-Saint-Georges. Vosne-Romanée Premier Cru Aux Reignots is one of the family's original holdings and one of my favorite Premiers Crus from Liger-Belair. Its other two Vosne-Romanée Premiers Crus, Les Suchots and the tiny, impossible-to-find Aux Brûlées, can be fantastic, but they are less consistent and more difficult to find than Aux Reignots. Liger-Belair has small holdings in most Premiers Crus, with one-fifth of a hectare or less, but Aux Reignots is four-fifths of a hectare. It lies on a fairly steep slope just above La Romanée, and its shallow soil over hard limestone produces wines of much **finesse** and intensity. Reignots doesn't have a reputation as one of the top Premier Cru vineyards in Vosne-Romanée, but Liger-Belair, which owns 40% of this vineyard, is bringing up its prestige. If the estate keeps producing vintages like 2015, 2012, and 2009, its reputation is sure to escalate.

IN THREE WORDS *Balanced, compelling, beautiful.*

DOMAINE DUGAT-PY

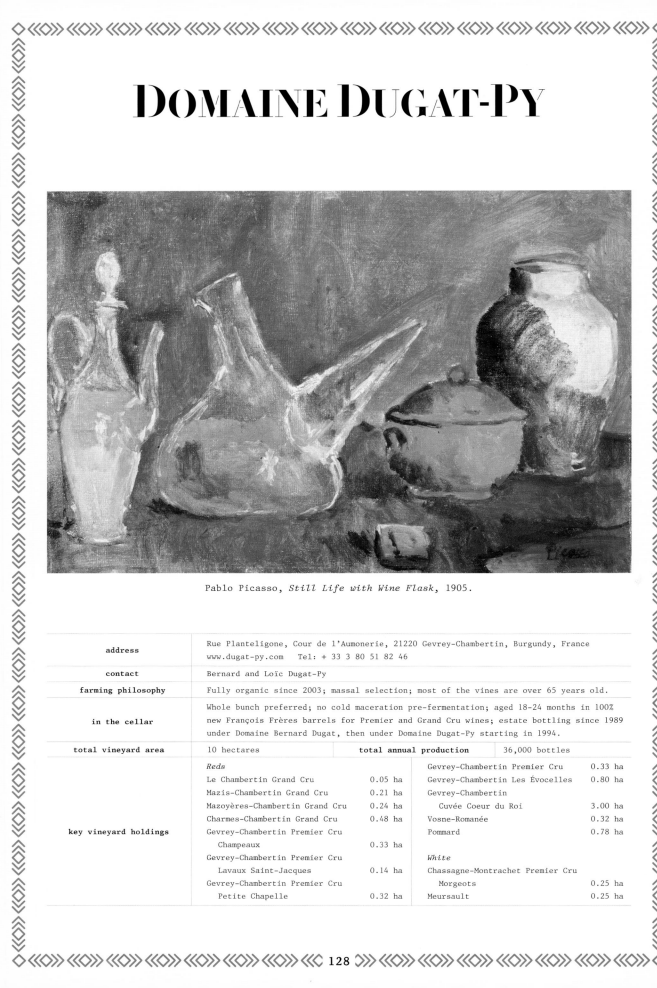

Pablo Picasso, *Still Life with Wine Flask*, 1905.

address	Rue Planteligone, Cour de l'Aumonerie, 21220 Gevrey-Chambertin, Burgundy, France www.dugat-py.com Tel: + 33 3 80 51 82 46
contact	Bernard and Loïc Dugat-Py
farming philosophy	Fully organic since 2003; massal selection; most of the vines are over 65 years old.
in the cellar	Whole bunch preferred; no cold maceration pre-fermentation; aged 18-24 months in 100% new François Frères barrels for Premier and Grand Cru wines; estate bottling since 1989 under Domaine Bernard Dugat, then under Domaine Dugat-Py starting in 1994.

total vineyard area	10 hectares	**total annual production**	36,000 bottles

key vineyard holdings	*Reds*		Gevrey-Chambertin Premier Cru	0.33 ha	
	Le Chambertin Grand Cru	0.05 ha	Gevrey-Chambertin Les Évocelles	0.80 ha	
	Mazis-Chambertin Grand Cru	0.21 ha	Gevrey-Chambertin		
	Mazoyères-Chambertin Grand Cru	0.24 ha	Cuvée Coeur du Roi	3.00 ha	
	Charmes-Chambertin Grand Cru	0.48 ha	Vosne-Romanée	0.32 ha	
	Gevrey-Chambertin Premier Cru		Pommard	0.78 ha	
	Champeaux	0.33 ha			
	Gevrey-Chambertin Premier Cru		*White*		
	Lavaux Saint-Jacques	0.14 ha	Chassagne-Montrachet Premier Cru		
	Gevrey-Chambertin Premier Cru		Morgeots	0.25 ha	
	Petite Chapelle	0.32 ha	Meursault	0.25 ha	

LE CHAMBERTIN GRAND CRU, GEVREY-CHAMBERTIN

Dugat-Py is the classic Burgundian tale of growers who became winemakers. The Dugat family were growers in Gevrey-Chambertin since the 17th century, but it was only with the 12th generation, some 300 years later, that Bernard Dugat decided to move into winemaking and bottle wines under the family name. (This winery should not be confused with Domaine Dugat, owned by Claude Dugat, who is Bernard's cousin.) Dugat-Py quickly rose to stardom with a range of sumptuous, dense wines made in the 1990s that garnered praise from American critics and collectors. His style has toned down since the early 2000s, but since his son, Loïc Dugat-Py, took over in 2014, the wines are considerably more elegant, less extracted, and more refined. The estate's small parcels of four Grand Cru wines are on strict allocation around the world, and even its latest-release Village Gevrey-Chambertin is sold for well over US$100 a bottle. All the Grands Crus are powerful, each expressing its own terroir, and the tiny Chambertin is the most *impressive* of them all. There is only one barrel made per year, from 100-year-old vines that are replanted one by one. The wines are so powerful that the rare bottles I have been able to taste, such as the fabulous 2005 and 2002 vintages, thanks to the generosity of an avid Hong Kong collector, are still painfully young. It appears these wines will need at least 20 years of aging before they can be approached; in their youth they are tightly knit, intense, *brooding*, wines that convey their stature but not yet their complexity and nuances. The 2017 is a great vintage for Dugat-Py, intense and fleshy yet elegant and detailed. The Chambertin is *majestic* and complex, but so is the Mazoyères-Chambertin, a knockout in this vintage. For a taste of Dugat-Py's style, try its more affordable Bourgogne Rouge or Village Gevrey-Chambertin. IN THREE WORDS *Intense, concentrated, powerful.*

> ❝ **Dugat-Py is the classic Burgundian tale of growers who became winemakers. The family were growers in Gevrey-Chambertin since the 17th century.** ❞

> 66 **Nothing makes the future look so rosy as to contemplate it through a glass of Chambertin.** 99

Napoleon Bonaparte

Patrick Caulfield, *Picnic Set*, 1978.

DOMAINE DUJAC

Dujac is one of the iconic estates in Morey-Saint-Denis, established by Jacques Seysses in 1968, but the vintage was such a disaster that he sold off the wines to négociants. The estate is now run by Jacques' sons Jeremy and Alec, as well as Jeremy's wife, Diana, a trained winemaker and graduate of the University of California Davis. The trio continues the tradition of making quality-focused, soulful wines from their expanding holdings that now total over 17 hectares and include seven Grand Cru vineyards.

In the cellar, Jacques Seysses has been unique in vinifying all the vintages he produced until 1999 with whole bunches rather than opting to destem. This is a perennial Burgundian debate (see page 37), but those who favor whole bunch are staunch supporters and include some of the top domaines, such as DRC, Leroy, and de Montille. Often, adding stems into the fermentation vat reduces color, alcohol, and acidity, but Jacques has successfully added stems and created wines of finesse, depth, and harmony.

Jeremy and Diana respect this tradition but are no longer so strict and may include a small percentage of destemmed grapes, which varies by vintage. The percentage of new oak used at Dujac is fairly high—for the Grands Crus, 100% new oak is used, while the Premiers Crus get about 50% new oak. Despite generous new oak use, there is barely a trace of toasty oak flavors in the wine. According to Jeremy, the oak is seasoned, air-dried for a minimum of 30 months, and toasted very lightly to prevent

imparting oak flavors. The wines are refined, always pale, beautifully perfumed, with layers of detail and silky tannins.

I find Jeremy a breath of fresh air in Burgundy, where growers can be closed and less candid. The first time I visited Dujac as a Master of Wine student nearly 20 years ago, I grilled Jeremy about the differences between whole bunch and destemming for Pinot Noir, and he blurted, "We often use tartaric acid during fermentation, because the stems reduce total acidity." Then he smiled, put his hand over his mouth, and said, "I don't think I was supposed to reveal that much." Over the years, I have come to look forward to his frank observations and his hypercritical comments about his own wine. If you are your own worst critic, there is no doubt that improvements are constantly being made, and this is clear in the wines he and Diana are producing today at Dujac.

Jacques Seysses's strong connections with top restaurants along with the family's close ties to the United States—Jeremy's mother and wife are both American—mean that its wines are in high demand. These delicate wines of finesse and elegance are on limited allocation, but are well worth experiencing. Apart from its seven impressive Grand Cru wines, its Premiers Crus are also worth seeking—I especially enjoy its Vosne-Romanée Beaux Monts and Malconsorts, and Gevrey-Chambertin Aux Combottes. Even at the Village level there is clear attention to detail, and I am a fan of its Village Morey-Saint-Denis.

address	7 Rue de Bussière, 21220 Morey-Saint-Denis, Burgundy, France www.dujac.com Tel: + 33 3 80 34 01 00			
contact	Jeremy, Diana, and Alec Seysses			
farming philosophy	Organic and biodynamic farming since 2001; massal selection.			
in the cellar	Mostly whole bunch, depending on vintage; aged 16-18 months in lightly toasted oak, 60-80% new for Grands Crus, 40-60% new for the Premiers Crus.			
total vineyard area	17.3 hectares		total annual production	90,000 bottles
key vineyard holdings	*Red*		Vosne-Romanée Premier Cru	
	Le Chambertin Grand Cru	0.29 ha	Les Beaux Monts	0.73 ha
	Charmes-Chambertin Grand Cru	0.70 ha	Morey-Saint-Denis Premier Cru	0.79 ha
	Clos de la Roche Grand Cru	1.95 ha	Chambolle-Musigny	0.64 ha
	Clos Saint-Denis Grand Cru	1.47 ha	Morey-Saint-Denis	2.93 ha
	Bonnes-Mares Grand Cru	0.59 ha		
	Romanée-Saint-Vivant Grand Cru	0.17 ha	*White*	
	Échezeaux Grand Cru	0.69 ha	Puligny-Montrachet Premier Cru	
	Chambolle-Musigny Premier Cru		Les Combettes	0.62 ha
	Les Gruenchers	0.33 ha	Puligny-Montrachet Les Folatières	1.17 ha
	Gevrey-Chambertin Premier Cru		Morey-Saint-Denis Premier Cru	
	Aux Combottes	1.16 ha	Les Monts Luisants	0.60 ha
	Vosne-Romanée Premier Cru		Morey-Saint-Denis	0.66 ha
	Aux Malconsorts	1.57 ha		

CLOS DE LA ROCHE GRAND CRU, MOREY-SAINT-DENIS

Dujac owns nearly 2 hectares of this prominent Grand Cru vineyard, slowly building up to its current size. Jacques Seysses acquired the original half-hectare parcel in 1968 from Marcel Graillet, and other acquisitions followed in the 1970s. Around nine plots are scattered throughout this nearly 17-hectare vineyard, making the final blend quite complex and layered. Within Dujac's portfolio, Clos de la Roche is *structured* and intense, but when compared with other producers of this vineyard, such as Ponsot (the largest owner in this vineyard), Coquard-Loison-Fleurot, or Hubert Lignier, Dujac's version is more sensual, hedonistic, and elegant. The second-largest owner of this vineyard, Dujac's Clos de la Roche is a benchmark style alongside Ponsot's more structured, riper, and muscular rendition. The 1985 is an experience to cherish, with its dazzling *aromatic* intensity and finesse; the 1990 is another beauty, with spectacular depth and *sublime* bouquet; the 1995 is drinking beautifully now and so is the 1997, both modest vintages but with high marks for delicious drinkability. If I had to choose just a handful of vintages to lay down in my cellar, it would be the 2005, 2010, 2012, and 2015.

IN THREE WORDS   *Complex, minerally, penetrating.*

CLOS SAINT-DENIS GRAND CRU, MOREY-SAINT-DENIS

Clos Saint-Denis is often more delicate, intellectual yet approachable compared with Dujac's other Grands Crus. Dujac owns nearly 1.5 hectares here, the second-largest owner, just behind Georges Lignier. In my experience, Dujac makes the best Clos Saint-Denis and sets the standard for this 6.6-hectare vineyard. Ponsot, Arlaud, and Jadot make wonderful expressions of this *clos,* but Dujac brings out its *sensuality*, the complex interplay between sweet spices, fruit, fine-grained tannins, and acidity. This is a *charismatic* wine that relies on its delicacy, exquisite detail, and finesse rather than intensity or power; older vintages of Clos Saint-Denis such as the 1985 and 1988 prove that *subtle*, fine, quiet wines can have a lifespan that is as long as the louder ones.

IN THREE WORDS   *Refined, elegant, alluring.*

Winemaking in Burgundy, removing grapes from clusters, engraving from *Grands hommes et grands faits de l'industrie*, France, c. 1880.

Domaine Duroché

GRANDS VINS

DE BOURGOGNE

Chambertin Clos de Bèze

"GRAND CRU"

APPELLATION CHAMBERTIN CLOS DE BÈZE GRAND CRU CONTRÔLÉE

2016

DOMAINE DUROCHÉ

13,5% vol.

L.1613

address	7 Place du Monument, 21220 Gevrey-Chambertin, Burgundy, France http://domaine-duroche.com Tel: +33 3 80 51 82 77
contact	Pierre Duroché
farming philosophy	Organic principles; minimal spraying.
in the cellar	Mostly destemmed, keeping whole berries, although some wines may have whole bunches; matured in minimal new oak, with only 10% new for all wines.

total vineyard area	8.3 hectares	**total annual production**	40,000 bottles

key vineyard holdings			
Charmes-Chambertin Grand Cru	0.41 ha	Gevrey-Chambertin Premier Cru	
Latricières-Chambertin Grand Cru	0.28 ha	Champeaux	0.13 ha
Chambertin-Clos de Bèze Grand Cru	0.25 ha	Gevrey-Chambertin Aux Ételois	0.35 ha
Griotte-Chambertin Grand Cru	0.02 ha	Gevrey-Chambertin Les Jeunes Rois	0.65 ha
Gevrey-Chambertin Premier Cru		Gevrey-Chambertin Champ	0.98 ha
Lavaut Saint-Jacques	1.20 ha	Gevrey-Chambertin Le Clos	0.39 ha
Gevrey-Chambertin Premier Cru		Gevrey-Chambertin	2.59 ha
Estournelles-Saint-Jacques	0.13 ha		

CHAMBERTIN–CLOS DE BÈZE GRAND CRU, GEVREY-CHAMBERTIN

Pierre Duroché is the fifth-generation vigneron in his family, with over 8 hectares of prime vineyards throughout Gevrey-Chambertin, yet not many Burgundy lovers are familiar with his domaine. His father, Gilles, who made the wines from the late 1980s until 2003, produced good, solid wines but not up to the potential of the great vineyards he farmed. It was only after his son Pierre took over in 2005 that there were whispers about the estate finally making the most of its four Grand Cru and three top Premier Cru vineyards. There is a purity and authenticity to Pierre's wines that allow the vineyards to express themselves more precisely. There were no dramatic changes but hundreds of small, minor refinements, details that can turn good wines into great ones. Pierre is humble and quite shy but becomes animated when he talks about how he is constantly learning with each successive vintage and experimenting with all the traditions that were handed down to him to see empirically if they work and make sense for the vineyards he farms. There is no rule about the use of whole bunches; he takes an "It depends" approach to everything he does. At the top of its vineyard holdings sits the family jewel: Clos de Bèze. It is only a quarter-hectare, in the heart of the vineyard, just above Chapelle-Chambertin, yielding just four, or in generous years five barrels, from vines planted in the 1920s. Under Pierre's watchful eye, these Grand Cru wines have glorious purity, subtle ***intensity***, and a silky texture. This is a serious wine, despite its delicate initial impression and sweet, spicy aromatics; the flavors are ***graceful*** but layered and intense with a minerally framework that reveals itself in the long finish. The 2010 is when Pierre really made his mark with this wine: It is ***exceptional***, and successive vintages such as the 2015 and 2016 show immense promise.

IN THREE WORDS ***Striking, pure, brilliant.***

DOMAINE EMMANUEL ROUGET

address
18 Route de Gilly, 21640 Flagey-Échezeaux, Burgundy, France
Tel: + 33 3 80 62 86 61

contact
Guillaume Rouget

farming philosophy
Lutte raisonnée, with minimal spraying, no herbicides.

in the cellar
Grapes are fully destemmed; cold pre-fermentation maceration; pump over preferred vs. punch down; aged up to 18 months in 100% new oak barrels, depending on the wine.

total vineyard area
9.5 hectares

total annual production
50,000 bottles

key vineyard holdings

Red

Échezeaux Grand Cru	1.42 ha
Vosne-Romanée Premier Cru Les Beaumonts	0.23 ha
Vosne-Romanée Premier Cru Cros Parantoux	0.72 ha
Savigny-Les-Beaune Premier Cru Les Lavières	0.14 ha
Vosne-Romanée	1.42 ha
Nuits-Saint-Georges	0.90 ha
Savigny-Les-Beaune	0.68 ha
Côte de Nuits Villages Les Chaillots	0.22 ha
Chorey-Les-Beaune	0.25 ha
Bourgogne Hautes Côtes de Nuits Rouge	0.33 ha
Bourgogne Passetougrain	1.00 ha

White

Bourgogne Hautes Côtes de Beaune Blanc	0.95 ha
Bourgogne Aligoté	0.42 ha
Crémant de Bourgogne	0.32 ha

VOSNE-ROMANÉE PREMIER CRU CROS PARANTOUX, VOSNE-ROMANÉE

Emmanuel Rouget was the chosen one, handpicked by the legendary Henri Jayer, because he happened to show interest in winemaking in the 1970s and because he was Henri's nephew by marriage. Emmanuel worked alongside Henri starting in 1976 until he set up his own operation in 1985, farming the vineyards and making the wines for his other two uncles, Lucien and Georges Jayer. During the 1980s and 1990s, Henri slowly started to hand over his vines for his nephew to manage, officially transferring all the vineyards to him in 1996, though Henri continued to bottle some wines under his own name. My first visit to Emmanuel Rouget over 10 years ago was underwhelming. My disappointment was no doubt partly due to my high expectations for Henri Jayer's successor, but the wines, except for Cros Parantoux, were ordinary. The cellar was musty and dirty, and Emmanuel was gruff, uttering short phrases rather than full sentences to my queries. It felt like the last thing he wanted to be doing was barrel tasting with an Asian woman in his cold cellar. I left feeling sad that somehow Henri Jayer's touch in the vineyard and the cellar had not been transmitted to his nephew—there was no magic in that cellar. I decided not to visit again until I heard that his two sons, Nicolas and Guillaume, were taking more responsibility, and I started to

taste with Guillaume. The generational shift is huge at this domaine, and now it is on my radar as an estate to watch. The few times I tasted with Emmanuel, the Cros Parantoux was magnificent; this is a vineyard that had the loving care of someone who had painstakingly planted it, and understood it so well that its **brilliant** voice rang clear and true. I have tasted wonderful vintages of this wine from the 1990s, which were clearly influenced by Henri Jayer, the workaholic who could not fully retire during this period. Recent vintages like the 2015 and 2016 are **gorgeous** and show promise; they have greater purity and **precision** than in the 2000s.

IN THREE WORDS *Glorious, exquisite, multifaceted.*

DOMAINE FAIVELEY

address	8 Rue du Tribourg, 21700 Nuits-Saint-Georges, Burgundy, France www.domaine-faiveley.com Tel: +33 3 80 61 04 55
contact	Erwan Faiveley
farming philosophy	Traditional farming, with minimal spraying.
in the cellar	Red grapes all destemmed, gentle extraction, matured 18 months in up to two-thirds new oak; top whites barrel-fermented, with minimal lees stirring.
total vineyard area	127 hectares (40% in Côte d'Or, 60% in Côte Chalonnaise)
total annual production	Undisclosed (estimated at several million bottles)

key vineyard holdings

Reds

Chambertin–Clos de Bèze Grand Cru Les Ouvrées Rodin	0.02 ha
Chambertin–Clos de Bèze Grand Cru	1.29 ha
Corton Grand Cru Clos des Cortons Faiveley Monopole	2.77 ha
Charmes-Chambertin Grand Cru	0.81 ha
Mazis-Chambertin Grand Cru	1.56 ha
Latricières-Chambertin Grand Cru	1.21 ha
Clos de Vougeot Grand Cru	1.27 ha
Échezeaux Grand Cru En Orveaux	0.83 ha
Musigny Grand Cru	0.13 ha
Gevrey-Chambertin Premier Cru La Perrière	3.02 ha
Gevrey-Chambertin Premier Cru Les Cazetiers	2.05 ha
Gevrey-Chambertin Premier Cru Champonnets	0.42 ha
Gevrey-Chambertin Premier Cru Clos des Issarts Monopole	0.61 ha
Gevrey-Chambertin Premier Cru Craipillot	0.14 ha
Gevrey-Chambertin Premier Cru Lavaux Saint-Jacques	0.98 ha
Gevrey-Chambertin Premier Cru La Combe aux Moines	1.24 ha
Chambolle-Musigny Premier Cru La Combe d'Orveau	0.26 ha
Chambolle-Musigny Premier Cru Les Fuées	0.19 ha

Nuits-Saint-Georges Premier Cru Les Saint-Georges	0.23 ha
Nuits-Saint-Georges Premier Cru Les Porêts Saint-Georges	1.69 ha
Nuits-Saint-Georges Premier Cru Aux Chaignots	0.73 ha
Nuits-Saint-Georges Premier Cru Aux Vignerondes	0.46 ha
Nuits-Saint-Georges Premier Cru Les Damodes	0.81 ha
Beaune Premier Cru Clos de l'Écu Monopole	2.37 ha
Pommard Premier Cru Les Rugiens	0.50 ha
Volnay Premier Cru Frémiets	0.74 ha

White

Corton-Charlemagne Grand Cru	0.87 ha
Bâtard-Montrachet Grand Cru	0.35 ha
Montagny Premier Cru Les Las	0.19 ha
Bienvenues-Bâtard-Montrachet Grand Cru	0.51 ha
Puligny-Montrachet Premier Cru Clos de la Garenne	0.19 ha
Puligny-Montrachet Premier Cru Les Referts	0.37 ha
Puligny-Montrachet Premier Cru Champ Gain	1.05 ha

CHAMBERTIN–CLOS DE BÈZE GRAND CRU LES OUVRÉES RODIN, GEVREY–CHAMBERTIN

Faiveley is one of the oldest and most respected négociants that have evolved with the times to become large landowners, not just brokers of wine. Since Erwan Faiveley took over in 2004, when he was just 25 years old, the company has been on a buying spree, acquiring vineyards across Burgundy, from Chablis to Gevrey-Chambertin. Recent purchases include Domaine Monnot vineyards, with parcels of Grands Crus vineyards Bienvenues-Bâtard-Montrachet and Bâtard-Montrachet; purchase of Domaine Dupont-Tisserandot's 20 hectares in Gevrey-Chambertin, and a recent purchase of a tiny piece of Musigny Grand Cru. When Faiveley was founded in 1825 by Pierre Faiveley, its primary focus was its négociant business, which grew over subsequent generations. Now, in its seventh generation, the focus has shifted toward the domaine business, and Erwan says only 20% of the wines are made from purchased grapes or wine. Erwan Faiveley may be young, but he is an impressive leader, with quite a clear vision of where he wants his family company to go. Currently, Faiveley owns 127 hectares, making it one of the largest and most important landowners in Burgundy. This includes 13 hectares of Grand Cru vineyards producing 12 different Grands Crus wines. Although Faiveley now has sizable white wine parcels, it is much better known for its reds. Musigny is arguably its flagship wine, but there is so little made that it is impossible to find; its Mazis-Chambertin and Latricières-Chambertin are wonderful examples of the vineyard. However, for me, the Clos de Bèze sits at the top of its portfolio, especially the *coveted* Les Ouvrées Rodin, which was first produced in 2009. Faiveley owns 1.3 hectares of Chambertin–Clos de Bèze, in four parcels. Les Ouvrées Rodin comes from a special plot, planted in 1966, and only four to five barrels are made each year. While the normal Clos de Bèze is impressive, Les Ouvrées Rodin is another step up in quality, with finer tannins, greater depth and *complexity*, and an incredible finish. This is a very special plot that Faiveley has done well to identify and bottle separately. All the vintages made since 2009 are consistently *extraordinary*, and best to cellar until at least 2025.

IN THREE WORDS *Magisterial, rich, intricate.*

DOMAINE FONTAINE-GAGNARD

---
address
19 Route de Santenay, 21190 Chassagne-Montrachet,
Burgundy, France   www.domaine-fontaine-gagnard.com
Tel: +33 3 80 21 35 50

contact
Céline Fontaine

farming philosophy
Lutte raisonnée, with plowing and minimal spraying.

in the cellar
White wines fermented and matured up to 12 months on the lees
in barrel, with minimal new oak, no more than 30%; red grapes
destemmed, aged up to 18 months with one-third new oak.

total vineyard area
12 hectares

total annual production
80,000 bottles

key vineyard holdings

Reds

Bâtard-Montrachet Grand Cru	0.30 ha
Criots-Bâtard-Montrachet Grand Cru	0.33 ha
Le Montrachet Grand Cru	0.08 ha
Chassagne-Montrachet Premier Cru Clos Saint-Jean	0.30 ha
Chassagne-Montrachet Premier Cru Morgeot	0.31 ha
Volnay Premier Cru Clos des Chênes	0.37 ha
Pommard Premier Cru Les Rugiens	0.22 ha
Chassagne-Montrachet	1.50 ha
Bourgogne	0.92 ha
Bourgogne Passetoutgrain	0.53 ha

White

Le Montrachet Grand Cru	0.08 ha
Bâtard-Montrachet Grand Cru	0.43 ha
Criots-Bâtard-Montrachet Grand Cru	0.33 ha
Chassagne-Montrachet Premier Cru La Boudriotte	0.80 ha
Chassagne-Montrachet Premier Cru Les Caillerets	0.56 ha
Chassagne-Montrachet Premier Cru Les Chenevottes	0.08 ha
Chassagne-Montrachet Premier Cru Clos de Murées	0.34 ha
Chassagne-Montrachet Premier Cru Clos Saint-Jean	0.36 ha
Chassagne-Montrachet Premier Cru La Grande Montagne	0.23 ha
Chassagne-Montrachet Premier Cru La Maltorie	0.76 ha
Chassagne-Montrachet Premier Cru Morgeot	0.70 ha
Chassagne-Montrachet Premier Cru La Romanée	0.36 ha
Chassagne-Montrachet Premier Cru Les Vergers	0.72 ha
Chassagne-Montrachet	1.69 ha
Bourgogne	0.21 ha

CRIOTS–BÂTARD–MONTRACHET GRAND CRU, CHASSAGNE–MONTRACHET

This domaine is the perfect place to discover the differences in Chassagne-Montrachet's Premier Cru vineyards. Fontaine-Gagnard makes no less than ten white Chassagne-Montrachet and two red Chassagne-Montrachet Premiers Crus. This is a young domaine, established in 1985 by Laurence Gagnard and her husband, Richard Fontaine. The vineyards were formed from parcels Laurence inherited from her father, Jacques Gagnard, and her mother, Marie-Joseph Delagrange, whose vineyards were split between Laurence and her younger sister, Claudine (Domaine Blain-Gagnard). The Gagnards and Delagranges have extensive ties in Chassagne-Montrachet and have always been regarded as quality-conscious producers. Under Richard Fontaine, the estate produced very good white wines and supple reds that fell under the radar of most Burgundy lovers. Since Richard's daughter Céline Fontaine joined the estate in 2007, the wines are becoming more precise and detailed. While the large number of Chassagne-Montrachet Premiers Crus are worth exploring, especially La Romanée and Les Caillerets, its three Grands Crus are exemplary. I am especially enamored of the small Grand Cru vineyard Criots-Bâtard-Montrachet, probably because I see so little of it. The total size of this Grand Cru vineyard is only 1.5 hectares, with each of the growers owning just a tiny parcel; Fontaine-Gagnard has one-third of a hectare, with vines dating back to the 1930s. The soil is stonier than at Bâtard and the wines usually more delicate and floral. Fontaine-Gagnard's Criots is a reference style—spicy, *layered*, and intense when young, and *sumptuous* and complex after ten years of age. Under Céline's watchful eye, the wines are now more *elegant* while still retaining their firm presence. IN THREE WORDS *Intense, focused, complex.*

66 Under Céline's watchful eye, the wines are becoming more precise and detailed. 99

> **66** Music is the wine which inspires one to new generative processes, and I am Bacchus who presses out this glorious wine for mankind and makes them spiritually drunken. **99**

Ludwig von Beethoven

Caravaggio, *Young Bacchus*, 1596–97.

DOMAINE FOURRIER

At a young age, Jean-Marie Fourrier committed himself to learning about winemaking and becoming a vigneron. It runs in his blood, with family ties to the vineyard dating back nearly a hundred years. Starting in his teens, he worked with his father and completed internships at Domaine Drouhin in Oregon and with the legendary Henri Jayer. By 1995, when he was only 23 years old, he took over the winemaking and management of the estate from his father, Jean-Claude.

When I first met Jean-Marie, I was impressed with his fluent English, and subsequently discovered he had married a lovely English lady, Vicki, who helps him manage the estate. He was unlike other Burgundian owners, who can be aloof, wary, or reserved during tastings. He loves to share his experience and winemaking philosophy and answer any questions with detail and examples. He is a down-to-earth, confident, yet humble man who has singlehandedly put his family estate on the fine wine map within two decades.

Over the past 23 years under his stewardship, Fourrier wines have become renowned and highly coveted among collectors. He was fortunate to inherit very old vines, some of which were planted more than 100 years ago, affording him great material as the base. However, the vast majority of the vineyards he farms is at the Village and Premier Cru levels, with only a tiny quarter-hectare holding in Griotte-Chambertin, a small Grand Cru vineyard.

Fourrier's reputation lies in the wines' ability to express even Village-level vineyards with remarkable clarity, depth, and precision. Jean-Marie doesn't have any secrets about how he is able to accomplish this: Reduce yields, plow the vineyards, debud rather than green harvest, introduce sorting tables, destem the grapes very slowly (like Henri Jayer), keep berries whole, use gravity rather than pumps, strict temperature control, minimal racking and sulfur use, reduce oak aging to 18 months, minimal new oak use. These are some of the obvious changes Jean-Marie made, but there is a much longer list of small refinements. He has fine-tuned every detail of grape growing and winemaking to what he believes would best express the vineyards in the purest voice.

In keeping with this philosophy, the Gevrey Premier Cru vineyards that his father used to blend together are now vinified and bottled separately. Among the six Premiers Crus, the Clos Saint-Jacques stands out as an exceptional wine, a fine example of this top vineyard that I consider

to be of Grand Cru level. Fourrier's Griotte-Chambertin is extremely rare but well worth seeking—this is a wine of magisterial proportions and incredible depth. At the other end of the price spectrum, the Village Gevrey-Chambertin, with over 3 hectares, is more widely available and is a great introduction to Fourrier.

address
7 Route de Dijon, 21220 Gevrey-Chambertin, Burgundy, France
Tel: + 33 3 80 34 33 99

contact
Jean-Marie Fourrier

farming philosophy
Lutte raisonnée, no herbicides, minimal spraying;
only grapes from vines more than 40 years old are used.

in the cellar
Grapes are all destemmed; minimal racking during *élevage*;
matured 18 months with minimal oak use, maximum 20% new.

total vineyard area
10 hectares

total annual production
45,000 bottles

key vineyard holdings

Griotte-Chambertin Grand Cru	0.26 ha
Gevrey-Chambertin Premier Cru Clos Saint-Jacques	0.89 ha
Gevrey-Chambertin Premier Cru La Combe aux Moines	0.87 ha
Gevrey-Chambertin Premier Cru Les Champeaux	0.21 ha
Gevrey-Chambertin Premier Cru Les Cherbaudes	0.67 ha
Gevrey-Chambertin Premier Cru Les Goulots	0.34 ha
Gevrey-Chambertin Premier Cru Les Gruenchers	0.29 ha
Morey-Saint-Denis Clos Solon	0.55 ha
Vougeot Premier Cru Les Petits Vougeot	0.34 ha
Gevrey-Chambertin Aux Échezeaux	0.47 ha
Chambolle-Musigny	0.39 ha
Gevrey-Chambertin	3.30 ha

GEVREY-CHAMBERTIN PREMIER CRU CLOS SAINT-JACQUES, GEVREY-CHAMBERTIN

Clos Saint-Jacques is one of the most picturesque vineyards in the Côte de Nuits. This 6.7-hectare walled vineyard lies on a steep, southeast-facing slope, with each of the five owners holding strips that run the entire length of the slope. The soil is very different at the top of the slope, where the wines can be more elegant and silky, compared with the bottom of the slope, where the soil is darker and the wines more muscular. Jasper Morris suggests in his book *Inside Burgundy* that perhaps the reason why the clos should have but did not receive Grand Cru status was because of its previous arrogant owner. Fourrier's Clos Saint-Jacques is a very unique parcel. The vines were planted in 1910, making it the oldest vineyard at Fourrier and one of the oldest vineyards in Burgundy. Vine age contributes to the wine's **haunting** depth, sumptuous tannins, **lingering** finish, and a **beguiling** array of flavors that range from graphite and earth to wild herbs and blackberries. In vintages like 1999, 2005, 2010, 2012, and 2015, the wine easily reaches Grand Cru quality. Only around 4,000 bottles are made per year.

IN THREE WORDS   *Captivating, classic, seamless.*

GRIOTTE-CHAMBERTIN GRAND CRU VIEILLE VIGNE, GEVREY-CHAMBERTIN

This is such a difficult wine to find, with only a few barrels made every year, that I hesitated to include it in this list. However, Fourrier's Griotte is such a great example of this tiny Grand Cru vineyard that I felt it merited inclusion. Griotte-Chambertin is a mere 2.7 hectares, split among nine growers, and the wines tend to be more aromatic, lifted, and less muscular than Chambertin or Clos de Bèze. It lies on an old quarry with plenty of active limestone, contributing to the wine's elegance and finesse. Fourrier's Griotte has lovely purity and **precision** in its flavors, each vintage reflecting both the site as well as the unique weather conditions of that year. However, there isn't a lot of vintage variation—what changes is the wine's personality more than

any substantial quality difference. I especially love the recent vintages from 2010, 2015, and 2016. There is natural concentration and *intensity* in this wine from ancient vines that are nearly 90 years old; the finish is incredibly long. Unlike many concentrated Grands Crus, Fourrier's Griotte is not impenetrable in its youth. There is enough to love and enjoy even if the wine is not yet 10 years old: lovely aromatics, ripe fruit sweetness, and *lush* tannins. However, the best vintages will warrant longer bottle age, and ideally even modest vintages shouldn't be approached for at least 10 to 15 years.

IN THREE WORDS *Compelling, intricate, lingering.*

66 **At a young age, Jean-Marie Fourrier committed himself to learning about winemaking and becoming a vigneron. It runs in his blood, with family ties to the vineyard dating back nearly a hundred years.** 99

DOMAINE FRANÇOIS LAMARCHE

address

9 Rue des Communes, 21700 Vosne-Romanée, Burgundy, France
Tel: +33 3 80 61 07 94

contact

Nicole Lamarche

farming philosophy

Organic cultivation since 2010.

in the cellar

Mostly destemmed, keeping whole berries, a small percentage of whole bunches may be added depending on vintage and wine; several days' cold maceration pre-fermentation; aged up to 20 months in oak; reduction of new oak from 100% in the past, up to 50% or none at all (e.g., 2016) depending on vintage.

total vineyard area

11 hectares

total annual production

60,000 bottles

key vineyard holdings

La Grande Rue Grand Cru Monopole	1.65 ha
Clos de Vougeot Grand Cru	1.35 ha
Grands Échezeaux Grand Cru	0.30 ha
Échezeaux Grand Cru	1.32 ha
Vosne-Romanée Premier Cru Les Chaumes	0.56 ha
Vosne-Romanée Premier Cru La Croix Rameau	0.21 ha
Vosne-Romanée Premier Cru Les Malconsorts	0.50 ha
Vosne-Romanée Premier Cru Les Suchots	0.58 ha
Nuits-Saint-Georges Premier Cru Les Cras	0.38 ha
Vosne-Romanée	0.89 ha

LA GRANDE RUE GRAND CRU MONOPOLE, VOSNE-ROMANÉE

La Grande Rue is a narrow strip ideally wedged between La Tâche to its south and Romanée-Conti to its north. This parcel was a wedding present given to Henri Lamarche in 1933 from his wealthy uncle Édouard, who was childless. However, it was not a Grand Cru until 1992, since at that time Henri did not see the necessity of paying the higher taxes for this status and did not bother to apply. Sixty years later, his son François made the appeal and was granted the status, given its geology, exposition, and ideal location. La Grande Rue became the youngest and the 33rd Grand Cru of Burgundy. Tragically, François Lamarche, who joined his father at the estate in 1985, died in 2013 in a tractor accident. Fortunately, the transition to the sixth generation had already occurred in 2007, when his daughter Nicole took sole charge over the winemaking. It is fantastic to see a strong group of women currently managing a top Vosne-Romanée estate: Nicole; her mother, Marie-Blanche; her cousin Nathalie; and Nathalie's mother, Geneviève. The estate has enviable parcels throughout the commune, making 14 different wines, including five Premiers Crus and four

Grands Crus. The family jewel is La Grande Rue, a small 1.6-hectare monopole, with its slope running nearly the full length as La Tâche. During the 1960s, until the mid-1990s, the wines were regarded and positioned like a Premier Cru. It was after the Grand Cru upgrade that effort was made to bring the wines up to Grand Cru level, including decreasing yields, more careful sorting, and building a new modern cellar, completed in 2000. The next jump came when Nicole Lamarche took charge and started refining the wines, making numerous small changes that have added up to more transparent wines that have *clarity*, elegance, and *grace*. La Grande Rue is a wine that favors finesse and subtlety over power, thus it never has the structure of La Tâche nor the brooding minerality of Romanée-Conti. Recent vintages of La Grande Rue, especially the 2005, 2010, 2014, and 2017, are *magnificent* and worthy of Grand Cru status. Given the stratospheric prices commanded by its two adjacent neighbors, La Grande Rue looks like a bargain.

IN THREE WORDS *Exceptional, transparent, tender.*

CHABLIS GRAND CRU LES CLOS, CHABLIS

Domaine Raveneau has been the reference standard for quality Chablis since the late François Raveneau established it in 1948. When François married Andrée Dauvissat (sister of Domaine Dauvissat's founder, René Dauvissat), it was the union of the two greatest names in Chablis. The modest holding, for Chablis, is barely 10 hectares, but it is nearly all in Grand Cru or Premier Cru vineyards. François retired in 1995, handing over the estate to his two capable sons, Jean-Marie and Bernard, joined by the next generation, Bernard's charming daughter Isabelle, since 2010. This is a simple cellar along a quiet street, and tasting with Bernard in the past and recently with Isabelle is a delightful experience. Bernard is inquisitive about the Asian market and the global perception of Chablis wines, and Isabelle is refreshingly candid about viticultural challenges and her winemaking decisions. Tasting Raveneau's entire range of wines is a lesson in minerality and a struggle to find words apart from crushed stone, slate, graphite, and salt. Yields are kept low and there is very little "winemaking" present in the wine; no hint of oak or butteriness, just complete *transparency* of the vintage and the terroir; one can almost taste Chablis' Kimmeridgian chalky-marl soil laden with marine sediment and fossils in the wine. If any dry white wine can challenge the best Burgundian reds for longevity, it would be Raveneau's Les Clos. This is the king of Chablis, the finest of the seven Grand Cru vineyards, with *sizzling* acidity, and minerality that gains in stature and depth with time in bottle. The 2008, 2010, and 2014 are bottled poetry. They are *inspiring* now in their youth but will be phenomenal with at least 15 years of bottle age.

IN THREE WORDS *Authentic, crystalline, poetic.*

DOMAINE FRANÇOIS RAVENEAU

address	9 Rue de Chichée, 89800 Chablis, Burgundy, France Tel: +33 3 86 42 17 46
contact	Isabelle Raveneau, Maxime Raveneau
farming philosophy	Sustainable and organic viticulture, with minimal spraying; low yields.
in the cellar	Matured 12 months in traditional old barrels; corks sealed with wax.

total vineyard area	10 hectares	**total annual production**	50,000 bottles

key vineyard holdings	Chablis Grand Cru Les Clos	0.50 ha	Chablis Premier Cru Montée de Tonnerre	3.12 ha
	Chablis Grand Cru Blanchot	0.67 ha		
	Chablis Grand Cru Valmur	0.75 ha	Chablis Premier Cru Monts-Mains	0.36 ha
	Chablis Premier Cru Vaillons	0.49 ha	Chablis	1.11 ha
	Chablis Premier Cru Butteaux	1.49 ha	Petit Chablis	0.82 ha
	Chablis Premier Cru Forêt	0.67 ha		

DOMAINE GEORGES MUGNERET-GIBOURG

(FORMERLY DOMAINE GEORGES MUGNERET)

address	5 Rue des Communes, 21700 Vosne-Romanée, Burgundy, France www.mugneret-gibourg.com Tel: +33 3 80 61 01 57
contact	Marie-Christine Mugneret, Marie-Andrée Mugneret
farming philosophy	Lutte raisonnée, plowing, no herbicides or insecticides.
in the cellar	Grapes mostly destemmed, up to 20% whole bunch depending on vintage and wine; 4–5 days' cold maceration; matured 18 months in oak barrels, two-thirds new for Grands Crus, one-third for Premiers Crus.

total vineyard area	8 hectares	**total annual production**	30,000 bottles

key vineyard holdings	Ruchottes-Chambertin Grand Cru	0.64 ha	Chambolle-Musigny Premier Cru	
	Clos de Vougeot Grand Cru	0.34 ha	Les Feusselottes	0.46 ha
	Échezeaux Grand Cru	1.24 ha	Vosne-Romanée	3.08 ha
	Nuits-Saint-Georges Premier Cru		Nuits-Saint-Georges	0.21 ha
	Les Chaignots	1.27 ha	Bourgogne	0.85 ha
	Nuits-Saint-Georges Premier Cru			
	Les Vignes Rondes	0.27 ha		

RUCHOTTES-CHAMBERTIN GRAND CRU, GEVREY-CHAMBERTIN

Since the death of Dr. Georges Mugneret in 1988, the three most important women in his life have come together to continue his legacy. Currently his two daughters, Marie-Christine, who has a doctorate in pharmaceutical studies, and Marie-Andrée, have made minor refinements in the vineyard and cellar. Marie-Christine, who is in charge of the winemaking, is committed to retaining the elegant style of wine that her father made. There are no firm and fast rules, and she is flexible both in the use of whole bunch (often up to 20%) as well as chaptalization (adding a bit of sugar to prolong fermentation and lightly increase alcohol levels). The use of new oak is also judicious among all its wines, from the three Premiers Crus to the Village Vosne-Romanée; no more than two-thirds is used for the Grands Crus. Its holdings may be modest, only 8 hectares total, but the majority is in Grand Cru and Premier Cru vineyards. Among its three Grand Cru holdings, Ruchottes-Chambertin is the most *sophisticated*, subtly layered with an intense mineral undertone. This small Grand Cru vineyard is only 3.3 hectares, with Mugneret-Gibourg owning just two-thirds of a hectare (Rousseau is the largest owner, with over 1 hectare). Ruchottes-Chambertin doesn't bloom and show its spicy, floral, and truffle flavors until it is at least 12 years old. One merely gets a whiff of it in its youth, when it is often so quiet that you wonder if it will ever speak. When it does express itself, it is an operetta—lively and *charming*, a wine that makes you smile. These wines are fairly consistent, with old vines dating back to the 1950s, but a few recent vintages stand out for their quality: 1999, 2005, 2009. Overall, Mugneret-Gibourg wines are about *harmony* and subtlety.

IN THREE WORDS *Stylish, harmonious, authentic.*

DOMAINE GEORGES ROUMIER

address	4 Rue de Vergy, 21220 Chambolle-Musigny, Burgundy, France www.roumier.com Tel: +33 3 80 62 86 37
contact	Christophe Roumier
farming philosophy	Organic principles, minimal treatments, no herbicides.
in the cellar	Mostly destemmed, proportion of whole bunch depending on vintage and wine; new oak used sparingly, one-third for Premiers Crus, and up to 50% for Grands Crus.
total vineyard area	12 hectares **total annual production** 52,000 bottles

key vinyeard holdings			
Red		Chambolle-Musigny Premier Cru	
Musigny Grand Cru	0.10 ha	Combottes	0.27 ha
Bonnes-Mares Grand Cru	1.89 ha	Morey-Saint-Denis Premier Cru	
Échezeaux (2016 first vintage)	0.13 ha	Clos de la Bussière Monopole	2.59 ha
Ruchottes-Chambertin Grand Cru	0.54 ha	Chambolle-Musigny	3.70 ha
Charmes-Chambertin Grand Cru	0.28 ha	Bourgogne	0.45 ha
Chambolle-Musigny Premier Cru			
Les Amoureuses	0.40 ha	*White*	
Chambolle-Musigny Premier Cru		Corton-Charlemagne Grand Cru	0.20 ha
Les Cras	1.75 ha		

Since Christophe Roumier took over fully from his father in 1990, the wines have become more refined, with wonderful detail and precision. Roumier wines have always been elegant, as vintages from the 1960s and 1970s reveal. The wines made by his grandfather then his father were good, and the best vintages great, but the quality jump came when Christophe, with an oenology degree from Dijon University, started to make changes in the vineyard and cellar.

The estate is now farming largely under organic principles, with no herbicides used, no chemical fertilizers, and minimal spraying. Sorting is done both in the vineyard and the winery with only perfectly ripe berries going into the vat. In the cellar, refinements include the addition of sorting tables and very gentle extraction.

I have been fortunate to taste numerous verticals of Roumier's Bonnes-Mares, Musigny, and Les Amoureuses. Despite their subtle personality, Roumier wines are built to age. Young wines tasted in the cellar don't do justice to the gorgeous beauties they become when they are fully open and expressive—even his Village Chambolle-Musigny benefits from around 8 years of bottle age. In their youth the wines are tightly wound, tense, light, and linear in shape; with age the wines gain in stature and detail, with the most seductive aromatics and delicately layered palate.

Nearly all the wines in Roumier's portfolio are benchmark wines—if you want to understand the depth and quality of Musigny or Bonnes-Mares, its wines define the terroir. While its Musigny is nearly impossible to find—one-tenth of a hectare produces just one barrel every year—the Bonnes-Mares is a lot easier to find, with 1.9 hectares producing around 6,000 bottles per year. If I had space to include one more wine from Roumier's portfolio, it would be the Chambolle-Musigny Premier Cru Les Amoureuses ("the lovers"). Here, the wine's intensity, elegance, and quality confer it Grand Cru status, and the market has priced it accordingly. The wine is consistently silky-textured, precise, with an astonishing array of flavors. The soil type in this 5-hectare Premier Cru site is very similar to Musigny, with the active limestone providing finesse and fine-grained, polished tannins.

Roumier's Village and Premier Cru wines are beautiful too—the Chambolle-Musigny is charming and classic, while all of its Chambolle Premier Cru wines are superb; besides Les Amoureuses, Les Cras, more widely available, is exquisite. I also like its Morey-Saint-Denis Premier Cru Clos de la Bussière, a monopole walled vineyard of good size, also more easily found in the market. At every level, Roumier makes detailed, elegant wines; Christophe has clearly perfected the formula for combining precise intensity with finesse.

BONNES-MARES GRAND CRU, CHAMBOLLE-MUSIGNY

There is impressive consistency in Roumier's Bonnes-Mares; even in lighter vintages, like 2007 and 2011, I find the wines ***profound*** and ***persistent***. Roumier is one of the top three farmers of this 15-hectare Grand Cru vineyard, with 1.9 hectares. The Roumier Bonnes-Mares is often compared with Vogüé, which has almost 2.7 hectares; Roumier's rendition is more floral, with less exotic spice than Vogüé's. Many plots scattered throughout the Grand Cru vineyard have been added over the years; the most recent addition is a 0.5-hectare section that Roumier is farming under a share-cropping agreement, or *métayage.* The original parcel came from Roumier's family in 1924, when Georges Roumier married Geneviève Quanquin and received it as dowry. The scattered holdings mean that each parcel produces a different style depending on the soil, the most noticeable being whether it is from *terres rouges* (red) or *terres blanches* (white marl) soil. Most of Roumier's plots come from the white soil, thus giving greater florality and minerality to the wine. Due to the wine's ***consistency***, I would happily recommend nearly all the vintages from 1999 onward, perhaps with the exception of 2003 (too broad) and 2004 (a bit green).

IN THREE WORDS ***Gorgeous, intricate, layered.***

MUSIGNY GRAND CRU, CHAMBOLLE-MUSIGNY

Musigny is mythical by reputation, with its vineyard dating back a thousand years, but it's even more so at Roumier. The total size of Musigny vineyard is about 10 hectares, with the majority owned by Vogüé; the other sixteen owners farm tiny parcels, and even one hectare is considered a good-size parcel. With only 300 bottles of Musigny on average produced per year, this wine from Roumier is impossible to find. Those fortunate enough to have allocations treasure it, and thus finding them at auction is also challenging. Beware of large quantities of this wine being offered at auction or from brokers, since numerous fakes have been found circulating in the market. With rarity comes ever-increasing demand (and prices) to experience this **seductive**, graceful wine. At its peak, with at least 12 years of bottle age, the bouquet is explosive and **captivating**—a mix of rose petals, crushed violets, and forest floor that changes with each swirl and sip. The palate combines elegance, finesse, and delicate intensity, with an **unforgettable** finish. The old vines and excellent terroir—the parcel is located in the Les Musigny *climat*—offer wonderful consistency. Perhaps that explains why, in some ways, Christophe's influence in this vineyard is the lightest; the wines made by his father in the 1980s and 1970s are equally sublime.

IN THREE WORDS *Exquisite, magnificent, magical.*

> **"Roumier wines have always been elegant, as vintages from the 1960s and 1970s reveal. Since Christophe Roumier took over fully from his father in 1990, the wines have become more refined, with wonderful detail and precision. Nearly all the wines in Roumier's portfolio are benchmark wines— they define the terroir."**

66 What though youth gave love and roses, Age still leaves us friends and wine. 99

Thomas More

Dinner aboard the ocean liner *Leviathan*, c. 1920s.

CHAMBOLLE-MUSIGNY PREMIER CRU LES CRAS, CHAMBOLLE-MUSIGNY

Ghislaine Barthod was a pioneer in the 1980s, taking over an important family property in 1986, in what was then a man's world. The vineyards were from her mother Madeleine Noëllat's side of the family, whose parents owned an estate in Chambolle-Musigny. Together with her husband, Louis Boillot, who runs his own domaine, they built a winery and cellar where both wines are housed but vinified and marketed separately. Barthod's holdings are unusual in that she has no Grand Cru, but nine small parcels of Chambolle-Musigny Premiers Crus. During her father's time, many were blended together and sold as Premier Cru without a vineyard designation, but Ghislaine has chosen to distinguish each plot's character and personality by keeping them separate. This is a wonderful property to explore nine out of the 24 total Premiers Crus in Chambolle-Musigny. Thanks to friends who are avid collectors, I have had the chance to taste several horizontals of these Premiers Crus, namely the 1999, 1996, and 1990 vintages. In the 1996 horizontal, which was blind and consisted of four Barthod Premiers Crus, we were not told they were from the same producer. The wines had such different personalities that I was convinced it had to be at least two producers. I loved the Les Cras and the Les Fuées the most, which was consistent with my conclusions from other horizontals of Barthod wines in different vintages. While Les Fuées is rich, generous, and sensual, I love Les Cras for its taut **structure**, tension, and **depth**. Vintages like 1990 and 1996 are **glorious** now, and look out for the trilogy of three great vintages for Les Cras: 2008, 2009, and 2010. | IN THREE WORDS | *Elegant, noble, profound.*

DOMAINE GHISLAINE BARTHOD

address	4 Ruelle du Lavoir, 21220 Chambolle-Musigny, Burgundy, France
contact	Ghislaine Barthod
farming philosophy	Lutte raisonnée, no herbicides or pesticides; minimal treatments; vineyards are plowed.
in the cellar	Bunches mostly destemmed; several days' natural cold maceration; matured 18 months in oak, with one-quarter new oak for Premiers Crus.

total vineyard area	7 hectares	total annual production	35,000 bottles

key vineyard holdings	Chambolle-Musigny Premier Cru 　Les Baudes	0.22 ha	Chambolle-Musigny Premier Cru 　Les Gruenchers	0.18 ha
	Chambolle-Musigny Premier Cru 　Aux Beaux Bruns	0.72 ha	Chambolle-Musigny Premier Cru 　Les Cras	0.86 ha
	Chambolle-Musigny Premier Cru 　Les Charmes	0.26 ha	Chambolle-Musigny Premier Cru 　Les Fuées	0.25 ha
	Chambolle-Musigny Premier Cru 　Les Châtelots	0.33 ha	Chambolle-Musigny Premier Cru 　Les Veroilles	0.37 ha
	Chambolle-Musigny Premier Cru 　Les Combottes	0.12 ha	Chambolle-Musigny	1.75 ha
			Bourgogne Rouge Les Bons Bâtons	2.00 ha

DOMAINE HENRI BOILLOT

(FORMERLY DOMAINE JEAN BOILLOT)

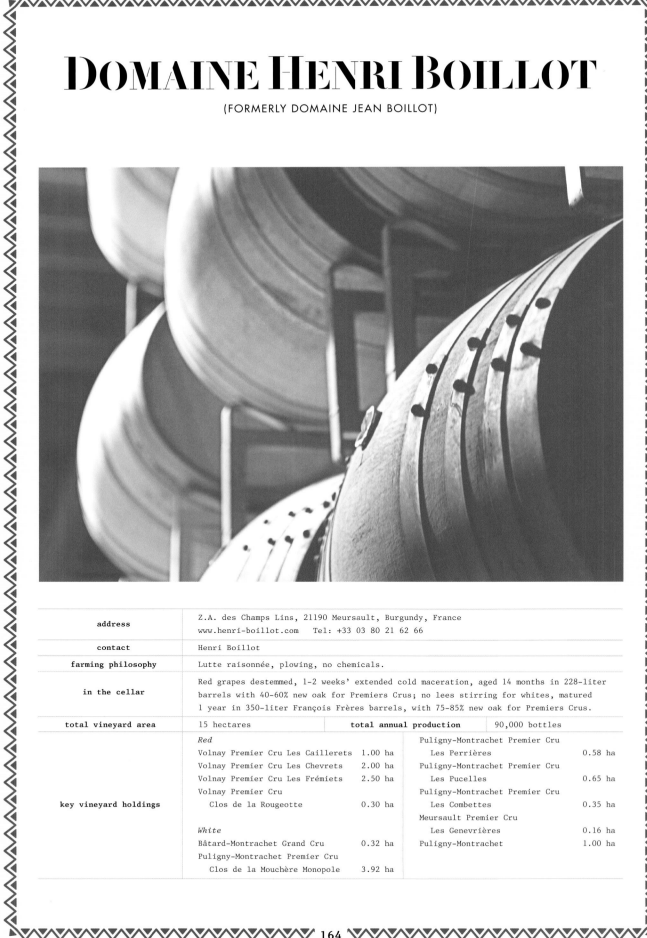

address	Z.A. des Champs Lins, 21190 Meursault, Burgundy, France www.henri-boillot.com Tel: +33 03 80 21 62 66
contact	Henri Boillot
farming philosophy	Lutte raisonnée, plowing, no chemicals.
in the cellar	Red grapes destemmed, 1–2 weeks' extended cold maceration, aged 14 months in 228-liter barrels with 40–60% new oak for Premiers Crus; no lees stirring for whites, matured 1 year in 350-liter François Frères barrels, with 75–85% new oak for Premiers Crus.

total vineyard area	15 hectares	**total annual production**	90,000 bottles

key vineyard holdings	*Red*		Puligny-Montrachet Premier Cru	
	Volnay Premier Cru Les Caillerets	1.00 ha	Les Perrières	0.58 ha
	Volnay Premier Cru Les Chevrets	2.00 ha	Puligny-Montrachet Premier Cru	
	Volnay Premier Cru Les Frémiets	2.50 ha	Les Pucelles	0.65 ha
	Volnay Premier Cru		Puligny-Montrachet Premier Cru	
	Clos de la Rougeotte	0.30 ha	Les Combettes	0.35 ha
			Meursault Premier Cru	
	White		Les Genevrières	0.16 ha
	Bâtard-Montrachet Grand Cru	0.32 ha	Puligny-Montrachet	1.00 ha
	Puligny-Montrachet Premier Cru			
	Clos de la Mouchère Monopole	3.92 ha		

PULIGNY-MONTRACHET PREMIER CRU CLOS DE LA MOUCHÈRE MONOPOLE, PULIGNY-MONTRACHET

Henri Boillot comes from a long line of distinguished vignerons whose roots can be traced back to the mid-19th century in Burgundy. Over several generations, the extended family married into other illustrious wine families, such as the Sauzets, and so, confusingly, there are several estates that bear the Boillot name: Jean-Marc Boillot is Henri's brother, while Pierre Boillot (who runs Domaine Lucien Boillot) and Louis Boillot are both his cousins. Henri Boillot's holdings are from his father Jean Boillot, and he changed the estate name to Henri Boillot after buying out his sister's and brother's shares in 2005. I first tasted with Henri Boillot in 2001 not too long after he moved into the modern premises in Meursault. I was very impressed with his minerally white wines, with their finely etched detail and focused acidity. While his négociant business remains successful, offering a range of very good white wines, the 15-hectare domaine based in Volnay has made bigger strides, consistently producing exceptional wines. The estate is split roughly into half red and half white wine production, although most people associate Henri Boillot with whites, due to his négociant business. He has wonderful parcels of Volnay Premiers Crus, including Les Caillerets, and the wines are lovely and delicious—pure, fruity, and quite modern in style. I have to confess that I find his whites much more exciting, and my two favorites are two of his Premier Cru Puligny-Montrachets, Les Pucelles and Clos de la Mouchère, which is a monopole. I chose the Clos for inclusion here because it is more widely available, since Henri owns nearly 4 hectares versus only two-thirds of a hectare for the Pucelles. While Pucelles is all finesse and purity, the Clos de la Mouchère, with vines that date back to the 1940s, is complex, creamy, and **striking** in its energy. Recent vintages have been excellent, and the 2014 and 2012 look especially promising, with the 2017 and 2011 not far behind; but the **beauty** of this wine is that it offers **pleasure** at all periods of its long life.

IN THREE WORDS *Vivacious, intense, delicious.*

NUITS-SAINT-GEORGES PREMIER CRU LES SAINT-GEORGES, NUITS-SAINT-GEORGES

Henri Gouges played an important role in local politics and in the development of the wine industry in Burgundy at a crucial time. He was the mayor of Nuits-Saint-Georges during the creation of the AOC system in the 1930s and was the person who effectively advocated that no Grands Crus be awarded in the commune. It is not clear why he took this position, although for other communes it was mainly due to financial reasons, to avoid Grand Cru taxes, which were higher than for Premiers Crus. There is now a movement among key Nuits growers to have several Premier Cru parcels upgraded to Grand Cru status. Henri Gouges was also instrumental in the movement toward domaine bottling as a response to négociants tampering with wines. Even now, this 15-hectare domaine continues to play a leading role in Nuits-Saint-Georges, in defining high standards and not being swayed by market trends and demands. Currently, the fourth generation is at the helm, and the wines continue to be built for aging: wiry, intense, and serious in their youth, with a kaleidoscopic array of flavors emerging after sufficient bottle age, normally at least 10 years for the Premiers Crus. Tasting with Gregory Gouges, or his cousin Antoine Gouges, the fourth-generation family members crafting these wines, is always a calming experience; he is thoughtful, articulate, and open about what they do in the cellar and the winery, explaining his decisions and choices. Nuits has a reputation for hard, structured, gutsy red wines, but this is no longer the case at Gouges, as well as elsewhere in the commune. Tannin management is much more sophisticated now, and combined with warmer vintages and more precise winemaking, the wines are ample, velvety, and can be quite fruity, such as the young 2017. Gouges makes a *beautiful* range of Premier Cru Nuits, and my favorite, which is not a surprise, is Les Saint-Georges. This 1-hectare parcel has vines dating back to the 1960s and is consistently the most complex and complete wine in Gouges' portfolio. Its 2010 is *stunning* and its 2015 even better still; but the vintages to drink now of Les Saint-Georges are those in the 1980s and 1990s, if you can find them. The 1999 is *superb* and the 1985 magnificent.

IN THREE WORDS *Classic, persistent, complex.*

DOMAINE HENRI GOUGES

address	7 Rue du Moulin, 21700 Nuits-Saint-Georges, Burgundy, France		
	www.gouges.com Tel: +33 3 80 61 04 40		
contact	Grégory Gouges		
farming philosophy	Organic since 2008.		
in the cellar	Grapes are destemmed, with a period of cold maceration; matured 18 months in barrels		
	with no more than one-fifth new oak.		
total vineyard area	14.5 hectares	total annual production	50,000 bottles

key vineyard holdings	Red			
	Nuits-Saint-Georges Premier Cru		Nuits-Saint-Georges Premier Cru	
	Les Saint-Georges	1.08 ha	Les Chaignots	0.46 ha
	Nuits-Saint-Georges Premier Cru		Nuits-Saint-Georges Premier Cru Les	
	Les Vaucrains	0.98 ha	Chênes Carteaux	1.01 ha
	Nuits-Saint-Georges Premier Cru		Nuits-Saint-Georges	3.20 ha
	Clos des Porrets-Saint-Georges	3.57 ha		
	Nuits-Saint-Georges Premier Cru		White	
	Les Pruliers	1.88 ha	Nuits-Saint-Georges Premier Cru	
			La Perrière Blanc	0.41 ha

DOMAINE JACQUES CARILLON

(FORMERLY LOUIS CARILLON ET FILS)

Georges de la Tour, *The Cheat with the Ace of Diamonds*, detail, c. 1635-40.

address	1 Rue Drouhin, 21190 Puligny-Montrachet, Burgundy, France www.jacques-carillon.com Tel: + 33 3 80 21 01 30		
contact	Jacques Carillon		
farming philosophy	Lutte raisonnée, plowing, minimal treatments, no herbicides.		
in the cellar	Whites and reds matured 1 year in barrel on fine lees; minimal new oak, up to 20% maximum.		
total vineyard area	5.2 hectares	**total annual production**	35,000 bottles

key vineyard holdings	*White*
	Bienvenues-Bâtard-Montrachet
	  Grand Cru
	Puligny-Montrachet Premier Cru
	  Champs Canet
	Puligny-Montrachet Premier Cru
	  Les Perrières
	Puligny-Montrachet Premier Cru
	  Les Referts
		0.12 ha
		
		0.55 ha
		
		0.61 ha
		
		0.24 ha
			Puligny-Montrachet
			Chassagne-Montrachet
			
			Red
			Saint-Aubin Premier Cru
			  Les Pitangerets
			Saint-Aubin Rouge
				2.71 ha
				0.27 ha
				
				0.45 ha
				0.28 ha

BIENVENUES-BÂTARD-MONTRACHET GRAND CRU, PULIGNY-MONTRACHET

I have always been a big fan of Louis Carillon's Puligny-Montrachets and was saddened to hear that his estate would be split between his two sons, Jacques and François, who would go their own ways. Jacques is the older, quieter one, who made the wines with his father, Louis; he seems happier walking in the vineyards than he does pouring wine for tasters to sample at his cellar. Not that he is unfriendly, but he is clearly a doer rather than a talker. Starting with the 2010 vintage, Jacques Carillon carries on his family's legacy in wine, going back to the 16th century, and makes wine solely from his 5-hectare estate. François, on the other hand, has been on an expansion plan since he split with his brother, without any qualms about being a négociant to supplement his share of the family vineyards. I tasted at both for many years and always preferred Jacques' wines, which are more **authentic** and pure, and closer to Louis Carillon's style

> " **Jacques Carillon carries on his family's legacy in wine, going back to the 16th century.** "

than François' wines. Jacques established this small domaine in 2010 with his wife, Sylvia, and employs very few people, opting to do everything himself. The vineyard is farmed sustainably and there is very little cellar work—minimal influence of lees or oak, just pure, fresh fruit harvested ripe but early enough to retain its natural acidity. The tiny parcel of Bienvenues-Bâtard-Montrachet is a rare gem. The entire Grand Cru vineyard is only 3.7 hectares, and Jacques Carillon farms just one-tenth of a hectare of vines that are more than 50 years old. The Bienvenues is seductively **layered** even in its youth, with its power perceptible in the minerality and acidity that form the backbone. Vintages like 1996, 1999, and 2005 from Louis Carillon and made by Jacques Carillon are **magical**, memorable experiences, and his recent vintages such as 2010, 2014, and 2015 are equally superb.

IN THREE WORDS   ***Pure, delicate, memorable.***

"When a man drinks wine at dinner, he begins to be better pleased with himself."

Plato

Edward Hopper, *In a Restaurant*, c. 1916–25.

MONTRACHET GRAND CRU, CHASSAGNE–MONTRACHET

Most domaines are stronger in either Côte de Beaune or Côte de Nuits, but Jacques Prieur is strong in both. The estate owns 21 hectares of some of the most prestigious vineyards in both côtes, producing nine Grands Crus and 15 Premier Cru wines. Established by Jacques Prieur in 1956, the estate was handed down to his six children after he and his wife passed away; but not long thereafter it was put up for sale, in the 1980s. The Labruyère family, together with four other French families, purchased the winery in 1988. They hired Nadine Gublin, who was the winemaker at Antonin Rodet, and put her in charge of winemaking in 1990. Together with Édouard Labruyère and Martin Prieur, Jacques Prieur's grandson, the trio slowly began to revitalize an estate that had a reputation for making solid but uninspiring wines. The wines are now riper, more **vibrant**, and better balanced than a few decades ago. The vineyards are being converted to organic farming, and the wines are made in an ample and expressive style, sleek and modern. Its Montrachet is almost always my favorite wine in its large portfolio. This is not a shy Montrachet; it is **sumptuous**, powerful, **exuberant**, layered with an abundance of fruit flavors. Jacques Prieur makes one of the most approachable Montrachets in its youth—happiness in a bottle.

IN THREE WORDS   *Opulent, expressive, joyful.*

DOMAINE JACQUES PRIEUR

address	6 Rue des Santenots, 21190 Meursault, Burgundy, France https://www.prieur.com Tel: + 33 3 80 21 23 85
contact	Édouard Labruyère
farming philosophy	Lutte raisonnée, plowing, minimal spraying; vineyards being converted to organic farming.
in the cellar	Red grapes mostly destemmed, with small percentage of whole bunch depending on wine and vintage; matured up to 18 months in oak, with one-third new oak for Premiers Crus and up to 100% new for Grands Crus; white grapes fermented in oak and matured 18 months on lees, with new oak use varying with wine and vintage.

total vineyard area	21 hectares	**total annual production**	120,000 bottles

key vineyard holdings	*Red*		*White*

Chambertin Grand Cru	0.49 ha	Montrachet Grand Cru	0.59 ha
Chambertin–Clos de Bèze Grand Cru	0.15 ha	Chevalier-Montrachet Grand Cru	0.14 ha
Musigny Grand Cru	0.77 ha	Corton-Charlemagne Grand Cru	0.22 ha
Clos de Vougeot Grand Cru	1.28 ha	Puligny-Montrachet Premier Cru	
Échezeaux Grand Cru	0.36 ha	Les Combettes	1.50 ha
Corton Bressandes Grand Cru	0.73 ha	Meursault Premier Cru Perrières	0.28 ha
Gevrey-Chambertin Premier Cru	0.49 ha	Meursault Premier Cru Santenots	0.08 ha
Beaune Premier Cru Champs Pimont	2.06 ha	Meursault Premier Cru Charmes	0.10 ha
Beaune Premier Cru		Beaune Premier Cru Champs Pimont	1.42 ha
Clos de la Féguine	1.59 ha	Beaune Premier Cru	
Beaune Premier Cru Grèves	1.17 ha	Clos de la Féguine	0.27 ha
Pommard Premier Cru Charmots	0.27 ha	Beaune Premier Cru Grèves	0.54 ha
Volnay Premier Cru Champans	0.35 ha	Meursault Clos de Mazeray	2.87 ha
Volnay Premier Cru Santenots	0.59 ha		
Volnay Premier Cru			
Clos des Santenots	1.19 ha		
Meursault Clos de Mazeray	0.25 ha		

DOMAINE JACQUES-FRÉDÉRIC MUGNIER

address	Château de Chambolle-Musigny, 21220 Chambolle-Musigny, Burgundy, France www.mugnier.fr Tel: + 33 3 80 62 85 39		
contact	Frédéric Mugnier		
farming philosophy	Organic principles; no fertilizers, herbicides, or insecticides used since early 1990s.		
in the cellar	Grapes are all destemmed; a few days' cool maceration at 15°C prior to fermentation; matured 18 months with minimal new oak, up to 20%.		
total vineyard area	14 hectares	**total annual production**	60,000 bottles

key vineyard holdings	*Red*
	Musigny Grand Cru 1.13 ha
	Bonnes-Mares Grand Cru 0.36 ha
	Chambolle-Musigny Premier Cru
	  Les Fuées 0.71 ha
			Chambolle-Musigny Premier Cru
			  Les Amoureuses 0.53 ha
			Nuits-Saint-Georges Premier Cru
			  Clos de la Maréchale 9.55 ha
			Chambolle-Musigny 1.35 ha

CHAMBOLLE–MUSIGNY PREMIER CRU LES AMOUREUSES, CHAMBOLLE–MUSIGNY

The 14 hectares of vineyards that make up this domaine have been in the family since 1863. However, no one in the family was interested in making wine until Jacques-Frédéric Mugnier took over the vineyard and estate in 1978; this was then passed down in 1985 to his son, Frédéric Mugnier, the fifth-generation family member. Vineyards that were leased out to Faiveley, Bruno Clair, and others were taken back, and by 2004 all the vineyards were reclaimed. Frédéric Mugnier makes classic Chambolle-Musigny—without much new oak, with very little intervention, no fining or filtration, and lots of humility. He is a soft-spoken man who talks about his wines with great respect. Frédéric was originally an engineer and then a commercial pilot before returning to the family domaine. The wines, from the Villages to the Grands Crus, are elegant, beautifully perfumed, with lovely tension and energy. While the Village wines, especially the Chambolle-Musigny, are excellent, it is Les Amoureuses and Musigny that are magical. I have always considered Les Amoureuses worthy of Grand Cru status, and at Mugnier the wines achieve the *purity*, precision, and depth to be among this elite category. Mugnier owns half a hectare in this vineyard with vines that were planted in the 1950s and 1960s. With vine age and high-limestone soil, the wines are *delicately* powerful, and vintages such as 2002, 2005, and 2009 prove that Les Amoureuses can be a sensual, *magical* experience.

IN THREE WORDS | *Enchanting, multifaceted, ethereal.*

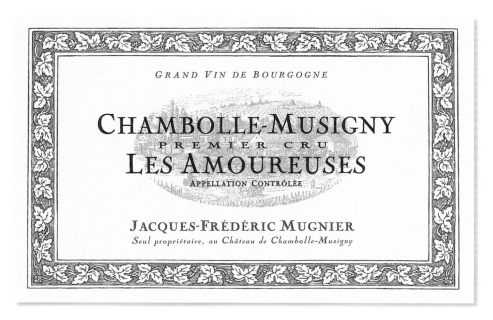

LE MUSIGNY GRAND CRU, CHAMBOLLE-MUSIGNY

Frédéric Mugnier makes subtle, complex wines with gorgeous aromatics and silky tannins; the wines are pale in color, aromatically seductive, and incredibly persistent on the palate. At the top of his portfolio sits Musigny, with over 1 hectare, making him the second-largest owner of this nearly 12-hectare Grand Cru vineyard, just after Vogüé. Mugnier's light touch in the cellar, with very little intervention and minimal new oak, means his Musigny appears delicate—light-colored, immensely *perfumed*, and gentle. However, this is just the initial surface impression. On the palate the wine offers *sensual*, layered floral flavors, while behind this delicacy lies a firm structure that is minerally, finely etched, and taut. This allows the wine to age and evolve for several decades easily. Mugnier destems and keeps the berries whole, so there is always *freshness* and incredible aromatic intensity. The low yields, combined with old-vine parcels that date back to 1947, mean these wines have great aging capability. There are no bad vintages of Mugnier's Musigny; even modest vintages like 2006 and 1998 produced great wines. However, two vintages stand out for their excellent quality: 2002 and 2005. Musigny is highly desirable and priced to match. A more affordable alternative is its Nuits-Saint-Georges Premier Cru Clos de la Maréchale: It is one of the most elegant, delicious Nuits Premiers Crus, with a touch of Chambolle charm and Mugnier's finesse.

| IN THREE WORDS | *Graceful, elegant, finely-etched.* |

> **"The low yields, combined with old-vine parcels that date back to 1947, mean these wines have great aging capability."**

Wine harvest in the French countryside, colored engraving, 1891.

DOMAINE JEAN GRIVOT

address	6 Rue de la Croix Rameau, 21700 Vosne-Romanée, Burgundy, France www.domainegrivot.fr Tel: +33 3 80 61 05 95
contact	Étienne Grivot
farming philosophy	Lutte raisonnée, minimal spraying; high-density planting, 11,000 vines per hectare.
in the cellar	Grapes destemmed; 1 week pre-fermentation cold maceration; matured 15 months in oak barrels, 20% new for Villages, 30-40% for Premiers Crus, and up to 50% for Grands Crus.

total vineyard area	15 hectares	**total annual production**	80,000 bottles

key vineyard holdings	*Red*		Vosne-Romanée Premier Cru	
	Richebourg Grand Cru	0.31 ha	Les Rouges	0.33 ha
	Clos de Vougeot Grand Cru	1.86 ha	Nuits-Saint-Georges Premier Cru	
	Échezeaux Grand Cru	0.84 ha	Aux Boudots	0.85 ha
	Vosne-Romanée Premier Cru		Nuits-Saint-Georges Premier Cru	
	Les Beaux Monts	0.93 ha	Les Pruliers	0.76 ha
	Vosne-Romanée Premier Cru		Nuits-Saint-Georges Premier Cru	
	Aux Brûlées	0.26 ha	Les Roncières	0.50 ha
	Vosne-Romanée Premier Cru		Nuits-Saint-Georges Aux Lavières	0.62 ha
	Les Chaumes	0.15 ha	Nuits-Saint-Georges Les Charmois	0.52 ha
	Vosne-Romanée Premier Cru		Chambolle-Musigny	
	Les Suchots	0.21 ha	La Combe d'Orveaux	0.62 ha
	Vosne-Romanée Premier Cru		Vosne-Romanée Bossières	0.73 ha
	Les/Aux Reignots	0.07 ha	Vosne-Romanée	2.97 ha

RICHEBOURG GRAND CRU, VOSNE-ROMANÉE

The Grivot family history and its vineyards date back to the 19th century. It is among the finest and most well regarded families, with enviable holdings in prime vineyards throughout the Côte de Nuits. Étienne Grivot, currently at the helm, took over from his father in 1982 and is now joined by his articulate and charming daughter, Mathilde. In the modern era, perhaps Domaine Grivot is most well known for its relationship with controversial consultant Guy Accad, who espoused long pre-fermentation cold maceration with huge doses of sulfur; this method has been long abandoned by the domaine, replaced with a week of cold soak with moderate sulfur additions. The period of experimentation from the late 1980s to the early 1990s meant that the wines during this period are not consistent, and tended to be modern, fruity, and somewhat extracted with grippy rather than suave tannins. Since the early 2000s, the wines have settled and become more consistently fine: Tannins are rounder and have lost their firm grip, the fruit is delicately layered rather than punchy, and the acidity is finer and better integrated into the wine. Tasting at Jean Grivot is a study in the terroirs of Vosne-Romanée. It has six Premiers Crus, two different bottlings of Vosne-Romanée, and no less than three Grands Crus, two from Vosne-Romanée and one from Vougeot. All three Grands Crus are excellent. I am in love with its 2010 Échezeaux, and its Vougeot is extremely charming. However, the jewel in its estate is clearly the Richebourg, made from over 80-year-old vines. This small plot, less than one-third of a hectare, produces wines of *finesse*, harmony, and breathtaking *beauty* at its peak. There are fewer than five barrels made per year, but it is worth the search to lay down the 2005, 2010, or the 2015 in the cellar. Mathilde's influence is increasingly present in the wines, with every vintage acquiring greater *purity* and precision.

IN THREE WORDS *Harmonious, plush, breathtaking.*

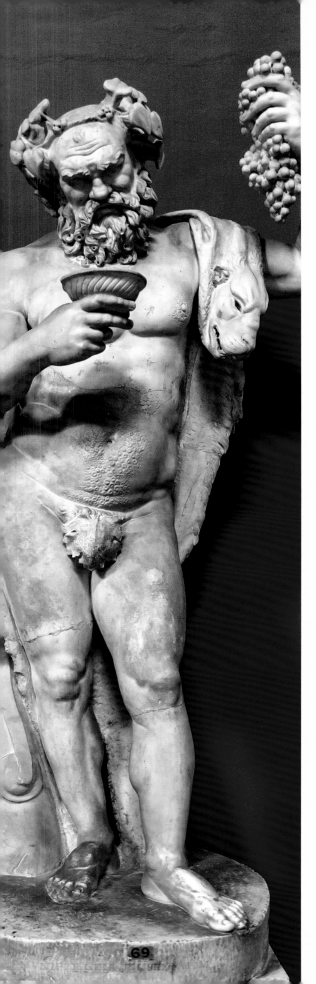

DOMAINE JEAN-JACQUES CONFURON

address

Les Vignottes D974, 21700 Premeaux-Prissey, Burgundy, France   Tel: + 33 3 80 62 31 08

contact

Sophie Meunier

farming philosophy

Fully organic since 1991, with some biodynamic methods employed.

in the cellar

Grapes destemmed; several days' cold maceration pre-fermentation; aged 16-18 months in oak, with half new oak for Villages and up to 80% new oak for Grands Crus.

total vineyard area

8.5 hectares

total annual production

45,000 bottles

key vineyard holdings

Red

Romanée-Saint-Vivant Grand Cru	0.50 ha
Clos de Vougeot Grand Cru	0.52 ha
Nuits-Saint-Georges Premier Cru Aux Boudots	0.30 ha
Nuits-Saint-Georges Premier Cru Les Chaboeufs	0.48 ha
Vosne-Romanée Premier Cru Les Beaux Monts	0.30 ha
Chambolle-Musigny Premier Cru	0.35 ha
Chambolle-Musigny	1.15 ha
Nuits-Saint-Georges Les Flurières	1.23 ha
Côte de Nuits-Villages Les Vignottes	1.26 ha
Côte de Nuits-Villages La Montagne	0.63 ha

Statue of Silenus, Pio-Clementine Museum, Room of Muses, Vatican Museums, Rome.

ROMANÉE–SAINT–VIVANT GRAND CRU, VOSNE–ROMANÉE

Sophie Meunier met her husband while studying wine, preparing to take over her family estate, when her father, Jean-Jacques Confuron, fell ill in 1982 (he died the following year). Since 1985, she and her husband, Alain Meunier, have been making the wine together. The vineyards under Sophie and Alain's care are enviable; handed down from both the maternal and paternal sides of her family. Its 8.5 hectares are scattered in Nuits-Saint-Georges, Chambolle-Musigny, and Vosne-Romanée, and include some ancient vines: The Romanée-Saint-Vivant, my favorite in its portfolio, was planted in 1929. Its minimal intervention philosophy and gentle hand in the cellar, combined with organic farming, produce wines of finesse that are filled with nuance and detail. All the wines in its entire portfolio are pale in color, with silky tannins, as light as a feather on the palate. These are wines of pleasure, with gorgeous perfume and delicacy. Some may find them *too* delicate, but if you are quiet enough and listen to the wines, they not only sing but also dance for you. The Romanée-Saint-Vivant in vintages like 1996 or 2005 is **sensual** and persistent. Typical of this Grand Cru, the bouquet is intoxicating, and Confuron's version **ethereal** and light, a wine that twirls on your tongue. Recent vintages like 2009 and 2012 are **harmonious** and complete, but unlike denser styles, Confuron's Romanée-Saint-Vivant can be approached at 8 or 9 years old. The 2009 and 2008 are delicious now, but will no doubt age for decades.

IN THREE WORDS *Tender, persistent, intoxicating.*

181

DOMAINE JEAN-MARC ET ANTONIN PILLOT

(FORMERLY JEAN-MARC PILLOT AND DOMAINE JEAN PILLOT ET FILS)

Raphaelle Peale, *Still Life with Fruit, Cakes and Wine*, 1821.

address	Le Haut des Champs, 21190 Chassagne-Montrachet, Burgundy, France Tel: + 33 3 80 21 92 96
contact	Jean-Marc Pillot
farming philosophy	Lutte raisonnée, plowing, no herbicides or pesticides.
in the cellar	Whites have minimal lees stirring, matured in mostly François Frères barrels, up to 18 months depending on wine, with very little new oak use, only up to 30%; reds are destemmed, several days' cold maceration, matured 1 year or more with minimal new oak.

total vineyard area	12 hectares	**total annual production**	100,000 bottles

key vineyard holdings		
Red		
Chassagne-Montrachet Premier Cru		
Clos Saint-Jean	0.45 ha	
Chassagne-Montrachet Premier Cru		
Les Macherelles	0.37 ha	
Chassagne-Montrachet Premier Cru		
Morgeot	0.65 ha	
Chassagne-Montrachet	1.40 ha	
Santenay Les Champs Claude	1.39 ha	
Bourgogne	1.03 ha	

White	
Chassagne-Montrachet Premier Cru	
Les Baudines	0.15 ha
Chassagne-Montrachet Premier Cru	
Les Caillerets	0.18 ha
Chassagne-Montrachet Premier Cru	
Les Champs Gains	0.25 ha
Chassagne-Montrachet Premier Cru	
Les Chenevottes	0.29 ha
Chassagne-Montrachet Premier Cru	
Clos Saint-Jean	0.38 ha

Chassagne-Montrachet Premier Cru	
Les Macherelles	0.28 ha
Chassagne-Montrachet Premier Cru	
La Maltroie	0.16 ha
Chassagne-Montrachet Premier Cru	
Morgeot	0.27 ha
Chassagne-Montrachet Premier Cru	
Les Vergers Clos Saint-Marc	0.49 ha
Rully Premier Cru Les Raclots	0.20 ha
Montagny Premier Cru Les Gouresses	0.40 ha
Chassagne-Montrachet Les Pierres	2.60 ha
Meursault Les Grands Charrons	0.16 ha
Puligny-Montrachet Noyer Bret	0.46 ha
Rully Les Gaudoirs	0.20 ha
Rully La Crée	0.25 ha
Rully La Chaume	0.28 ha
Montagny Les Bassets	0.50 ha
Bourgogne Chardonnay	
Le Haut des Champs	1.00 ha

CHASSAGNE-MONTRACHET PREMIER CRU LES VERGERS CLOS SAINT-MARC, CHASSAGNE-MONTRACHET

Jean-Marc Pillot has not only raised the reputation of his family's estate, but also doubled its size since he took over from his father in the early 1990s. The wines have changed in style too, from the appealing, juicy, ripe reds and whites to serious, harmonious wines that have more depth and tension. Over the past 15 years, there has been a thoughtful decision to use less new oak, to capture more mineral notes and retain freshness by making changes in both the cellar as well as the vineyard. These refinements since the early 2000s are now in bottle and the results are striking. The reds are vibrant, balanced, and elegant; the whites are taut and display greater precision. While most Chassagne producers focus on white wines, Pillot spends as much time and effort on its reds. Its Chassagne Clos Saint-Jean Rouge and Morgeot Rouge are lovely—silky-textured and refined. As much as I appreciate its reds, I find the white wines in its portfolio much more *exciting*. Two special white wines in its portfolio worth seeking are Clos Saint-Jean Blanc and Clos Saint-Marc. Both vineyards have ancient vines nearly 100 years old, and the wines are *ethereal*, intense beauties. My favorite is the Clos Saint-Marc, which sits within the Premier Cru Les Vergers vineyard. The 2014 is a study in tension while the 2010 and 2015 are concentrated, *finely etched* examples of a great terroir and old vines in the hands of a talented winegrower.

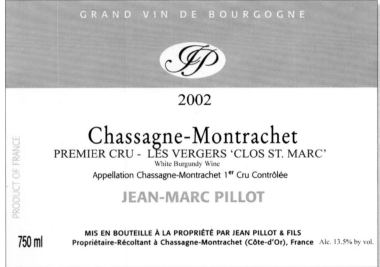

IN THREE WORDS *Compelling, minerally, dramatic.*

DOMAINE JEAN-NOËL GAGNARD

© Michel Joly

address	9 Place des Noyers, 21190 Chassagne-Montrachet, Burgundy, France www.domaine-gagnard.com Tel: +33 3 80 21 31 68
contact	Caroline Lestimé
farming philosophy	Certified organic since 2014, following biodynamic principles; massal selection.
in the cellar	Regular lees stirring; aged 18 months in lightly toasted François Frères barrels with minimal new oak, up to one-third.

total vineyard area	11.4 hectares	**total annual production**	65,000 bottles

key vineyard holdings	*Whites*
	Bâtard-Montrachet Grand Cru 0.36 ha
	Chassagne-Montrachet Premier Cru
	   Les Caillerets 1.06 ha
	Chassagne-Montrachet Premier Cru
	   Les Petits Clos 0.32 ha
	Chassagne-Montrachet Premier Cru
	   Les Boirettes 0.16 ha
	Chassagne-Montrachet Premier Cru
	   Blanchot-Dessus 0.12 ha
	Chassagne-Montrachet Premier Cru
	   Morgeots 0.16 ha
	Chassagne-Montrachet Premier Cru
	   La Boudriotte 0.48 ha
	Chassagne-Montrachet Premier Cru
	   Clos de la Maltroye 0.34 ha
	Chassagne-Montrachet Premier Cru
	   Les Champs Gains 0.22 ha
	Chassagne-Montrachet Premier Cru
	   Les Chaumées 0.59 ha
	Chassagne-Montrachet Les Masures 0.61 ha
		Chassagne-Montrachet Premier Cru
		   Les Chenevottes 0.49 ha
		Chassagne-Montrachet Les Chaumes 0.29 ha
		Chassagne-Montrachet Champ Derrière 0.44 ha
		Chassagne-Montrachet Pot Bios
		   (since 2009) 0.13 ha
		Bourgogne Hautes Côtes de Beaune
		   Blanc Sous Eugisons 1.07 ha
		
		Reds
		Chassagne-Montrachet Premier Cru
		   Morgeot 0.44 ha
		Chassagne-Montrachet Premier Cru
		   Clos Saint-Jean 0.33 ha
		Santenay Premier Cru
		   Clos de Tavannes 0.30 ha
		Chassagne-Montrachet
		   Cuvée L'Estimée 1.37 ha
		Bourgogne Hautes Côtes de Beaune
		   Clos Bortier 0.29 ha

BÂTARD–MONTRACHET GRAND CRU, CHASSAGNE–MONTRACHET

Caroline Lestimé took over from her father, Jean-Noël Gagnard, in 1989 and has been raising the reputation and standards of the family domaine. The Gagnard family were growers for many generations, but it was only during Jean-Noël's time that it started bottling wines under its own family label. Caroline studied business and took crash courses in oenology and viticulture in 1988, while working with her father, and took over just a year later. Most of the changes she has made have been in the vineyard rather than the cellar: All the plots are now farmed organically, and the estate received certification in 2014. Caroline prefers to harvest ripe grapes and keep intervention in the cellar to a minimum, with light toasting for the François Frères barrels, and only a small percentage of new oak. Tasting with Caroline is always a fun experience; she putters about the cellar like a mother hen in her coop. She makes wines that are ample, ripe, and round, with warmth and **generosity**, instead of the currently fashionable lean, gum-bracing acidity and tense style preferred by some growers. The dozen or so different Chassagne Premier Cru reds and whites that this estate makes are lively and distinctive. At the top of its portfolio sits one Grand Cru that is always in high demand, with only 200 cases made: the Bâtard-Montrachet. It owns just one-third of a hectare in an ideal plot in the middle of this Grand Cru appellation. The Bâtard-Montrachet here is like a field of yellow orchard fruits and white flowers—powerful, impressive, and very long on the finish. There is more new oak in this Grand Cru, up to 80%, because it can handle it. Behind the **amplitude**, however, there is firm acidity and structure along with **freshness**. I love the Bâtard in the 1999, 2011, and 2014 vintages.

IN THREE WORDS **Generous, concentrated, balanced.**

CHARMES-CHAMBERTIN GRAND CRU, CUVÉE TRÈS VIEILLES VIGNES, GEVREY-CHAMBERTIN

The Roty family is notorious for being extremely private and difficult to visit, and this only worsened when Philippe Roty, who had taken over from his father, Joseph Roty, in 2008, was diagnosed with cancer and died in 2015. The family's ties to Gevrey and its vineyard go back to the early 18th century, with the current generation being the 11th generation. Pierre-Jean Roty is a friendly young man with a cherubic face that belies the huge burden of carrying on his family estate quite unexpectedly. The 2015 and 2016 vintages, which is what this domaine is showing while everyone else releases the 2017, are remarkable. Joseph Roty wines are unique; they stand out in a blind tasting lineup, with their forthright, strong, unapologetic personality. The wines are intensely concentrated—the result of a combination of extremely old vines (vineyards are over 50 years old on average) that are made to a special Roty formula: Destem, cold macerate for a week, ferment slowly, age in high-toast, mostly new barrels for two full years, and release late. The **density** and power of the wines jumps out at you, whether they are only 10 years old or over 30. Roty does not allow barrel tastings, thus all my notes are from bottled wines. Each of its three Grands Crus is **immense** in concentration and size. In horizontal tastings of its Charmes-Chambertin, Griotte-Chambertin, and Mazy-Chambertin, I preferred the Charmes in the 1999 and 2002 vintages, while in the 1998 and 1996 vintages I preferred the Griotte. However, in most vintages, such as the recent 2016, I had a strong preference for the Charmes. The Charmes-Chambertin is a very special wine, because of the ancient vines, which were planted in the 1880s and are only replanted vine by vine when they die. Only around eight barrels of this wine are made per year, or 2,400 bottles. This wine is bottled **history**, and it belongs in every serious Burgundy lover's cellar.

IN THREE WORDS **Robust, impressive, distinctive.**

DOMAINE JOSEPH ROTY

(SOME VINTAGES SAY PHILIPPE ROTY)

Diego Rodriguez de Silva y Velazquez, *The Lunch*, 1620.
FOLLOWING PAGES Carolyn Hubbard-Ford, *A Theatrical Dinner*, 1998.

address	24 Rue Maréchal de Lattre de Tassigny, 21220 Gevrey-Chambertin, Burgundy, France Tel: + 33 3 80 34 13 59
contact	Pierre-Jean Roty
farming philosophy	Lutte raisonnée; hard pruning, leaving only six buds per vine; vines over 50 years old are preserved as long as possible.
in the cellar	Grapes are destemmed; 1 week cold maceration pre-fermentation; matured up to 2 years in barrels; generous use of high-toast new oak, one-third to half new for Village wines, up to 90% new for Premiers Crus, 100% for Grands Crus.

total vineyard area	15 hectares (estimated)	**total annual production**	70,000 bottles (estimated)

key vineyard holdings **(specific details undisclosed)**	*Red*		Gevrey-Chambertin Cuvée de la Brunelle	N/A
	Charmes-Chambertin Grand Cru	N/A	Gevrey-Chambertin	
	Griotte-Chambertin Grand Cru	N/A	Cuvée de Très Vieilles Vignes	N/A
	Mazy-Chambertin Grand Cru	N/A	Marsannay Rouge Clos de Jeu	N/A
	Gevrey-Chambertin Premier Cru Fonteni	N/A	Marsannay Rouge Champs Saint Étienne	N/A
	Gevrey-Chambertin Clos Prieurs Bas	N/A	Marsannay Rouge Cuvée de Boivin	N/A
	Gevrey-Chambertin		Marsannay Rouge Ouzelois	N/A
	Cuvée de Champs Chenys	N/A		

DOMAINE LEFLAIVE

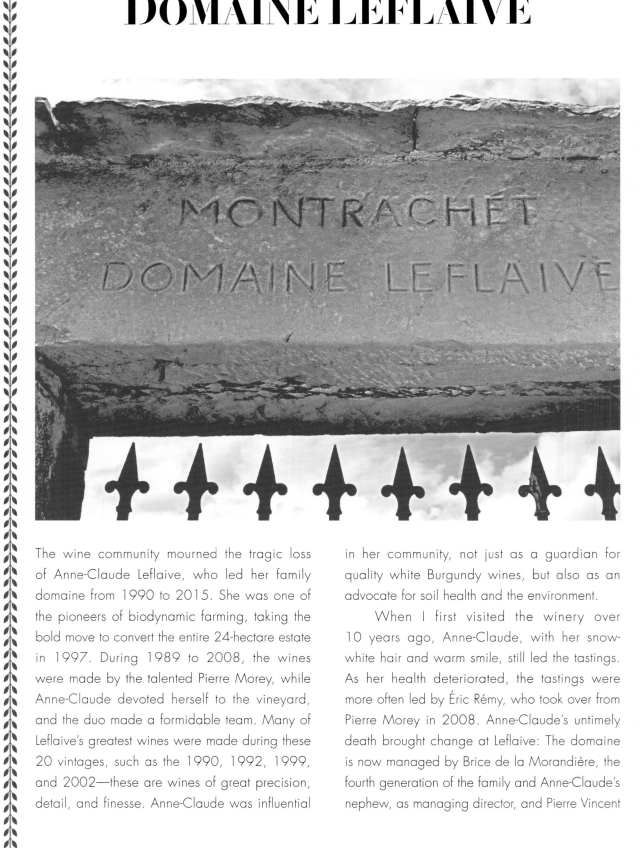

The wine community mourned the tragic loss of Anne-Claude Leflaive, who led her family domaine from 1990 to 2015. She was one of the pioneers of biodynamic farming, taking the bold move to convert the entire 24-hectare estate in 1997. During 1989 to 2008, the wines were made by the talented Pierre Morey, while Anne-Claude devoted herself to the vineyard, and the duo made a formidable team. Many of Leflaive's greatest wines were made during these 20 vintages, such as the 1990, 1992, 1999, and 2002—these are wines of great precision, detail, and finesse. Anne-Claude was influential in her community, not just as a guardian for quality white Burgundy wines, but also as an advocate for soil health and the environment.

When I first visited the winery over 10 years ago, Anne-Claude, with her snow-white hair and warm smile, still led the tastings. As her health deteriorated, the tastings were more often led by Éric Rémy, who took over from Pierre Morey in 2008. Anne-Claude's untimely death brought change at Leflaive: The domaine is now managed by Brice de la Morandière, the fourth generation of the family and Anne-Claude's nephew, as managing director, and Pierre Vincent replacing Rémy as the winemaker and general manager since 2017. Vincent's appointment is great news for Leflaive lovers, since he is a talented winemaker and was instrumental in lifting the quality of wines at Domaine de la Vougeraie and converting it to biodynamics as technical manager for 11 years.

Domaine Leflaive has a dream portfolio of some of the greatest white wine vineyards in Burgundy, mainly concentrated in Puligny-Montrachet. It owns no less than four Grand Cru vineyards, totaling 5 hectares, and numerous Premier Cru vineyards, making it the largest single owner of Premier and Grand Cru vineyards in Puligny. In Puligny-Montrachet Le Clavoillon alone, it owns nearly 5 hectares. These prestigious vineyards were acquired by the founder of the domaine, Joseph Leflaive, in the beginning of the 20th century.

There was a shift in style around the same time that the vineyard was moving toward biodynamic viticulture. In 1990, when Anne-Claude Leflaive was appointed manager of the estate, she began to conduct trials comparing the effect of traditional farming versus organic and biodynamic farming. The trials convinced the family that biodynamic viticulture was not only better for the vineyard but also added greater precision to the wines. In the cellar, there was a shift toward a lighter hand in winemaking, with the reduction of new oak use from over half new for the top wines to the current 20-25% for Grands Crus. The result is greater purity and minerality in the wines.

Pierre Vincent is already making small changes at the domaine, with upgrades in the cellar and the winemaking facilities; it is still early days for the new management team, but the signs are positive. By reputation and quality, and through its strong vineyard holdings, Domaine Leflaive defines Puligny-Montrachet and its top vineyards.

address	Place des Marronniers, 21190 Puligny-Montrachet, Burgundy, France www.leflaive.fr Tel: + 33 3 80 21 30 13		
contact	Brice de la Morandière, Pierre Vincent		
farming philosophy	Fully biodynamic since 1997.		
in the cellar	Matured 12 months in oak and 6 months in tanks; minimal new oak use, up to 25% for Grands Crus; Diam corks used for all wines starting with the 2014 vintage.		
total vineyard area	24 hectares	**total annual production**	140,000 bottles (excluding Mâcon)
key vineyard holdings	*White* Le Montrachet Grand Cru 0.08 ha Chevalier-Montrachet Grand Cru 1.92 ha Bâtard-Montrachet Grand Cru 1.91 ha Bienvenues-Bâtard-Montrachet Grand Cru 1.15 ha Puligny-Montrachet Premier Cru Pucelles 2.75 ha Puligny-Montrachet Premier Cru Combettes 0.73 ha		Puligny-Montrachet Premier Cru Folatières 1.06 ha Puligny-Montrachet Premier Cru Clavoillon 4.80 ha Meursault Premier Cru Sous le Dos d'Âne 1.26 ha Puligny-Montrachet 4.65 ha Bourgogne Blanc 4.06 ha

CHEVALIER-MONTRACHET GRAND CRU, PULIGNY-MONTRACHET

Two producers dominate at Chevalier-Montrachet—Bouchard and Leflaive, with combined holdings of 62% of the vineyard. Among the five Grand Cru vineyards with Montrachet in the name, Chevalier epitomizes purity and finesse. Bâtard and Bienvenues tend to be richer, while Le Montrachet is usually more powerful. Domaine Leflaive's Chevalier has long been the quality standard to which others are compared. As a benchmark, Chevalier-Montrachet is Leflaive's *signature* wine. In its youth, the wine is sinewy and racy, with a fine line of acidity running through it. With age this wine blossoms, offering *delicate* layers of toasted hazelnuts, graphite, and dried jasmine in one sip, another array of flavors in the next sip. Even with age, this wine remains trim, like a seasoned racehorse. A 30-year-old Chevalier-Montrachet from the 1980s, such as the gorgeous 1982 and the 1985, are still beautifully poised, *complex*, and intense. The combination of old vines, meticulous vineyard work, and careful handling in the cellar means the wines are incredibly consistent, except when tainted with premox issues. The best young vintages for cellaring are the 2005, 2010, 2014, and 2017.

IN THREE WORDS *Inspiring, poised, precise.*

PULIGNY-MONTRACHET PREMIER CRU LES PUCELLES, PULIGNY-MONTRACHET

Among the four Premier Cru Puligny-Montrachet vineyards that Leflaive owns, Les Pucelles is its second largest parcel, at 2.75 hectares; Clavoillon is nearly 5 hectares. Leflaive is the largest owner of this 6.6-hectare Premier Cru vineyard and sets high standards for the other half-dozen owners. Les Pucelles borders Bâtard-Montrachet and Bienvenues-Bâtard-Montrachet, and from the soil surface there is little difference, with Jurassic limestone as its base. However, soil depths vary widely, and like much of Burgundy, the geological variation is great. Leflaive is able to blend from its sizable parcel, creating a wine that combines intensity, *profundity*, and finesse. In vintages like 2012 and 2016, the wines are on par with Grands Crus wines. Domaine Leflaive's Pucelles makes a strong case for upgrading this vineyard to Grand Cru status. Pucelles at its best offers *alluring* floral aromatics and incredible *tension* with penetrating depth. Treat this wine like a Grand Cru and cellar it for 8 years or more, and you will be rewarded. The best vintages to enjoy now are 2002, 2004, and 2007.

IN THREE WORDS *Penetrating, graceful, multifaceted.*

Guido Reni, *Drinking Bacchus*, c. 1623.

DOMAINE LEROY

Domaine Leroy has a short 30-year history, and yet in this brief time the wines have become among the most collectible in Burgundy. The family has ties with the vineyard going back a few centuries, and its négociant company, Maison Leroy, celebrated its 150th year in 2018. The petite, formidable woman behind this estate is Lalou Bize-Leroy—a trailblazer with a strong vision of how to craft quality wine.

By 1955, when she was still in her 20s, she ran her family's négociant business, Maison Leroy, taking over from her father, Henri Leroy. By 1974, Bize-Leroy became co-director of Domaine de la Romanée-Conti (DRC), since her father owned half of this legendary domaine, and managed it together with Aubert de Villaine. In 1992, after a very public dispute widely reported in the press, she was ousted by the board of DRC, which included her own sister. Currently, her daughter Perrine Fenal is co-director at DRC.

The dispute centered around accusations about unauthorized sales of DRC wines by Maison Leroy to a Swiss exporting company, who was selling it in the gray market. This was the cause cited by DRC for the decision, but there were other underlying factors: The sale of one-third of Maison Leroy shares to the Takashimaya group, and the growing competition created by Domaine Leroy, formed in 1988 with vineyards purchased from Domaine Charles Noëllat. Maison Leroy distributed DRC wines, and being partially owned by a Japanese conglomerate did not sit well with the board of DRC.

Still retaining her 25% share in DRC, Bize-Leroy refocused her energy on Domaine Leroy,

attending to every detail in both the vineyard and the winery. Despite setbacks such as the disastrous 1993 vintage, when mildew ravaged her vineyards, she continued her path toward biodynamic farming, shunning all chemical use, increasing microbial life in the vineyard, and adhering to a strict calendar. Bize-Leroy was a pioneer in every sense of the word, embracing biodynamic viticulture before it became trendy in Burgundy, adhering to extremely low yields, employing unique vine training and very strict pruning techniques, and choosing to replant vine by vine rather than uproot an entire plot. She relies on intuition and listening to the land more than on science or numbers. It is easy to spot

her vineyards, with their wild, Medusa-like vines, whose canes are never cut or hedged, producing small, low-hanging grape clusters at less than half the yield of her neighbors.

Madame, as she is referred to by those around her, has more style in her mid-80s than most women half her age. She may be petite in size, but her intensity and charisma make most people feel small in her presence. She comes alive and her green-blue eyes sharpen when she speaks about her vineyards, her wines, or her favorite pastime, rock climbing. When I ask how she manages to get so much profundity, complexity, and energy in her wines, she replies, "It is simple, I love my vines more deeply than most people."

Bize-Leroy's wines are rarely found at auction, but despite this the wines are astronomically priced. Only two other domaines in Burgundy achieve similar price points: those from the late Henri Jayer and Domaine de la Romanée-Conti. The ever-increasing prices for Domaine Leroy wines have not dissuaded buyers or collectors; it has done the opposite and fueled their desire to want more.

Domaine Leroy wines in the past 20 years, once the vines fully adapted to biodynamic farming, are truly extraordinary. From the Village Vosne-Romanée to the rare Musigny Grand Cru, the wines are superb: They set new standards for their appellations and must be experienced to be truly appreciated; the vineyards sing through the wines, and their voices are joyful, loud, and clear. It is this domaine more than any other property that positions Lalou Bize-Leroy as one of the greatest custodians of Burgundian terroir.

address	15 Rue de la Fontaine, 21700 Vosne-Romanée, Burgundy, France www.domaine-leroy.com Tel: + 33 3 80 21 21 10
contact	Lalou Bize-Leroy
farming philosophy	100% biodynamic cultivation since 1988; very old vines are replanted individually; during the growing season, the shoots are not cut back (summer pruned) but curled over and tied to the trellis, requiring extensive manual labor.
in the cellar	Exclusively whole bunch, with cool temperatures preferred for fermentation; all reds and whites aged 14-18 months in 100% new oak.

total vineyard area	22 hectares		total annual production	20,000-45,000 bottles

	Red		Savigny-Les-Beaunes Premier Cru	
	Chambertin Grand Cru	0.70 ha	Narbantons	0.81 ha
	Latricières-Chambertin Grand Cru	0.57 ha	Nuits-Saint-Georges Aux Allots	0.52 ha
	Clos de la Roche Grand Cru	0.67 ha	Nuits-Saint-Georges Aux Lavières	0.69 ha
	Musigny Grand Cru	0.27 ha	Nuits-Saint-Georges	
	Clos de Vougeot Grand Cru	1.91 ha	Au Bas de Combe	0.15 ha
	Richebourg Grand Cru	0.78 ha	Vosne-Romanée Aux Genaivrières	1.23 ha
	Romanée-Saint-Vivant Grand Cru	0.99 ha	Chambolle-Musigny Les Fremières	0.35 ha
	Corton-Renardes Grand Cru	0.50 ha	Gevrey-Chambertin	0.11 ha
	Gevrey-Chambertin Premier Cru		Pommard Les Vignots	1.26 ha
key vineyard holdings	Les Combottes	0.46 ha	Pommard Les Trois Follots	0.07 ha
	Chambolle-Musigny Premier Cru		Côteaux Bourguignons Rouge	0.52 ha
	Les Charmes	0.23 ha		
	Nuits-Saint-Georges Aux Vignerondes	0.38 ha	*White*	
	Nuits-Saint-Georges Aux Boudots	1.20 ha	Corton-Charlemagne Grand Cru	0.43 ha
	Vosne-Romanée Premier Cru		Auxey-Duresses Les Lavières	0.35 ha
	Aux Brûlées	0.27 ha	Bourgogne Aligoté	2.58 ha
	Vosne-Romanée Premier Cru		Bourgogne Blanc	0.35 ha
	Aux Beaux Monts	2.61 ha	Côteaux Bourguignons Blanc	0.26 ha
	Volnay Santenots du Milieu	0.35 ha		

CHAMBERTIN GRAND CRU, GEVREY-CHAMBERTIN

Leroy's Chambertin is magisterial and profound. I recall numerous occasions when this wine moved me to tears: The 2010 vintage, with its incredible depth, chiseled form, great power and length. The wine is magnificent, and I was lost for words and nearly cried when told there were only two barrels, or 600 bottles, made in 2015. The 2012 and the 2009 vintages were both emotional wines for me; I scribbled "perfect," "classy," "majestic," while drinking their greatness, knowing it was like infanticide. Even the brilliant 1999 was much too young, and I noted that it should not be approached until at least 2022; the 1993 is just starting to be approachable at 25 years of age. Vintages that were sublime in their youth and best after 25 years include the 2001, 2005, and 2008. But there are really no weak recent vintages of Chambertin; even the 2011 and 2007 are penetrating, structured, and persistent. There are many who love Latricières-Chambertin, but every time I have tasted it side by side with the Chambertin, there is no doubt that Chambertin has the extra depth, the **_muscled_** finish, and intensity to outlive and outshine the Latricières. Leroy's Chambertin is so complex, with so many changing facets, that to describe it accurately would sound like incessant rambling. Leroy's

Chambertin is a *dramatic*, powerful wine that takes you on an emotionally *thrilling*, unforgettable ride. IN THREE WORDS *Profound, complex, assertive.*

CLOS DE LA ROCHE GRAND CRU, MOREY-SAINT-DENIS

Clos de la Roche is a large Grand Cru area by Burgundian standards, totaling nearly 17 hectares, with 8 climats. Domaine Leroy farms just a sliver of it—0.67 hectares, producing around 1,500 bottles a year. The largest vineyards are owned by Dujac, Ponsot, and Rousseau. Clos de la Roche was acquired by Lalou Bize-Leroy in 1989, when she bought vineyards from Domaine Philippe Rémy. The purchase included Chambertin, Latricières-Chambertin, and Clos de la Roche, the last being the largest of the three parcels. With so little produced, most Clos de la Roche comparisons do not include Domaine Leroy's version. However, in discussing the diverse expressions of this brown limestone vineyard, it would be a mistake to exclude Leroy's rendition. Since the 1999, I cannot remember tasting a weak or disappointing vintage of this wine. Perhaps it is the biodynamic farming or the extremely low yields or a hundred other details that contribute to the wine's extraordinary *concentration* and presence. In its youth the wine is lush, velvety-textured, with mocha, earth, and spice-infused flavors, and great young examples include 2002, 2008, 2012, and 2015; with age, approaching two decades, the wine acquires stature and length, and becomes lingering and more gently *persistent*. It is worth seeking the powerful 1996, the *seamless* 1998, or the beautiful 2001, which is just starting to open. Clos de la Roche is lucky to have so many great owners, including Domaine Leroy, who consistently produces one of the best examples. IN THREE WORDS *Formidable, extraordinary, energetic.*

RICHEBOURG GRAND CRU, VOSNE-ROMANÉE

Lalou Bize-Leroy knows the Richebourg vineyard well; she has over a decade of experience overseeing DRC's sizable 3.5-hectare holding during the 1980s. Domaine Leroy's share is tiny in comparison, barely 0.8 hectares, but it farms the second-largest portion of the total; ten other domaines farm even smaller shares. Lying mid-slope, with plenty of limestone scree deposits, the Richebourg vineyard is spread out over 8 hectares, ideally positioned to create robust, powerful wines that have richness and generosity. Leroy's Richebourg distinguishes itself in its concentration, depth, and *poise*. It's difficult not to compare it to DRC's Richebourg, and the two are very different. While both have similar characteristics, such as plush, firm tannins and towering presence, Leroy's Richebourg is more **chiseled**, its flavors more precise and well defined. DRC's Richebourg is often more muscular, not heavy but strong. Leroy's Richebourg has a wild and seductive side; there are more exotic spices on the nose, and the texture, while still **sumptuous**, is finer and silkier. This wine needs at least 20 to 25 years of cellaring—the vintages to enjoy now are from the early to mid-1990s, and the knockout vintages in recent years include the 2002, 2005, 2010, 2012, and 2015.

IN THREE WORDS *Magnificent, structured, sublime.*

ROMANÉE-SAINT-VIVANT GRAND CRU, VOSNE-ROMANÉE

No other Grand Cru vineyard in the Côte de Nuits offers the kind of intoxicating fragrance and sensual flavors combined with refined elegance like Romanée-Saint-Vivant. At its peak, this is wine perfume captured in a bottle. Structurally, it is at the opposite end of the spectrum compared with Richebourg—where Richebourg is sumptuous, muscular, and powerful, Romanée-Saint-Vivant is graceful, classy, and elegant. Leroy is just behind DRC in vineyard holdings, with nearly a hectare of vines; small compared to DRC's 5.3 hectares. Leroy's Romanée-Saint-Vivant is not shy, it is often the most expressive among the Grands Crus in its youth, with a **symphony** of flavors. Its strength

lies in its **seductive**, charming qualities, with an earlier drinking window: Lovely floral, spicy, and vibrant red fruits when young, and more delicate, forest floor flavors with age. Don't mistake its grace and lightness with lack of backbone or inability to age; Leroy's Romanée-Saint-Vivant possesses a sinewy body and exceptional longevity. Both the 1988 and the 1989 vintages are still going strong, their trim figures accentuated by complex aromatics and an astonishing array of flavors. The 2010 vintage is magnificent—it convinced me that perhaps **perfection** is possible in a wine. Other impressive young vintages include 2002, 2005, 2008, 2012, and 2015.

IN THREE WORDS *Sophisticated, alluring, sensual.*

VOSNE-ROMANÉE PREMIER CRU LES BEAUX MONTS, VOSNE-ROMANÉE

Leroy's Vosne-Romanée Premier Cru wines, the Brûlées and the Beaux Monts, are both excellent. I chose the Beaux Monts to highlight because of its wider accessibility—Leroy owns 2.6 hectares of the Beaux Monts, versus only 0.27 hectares for the Brûlées. In some years, like the 2015 and the 2014, I preferred the Brûlées, but in other vintages, such as the 2013 and 2011, I preferred the Beaux Monts. Leroy is the largest owner of this relatively large top Premier Cru vineyard, which totals 11.4 hectares. The soil is shallow, and the limestone-clay base offers good drainage and water retention balance. Leroy's Beaux Monts is considered the reference standard for this site. Even in lighter vintages, such as the 2007, Leroy's Beaux Monts is *intense*, with wonderful concentration. There are those who may find the wine too strong, but that is because it was built for the long haul. Recent vintages since 2000 have seen Beaux Monts gain more purity, detail, and *finesse*, and lose some of the brute power it had in the 1990s. Leroy coaxes

Grand Cru–level wines from this site, and thus it must be treated like a Grand Cru; approach it after at least 15 years of age. With time, the wine acquires elegance and becomes pure *energy* and minerals, with beautiful spices and dried flowers in the background. Be careful not to confuse the Premier Cru Beaux Monts with the two Village-level vineyards that bear its name—Les Hauts Beaux Monts and Les Beaux Monts Hauts Rougeots; look for the Premier Cru indication to ensure you are getting the correct wine.

IN THREE WORDS *Bold, classy, serious.*

VOLNAY PREMIER CRU
CLOS DES DUCS MONOPOLE, VOLNAY

Marquis d'Angerville is one of the preeminent estates in Burgundy, and its top cuvées have long been considered benchmarks for quality. For over 200 years this property has been in the d'Angerville family; it was already held in high regard by the dukes of Burgundy prior to the family purchasing it. The current family member to lead this property is Guillaume d'Angerville, a former merchant banker, who took over from his father, Jacques, in 2003. Guillaume's grandfather, Sem d'Angerville, was a prominent figure in Burgundy for being one of the first to promote the domaine-bottling movement and for his advocacy to set up the AOC system to protect producers against fraudulent and mislabeled Burgundy bottles. The estate is considered the "king of Volnay" for being the largest holder of Premier Cru parcels, over 10% of the total Premier Cru vineyards. All the wines are made in a purist style, with delicate, vibrant, intense flavors surrounding a firm structure that enables the wines to age. The entire vineyard has converted to biodynamics since 2009, and this has contributed to the wines' finesse and delicacy. All the Marquis d'Angerville's red wines are intense, but they are also pure and transparent: very little new oak, never overripe, with silky, fine-grained tannins. The jewel in its portfolio is the Clos des Ducs, a 2-hectare vineyard that still has vines dating back to the 1950s. This steep hillside vineyard, with white marl and limestone soil, produces wines of great **subtlety** and persistence. It is a wine of contradictions: At once delicate and powerful, gentle yet strong. The rose petal and violet bouquet is **intoxicating** in its youth and blossoms into **gorgeous** flavors of forest floor, white truffle, and sweet spices with age. Clos des Ducs vintages such as 1985, 1991, and 1993 are the epitome of great Volnay—perfumed, fine, intense, and beautifully transparent.

IN THREE WORDS *Aristocratic, exquisite, classic.*

Domaine Marquis d'Angerville

Detail of a mosaic in the House of Theseus, Nea Pafos, Cyprus.

address	Rue de Mont, 21190 Volnay, Burgundy, France www.domainedangerville.fr Tel: + 33 3 80 21 61 75
contact	Guillaume d'Angerville
farming philosophy	Biodynamic since 2009.
in the cellar	Grapes destemmed, cooled but not chilled; matured 16-18 months in barrels with no more than 20% new oak.

total vineyard area	14.5 hectares	**total annual production**	65,000 bottles

key vineyard holdings	*Red* Volnay Premier Cru Clos des Ducs Monopole — 2.15 ha Volnay Premier Cru Cailleret — 0.65 ha Volnay Premier Cru Champans — 3.98 ha Volnay Premier Cru Clos des Angles — 1.07 ha Volnay Premier Cru Frémiets — 1.57 ha Volnay Premier Cru Mitans — 0.65 ha	Volnay Premier Cru Pitures — 0.31 ha Volnay Premier Cru Taillepieds — 1.07 ha Pommard Combes Dessus — 0.38 ha Volnay Villages — 0.54 ha *White* Meursault Premier Cru Santenots — 1.05 ha

Domaine Méo-Camuzet

address	11 Rue des Grands Crus, 21700 Vosne-Romanée, Burgundy, France www.méo-camuzet.com Tel: + 33 3 80 62 48 80
contact	Jean-Nicolas Méo
farming philosophy	Majority of the vineyards farmed organically.
in the cellar	Grapes destemmed; several days' maceration cold pre-fermentation; matured 17 months in oak, two-thirds new for Premiers Crus and 100% for Grands Crus.
total vineyard area	nearly 20 hectares

total annual production	90,000 bottles

key vineyard holdings

Red		Vosne-Romanée Premier Cru	
Richebourg Grand Cru	0.34 ha	Cros Parantoux	0.30 ha
Échezeaux Grand Cru	0.44 ha	Nuits-Saint-Georges Premier Cru	
Clos de Vougeot Grand Cru	3.03 ha	Aux Boudots	1.05 ha
Corton Grand Cru Clos Rognet	0.45 ha	Nuits-Saint-Georges Premier Cru	
Corton Grand Cru Les Perrières	0.68 ha	Aux Murgers	0.73 ha
Corton Grand Cru La Vigne au Saint	0.19 ha	Nuits-Saint-Georges Bas de Combe	0.58 ha
Vosne-Romanée Premier Cru		Vosne-Romanée	1.38 ha
Les Chaumes	2.02 ha		
Vosne-Romanée Premier Cru		White	
Les Brûlées	0.72 ha	Hautes Côtes de Nuits	
		Clos Saint Philibert	3.54 ha

RICHEBOURG GRAND CRU, VOSNE-ROMANÉE

It is hard to believe that this renowned estate only began domaine bottling partially in 1983; it reclaimed most of its vineyards in 1988 and fully launched the estate Méo-Camuzet in 1989, with the arrival of Jean-Nicolas Méo. Part of Méo-Camuzet's rapid rise to fame is due to the family's long history in the region: Étienne Camuzet was a shrewd, well-connected politician who bought noteworthy vineyards throughout the region starting in the early 1900s. The other reason for the domaine's quick ascension was its association with Henri Jayer, who continued to consult at Méo-Camuzet and guided Jean-Nicolas Méo during the early part of his management. By 1989, when the domaine was just establishing itself, Henri Jayer was starting to develop a following and was known as a rising star in the United States, after launching Vosne-Romanée Premier Cru Cros Parantoux, starting with the 1978 vintage. Jean-Nicolas Méo initially sought out Jayer's advice and wisdom, but soon went his own way. Since the 1990s, Jean-Nicolas has been making incremental changes in the vineyard and cellar. The estate now farms under organic principles, and the vineyard work has increased, along with the quality. Méo-Camuzet still generally adheres to Henri Jayer's vinification methods: Destemming, cold maceration, indigenous yeast fermentation, and generous use of new oak for maturation. The wines have wonderful purity and depth; there is a polished modernity to Méo-Camuzet's wine style, with plenty of generous fruit and freshness. Jean-Nicolas represents the new generation of winegrowers in Burgundy, who are well-traveled, global in their outlook, but devoted and rooted to the land. His English is fluent, his office above the cellar is modern and chic. Méo-Camuzet is fortunate to own some of the best vineyards in Côte de Nuits, including several Grand Cru and Premier Cru vineyards in Vosne-Romanée and Nuits-Saint-Georges. Clos de Vougeot is its largest and most easily accessible, but the two most sought-after wines are its Cros Parantoux and its Richebourg. I selected the latter because Cros Parantoux would draw too many comparisons with Jayer's, which didn't seem fair. Both are glorious, special wines. Méo-Camuzet only has one-third of a hectare of Richebourg, so quantity is extremely small, while demand for this wine is growing every year. The wine epitomizes the awe-inspiring power of this vineyard and its undeniable nobility and class. The most *memorable* vintage of this wine is the 1985, a great vintage, made by Henri Jayer. Vintages like 1991 and 1999 are spiritual experiences; wines that leave you humble, speechless in the presence of beauty. Younger vintages like 2010 and 2015 are *striking* in their intensity and persistence, surrounded by a whirl of *tantalizing* aromatics and minerality. These youthful wines are taut, muscular, and focused—classic Richebourg from a remarkable estate.

IN THREE WORDS   *Noble, powerful, beautiful.*

66 Behold the rain which descends from heaven upon our vineyards; there it enters the roots of the vines, to be changed into wine; a constant proof that God loves us, and loves to see us happy. 99

Benjamin Franklin

DOMAINE MICHEL LAFARGE

address	15 Rue de la Combe, 21190 Volnay, Burgundy, France www.domainelafarge.com Tel: + 33 3 80 21 61 61
contact	Frédéric Lafarge
farming philosophy	Fully biodynamic since 2000.
in the cellar	Grapes destemmed; whole berries; matured 16 months in barrels with minimal new oak, no new oak for Villages, up to 20% for Premiers Crus in exceptional vintages.
total vineyard area	12 hectares	**total annual production**	50,000 bottles

key vineyard holdings				
Red		Beaune Premier Cru Les Aigrots	0.70 ha	
Volnay Premier Cru Clos du		Volnay (two cuvées)	2.48 ha	
Château des Ducs Monopole	0.57 ha	Côte de Beaune Villages (Meursault)	0.28 ha	
Volnay Premier Cru Clos des Chênes	0.90 ha	Bourgogne Passetoutgrains	1.56 ha	
Volnay Premier Cru Les Caillerets	0.30 ha	Bourgogne Pinot Noir	1.22 ha	
Volnay Premier Cru Les Mitans	0.40 ha			
Volnay Premier Cru Chanlins	0.26 ha	*White*		
Volnay Premier Cru	0.30 ha	Beaune Premier Cru Les Aigrots	0.25 ha	
Pommard Premier Cru Les Pézerolles	0.14 ha	Meursault	1.00 ha	
Beaune Premier Cru Les Grèves	0.38 ha	Bourgogne Aligoté	1.13 ha	

VOLNAY PREMIER CRU
CLOS DES CHÊNES, VOLNAY

Lafarge is one of the leading estates based in Volnay and often rivals Marquis d'Angerville and Pousse d'Or for producing the most elegant and longest-lived Volnays. The father-and-son duo managed the estate together since the mid-1980s until Michel Lafarge's death in 2020, aged 91. The 12-hectare estate has been in the family since the early 19th century and has been quietly making beautiful Volnays since the 1930s. The first vintage of Lafarge's Clos des Chênes was in 1934, made by Frédéric Lafarge's grandfather, and by the 1960s all the wines were domaine bottled. There have been gradual changes—the estate is fully biodynamic since 2000, but practicing biodynamics since the early 1990s. All red grapes are destemmed, and minimal new oak is used for aging. Both Frédéric and Michel agree on a minimalist approach to winemaking and can aptly be called "men of the earth." Its holdings have increased in recent years with Caillerets and Mitans vineyards added in 2000 and 2005, respectively. Lafarge wines are built for aging, although the pale color and delicate perfume may suggest otherwise. My favorite wine in its portfolio, not surprisingly, is the Clos des Chênes. Lafarge's rendition is often of Grand Cru quality. Vintages like 2002 and 2005 reveal a barely mature, intense wine, with a firm backbone of silky tannins surrounded by layers of **magnificent**, gentle flavors that linger on the palate. Recent vintages starting in 2009 have been terrific and far more consistent than the wines from the 1980s and 1990s. This impressive wine comes from a nearly 1-hectare plot located toward the bottom of the vineyard, just above the road, that is red in color from the high iron content, which seems to add a deeper, richer **dimension** to the wine. Soils higher up the slope are lighter, with more limestone, and tend to be more perfumed and lighter in weight. Clos des Chênes from Lafarge is a serious, **age-worthy** Volnay that rewards those with patience to wait at least 15 to 20 years. IN THREE WORDS *Impressive, lingering, complete.*

CHEVALIER-MONTRACHET GRAND CRU, PULIGNY-MONTRACHET

Michel Niellon is a small estate with a huge following. Its intense, precise Chassagne whites and glorious Bâtard-Montrachet and Chevalier-Montrachet are in high demand globally. The two Grands Crus are produced in such minute quantities that prices have escalated to incredible levels, especially for the older vintages found at auction.

Michel Niellon started working with his father at the family estate in the 1950s and has now handed over the reins to the next generation: Michel Coutoux, his son-in-law, married to his daughter Stéphanie. For many years they made the entire production in a tiny cellar beneath their house in Chassagne, but in 2009 they finally built a modern, spacious cellar at the edge of town. Niellon's wines are expressive, ripe, and intense, never shy or thin. Behind the fruit is wonderful *energy* and acid tension, which allows the wines to age beautifully. Both the Bâtard-Montrachet and Chevalier-Montrachet are capable of long aging: The Bâtard is more powerful and rich, while the Chevalier has greater refinement and class, in my opinion. Vintages of Chevalier-Montrachet from the 1980s, especially the 1985, 1989, and 1990, exemplify the cellaring potential of this incredible Grand Cru white, all enjoyed when they were over 25 years old. With less than a quarter-hectare, there is only about four barrels of the Chevalier made per year. The *intensity* comes partly from the old vines, which date back to the 1960s, and also from the low yields at Niellon.

I recommend its Chevalier-Montrachet with at least 12 years of age, when it becomes a *magical* sensory experience that you won't forget.

IN THREE WORDS *Gorgeous, persistent, linear.*

DOMAINE MICHEL NIELLON

Edward Cucuel, *In the Arbor*, c. 1900.

address	Le Haut des Champs, 21190 Chassagne-Montrachet, Burgundy, France Tel: + 33 3 80 24 70 17
contact	Michel Coutoux
farming philosophy	Lutte raisonnée, with minimal spraying.
in the cellar	Whites are barrel-fermented, with regular lees stirring, matured 1 year in oak, with up to one-third new barrels.

total vineyard area	7.5 hectares	**total annual production**	45,000 bottles

key vineyard holdings	*White*		Chassagne-Montrachet Premier Cru	
	Chevalier-Montrachet Grand Cru	0.23 ha	La Maltroie	0.95 ha
	Bâtard-Montrachet Grand Cru	0.12 ha	Chassagne-Montrachet	2.21 ha
	Chassagne-Montrachet Premier Cru			
	Les Chaumées	0.54 ha	*Red*	
	Chassagne-Montrachet Premier Cru		Chassagne-Montrachet Premier Cru	
	Clos Saint-Jean	0.52 ha	La Maltroie	0.13 ha
	Chassagne-Montrachet Premier Cru		Chassagne-Montrachet Premier Cru	
	Les Champgains	0.44 ha	Clos Saint-Jean	0.19 ha
	Chassagne-Montrachet Premier Cru		Chassagne-Montrachet	1.50 ha
	Les Vergers	0.39 ha		
	Chassagne-Montrachet Premier Cru			
	Les Chenevottes	0.18 ha		

DOMAINE PARENT

address	3 Rue de la Métairie, 21630 Pommard, Burgundy, France www.domaine-parent.com Tel: + 33 3 80 22 15 08
contact	Anne Parent, Catherine Parent
farming philosophy	Certified organic since 2013, working toward biodynamic principles.
in the cellar	Mostly destemmed, whole berries; several days' cold maceration; matured 14-18 months in barrels with one-third new oak for Villages, 40-60% new oak for Premiers Crus, 80-100% for Grands Crus, depending on wine and vintage.
total vineyard area	10 hectares
total annual production	130,000 bottles (including wine made from purchased grapes)
key vineyard holdings	*Red* Corton Grand Cru Les Renardes — 0.30 ha Pommard Premier Cru Les Épenots — 0.58 ha Pommard Premier Cru Les Croix Noires — 0.18 ha Pommard Premier Cru Chaponnières — 0.63 ha Pommard Premier Cru Les Chanlins — 0.35 ha Pommard Premier Cru Les Argillières — 0.29 ha Beaune Premier Cru Les Épenottes — 1.75 ha Ladoix Premier Cru Corvée — 0.39 ha Pommard La Croix Blanche — 0.32 ha Pommard Les Noizons — 0.12 ha

POMMARD PREMIER CRU LES ÉPENOTS, POMMARD

Anne and Catherine Parent, the sister duo who have run the estate since 1998, represent the 12th generation of Parents in the family business. (Their brother François took his portion of the estate to combine it with those of his wife, Anne-François Gros, and their wines are bottled as A.F. Gros & François Parent.) Here, Anne is in charge of winemaking while Catherine manages the business and commercial side. Anne is friendly, open, and candid about the refinements she has made over the past 20 years in the vineyard and the cellar. It has been a long road toward organic farming, but the estate received its accreditation in 2013. Pommard has had a rough time, with an onslaught of climatic challenges starting with the 2011 vintage, and like its neighbors, saw its yields plummet. The recent négociant business has increased its production, but even purchased grapes have been in low supply. Domaine Parent has had very little wine to sell from 2010 until 2016, so 2017 was a huge relief, with "back to normal" yields. Anne continues her family's tradition of being involved in the industry at different levels: Her ancestor Étienne Parent was a friend and wine advisor to Thomas Jefferson in the 18th century. Anne is a true ambassador for Burgundy, involved with the Burgundy Wine Board (BIVB) and instrumental in establishing the Femmes et Vins de Bourgogne to bring together women in the industry. Parent's wines are pure, elegant, and harmonious. The tannins are always beautifully managed and velvety, which is not always easy or often achieved in the case of Pommard. I am very impressed with Parent's recent vintages from 2005 onward, and the **dedication** to detail is noticeable in its top Premier Cru Pommard, Les Épenots. This wine stands out in its portfolio as a wine of great **finesse** and depth. As Anne explains, this vineyard was considered Grand Cru but the commune decided not to apply, given the higher taxes the superior classification entails. I love the 2015 Les Épenots, I think it is the best yet from the domaine— exuberant yet **profound**, with sumptuous tannins and layers of flavors that linger for a very long time. Older vintages that have been superb include the 2005, 2010, and 2013.

IN THREE WORDS | *Serious, polished, layered.*

DOMAINE PERROT-MINOT

address	11 Chemin des Petites Rues, 21220 Morey-Saint-Denis, Burgundy, France www.perrot-minot.com Tel: + 33 3 80 34 32 51
contact	Christophe Perrot-Minot
farming philosophy	Organic, no chemical fertilizers or herbicides.
in the cellar	Partially destemmed, 50-60% whole bunch on average, depending on wine and vintage; 1 week cold maceration; matured 14 months in barrels with one-fifth new oak or less for all wines, even Grands Crus.
total vineyard area	12 hectares
total annual production	50,000 bottles (includes wines from purchased grapes)

key vineyard holdings

Red

Charmes-Chambertin Grand Cru	0.91 ha		Morey-Saint-Denis Premier Cru	
Mazoyères-Chambertin Grand Cru	0.74 ha		La Riotte Vieilles Vignes	0.58 ha
Vosne-Romanée Premier Cru			Nuits-Saint-Georges Premier Cru	
Les Beaux Monts Vieilles Vignes	0.83 ha		La Richemone Vieilles Vignes	1.46 ha
Chambolle-Musigny Premier Cru			Nuits-Saint-Georges Premier Cru	
Combe d'Orveau Vieilles Vignes	0.47 ha		Les Cras Vieilles Vignes	0.08 ha
Chambolle-Musigny Premier Cru			Nuits-Saint-Georges Premier Cru	
Fuées Vieilles Vignes	0.13 ha		Les Murgers Vieilles Vignes	0.18 ha
Chambolle-Musigny Premier Cru			Vosne-Romanée Champs Perdrix	0.36 ha
Les Charmes Vieilles Vignes	0.09 ha		Vosne-Romanée	0.41 ha
Chambolle-Musigny Premier Cru			Chambolle-Musigny Vieilles Vignes	0.85 ha
Les Baudes Vieilles Vignes	0.04 ha		Morey-Saint-Denis La Rue de Vergy	1.39 ha
			Gevrey-Chambertin	1.51 ha

CHARMES-CHAMBERTIN GRAND CRU VIEILLES VIGNES, GEVREY-CHAMBERTIN

Christophe Perrot-Minot has been tinkering and refining the estate's wine style since taking over from his father in 1993. He is the first to admit that, looking back, he made some wrong calls when he began, but feels confident and happy about the new direction of the wines since 2005. Prior to Christophe's arrival, Perrot-Minot wines were solid but not performing to their vineyards' potential. Perrot-Minot has 12 hectares of wonderful parcels spread throughout Côte de Nuits, including two Grands Crus, as well as excellent Chambolle, Vosne, and Nuits Premier Cru parcels. I had many bottles of its Charmes-Chambertin from the 1990s, and some vintages like the 1996 and 1999 were good but not outstanding. Christophe Perrot-Minot is a suave, articulate man who is clearly devoted to increasing the estate's reputation and wine quality. From the tastings I have had in recent years, I think he has found the right formula. All the wines have wonderful transparency and clarity, which offers greater terroir *expression*. Christophe says that since 2005 he is very gentle with the grapes, calling it "infusion" rather than extraction, with only three to four punch-downs during the entire fermentation. Its Grands Crus, which number seven including those it makes from purchased grapes, are all pure, detailed, with wonderful intensity. Very little new oak is used, only up to 20%. The Chambertin and Clos de Bèze, both from purchased grapes, are glorious expressions of their place and have lovely purity. (The wines made from the purchased grapes have the same label but without the word "domaine.") I always rank these two as among my favorites in its Grand Cru lineup. However, for this book I chose its estate-grown Charmes-Chambertin because it has long been the domaine's flagship wine. It has a separate bottling of the Mazoyères, but I usually have a slight preference for the Charmes, which I find a bit deeper, more complex and **complete**. Recent vintages such as 2010, 2012, 2015, 2016, and 2017 are **superb**, and I can't wait to follow their lives as they mature and age. As wonderful as these vintages are, I have a feeling that Christophe's best wines are yet to be made. IN THREE WORDS *Pure, precise, impeccable.*

CLOS DE LA ROCHE GRAND CRU CUVÉE VIEILLES VIGNES, MOREY–SAINT–DENIS

The first parcels to make up Domaine Ponsot were purchased in 1872 by William Ponsot. Subsequent generations, highly accomplished in their respective professions, expanded the holdings to 11 hectares, including 12 Grands Crus. The family has been highly regarded for its innovative work through four generations: Hippolyte Ponsot was one of the first to domaine bottle all its wines starting in 1932, and as a lawyer he was also one of the founders of the AOC classification for Burgundy wines in 1936. Jean-Marie Ponsot was a pioneer of clonal selection in the 1960s, and many of the Pinot Noir clones used by top vintners around the world came from its Clos de la Roche vineyards. Most recently, Laurent Ponsot, as the fourth generation winemaker, made headlines as an evangelist against fake wines. His departure from the domaine in early 2017 came as a surprise to the wine community, and the estate is now managed by his sister Rose-Marie Ponsot and winemaker Alexandre Abel. The domaine's total vineyard size is now 8 hectares, and Chambertin, Clos Saint-Denis, and Griotte-Chambertin are no longer part of Domaine Ponsot. It is still too early to see if any dramatic changes will ensue with the new management team, but the Ponsot wines in the market for the coming several years will be those made by Laurent Ponsot. There is a unique signature that he imparted to all the domaine's wines: deep color, high extraction, sumptuous velvety-textured tannins from old vines and late harvest (no new oak is used), and a richness of flavors that make them majestic and distinctive. Ponsot defines Clos de la Roche just as Vogüé defines Musigny, and Rousseau defines Chambertin; its 3.4 hectares, which represents the lion's share of Clos de la Roche, sets a high bar for others to follow. This wine is *monumental*, and one can't help but be awe-struck by its *stature* and depth. I enjoy the cooler vintages, like the 2008 and 2012, often more than the warm ones, because it brings out more of Clos de la Roche's minerality and *tension*. One note of caution is the bottle variation one can encounter in Ponsot's wines, because it chooses not to add any sulfur dioxide, which protects wine during aging.

IN THREE WORDS   *Assertive, virile, majestic.*

DOMAINE PONSOT

Gaston Balande, *Lunch on the Banks of the Seine*, 1914.

address	21 Rue Montagne, 21220 Morey-Saint-Denis, Burgundy, France www.domaine-ponsot.com Tel: + 33 3 80 34 32 46		
contact	Rose-Marie Ponsot		
farming philosophy	Largely following biodynamic and organic principles, without certification; average vine age for Grand Cru vineyards is over 50 years; among the latest to harvest.		
in the cellar	Grapes destemmed; no fining, filtration, or sulfur addition; movement of grapes and wine via gravity; matured 2 years in used barrels, with no new oak; wines bottled with ArdeaSeal, a synthetic closure, except for magnums and large-format bottles.		
total vineyard area	8 hectares	**total annual production**	45,000 bottles

key vineyard holdings	*Red*
	Chapelle-Chambertin Grand Cru 0.47 ha
	Clos de la Roche Grand Cru
	  Cuvée Vieilles Vignes 3.36 ha
	Morey-Saint-Denis Premier Cru
	  Cuvée des Alouettes 1.05 ha
	Morey-Saint-Denis Cuvée des Crives 0.62 ha
			Gevrey-Chambertin
			  Cuvée de l'Abeille 0.51 ha
			
			White
			Morey-Saint-Denis Premier Cru
			  Blanc Clos des Monts Luisants 0.98 ha

CLOS SAINT-DENIS GRAND CRU CUVÉE TRÈS VIEILLES VIGNES, MOREY-SAINT-DENIS

(LAST VINTAGE 2017)

From the time Laurent Ponsot took charge of the estate in 1990, the wines became indelibly marked with his signature. Laurent is a controversial figure in Burgundy—he is not one to follow trends and is quite vocal about the things he believes in. In this small region, where nearly everyone is related to each another, it is quite unusual and makes him stand apart. At Domaine Ponsot he was equally headstrong with his unique philosophy, which included minimal treatments in the vineyard, late harvest, destemming, no fining, filtration, or sulfur dioxide addition, and no new oak. Laurent is the first to admit that in the 1960s and 1970s Domaine Ponsot wines were not consistent, since his father was mayor of the village and spent more time involved in politics than in the vineyard. Although Laurent Ponsot left the family domaine in 2017 to start his own wine company, his sisters continue with the same winemaking regimen and style. Ponsot wines from the 1990s garnered much praise and gained a huge following in the United States, where collectors admired his bold, concentrated, unique style of wines. Clos Saint-Denis is one of the lightest and most *elegant* of the Grands Crus in Ponsot's portfolio. In this 6.6-hectare Grand Cru vineyard, Ponsot is the third-largest owner, with less than 1 hectare. The vines, according to Laurent, are more than 120 years old, hence the words "Cuvée Très Vieilles Vignes" on the label. What I love about this wine is its incredible finesse and delicacy, combined with a lingering minerally finish. The flavors are restrained, *intricate*, and beautifully layered, *seamless* and complete. Perhaps it is the combination of ancient vines and little intervention that makes this wine sing so beautifully, especially in vintages like 1999, 2005, and 2009. IN THREE WORDS *Deep, harmonious, opulent.*

Harvest scene, detail of a capital carved in relief, c. 1125, Burgundy.

Domaine Rossignol-Trapet

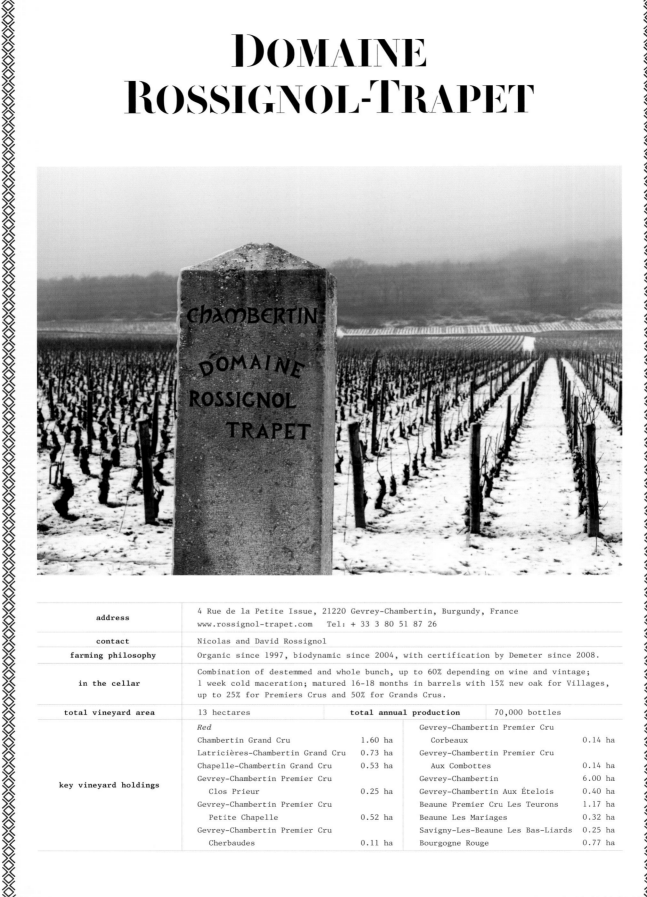

address	4 Rue de la Petite Issue, 21220 Gevrey-Chambertin, Burgundy, France www.rossignol-trapet.com Tel: + 33 3 80 51 87 26
contact	Nicolas and David Rossignol
farming philosophy	Organic since 1997, biodynamic since 2004, with certification by Demeter since 2008.
in the cellar	Combination of destemmed and whole bunch, up to 60% depending on wine and vintage; 1 week cold maceration; matured 16-18 months in barrels with 15% new oak for Villages, up to 25% for Premiers Crus and 50% for Grands Crus.

total vineyard area	13 hectares	**total annual production**	70,000 bottles

key vineyard holdings			
Red		Gevrey-Chambertin Premier Cru	
Chambertin Grand Cru	1.60 ha	Corbeaux	0.14 ha
Latricières-Chambertin Grand Cru	0.73 ha	Gevrey-Chambertin Premier Cru	
Chapelle-Chambertin Grand Cru	0.53 ha	Aux Combottes	0.14 ha
Gevrey-Chambertin Premier Cru		Gevrey-Chambertin	6.00 ha
Clos Prieur	0.25 ha	Gevrey-Chambertin Aux Ételois	0.40 ha
Gevrey-Chambertin Premier Cru		Beaune Premier Cru Les Teurons	1.17 ha
Petite Chapelle	0.52 ha	Beaune Les Mariages	0.32 ha
Gevrey-Chambertin Premier Cru		Savigny-Les-Beaune Les Bas-Liards	0.25 ha
Cherbaudes	0.11 ha	Bourgogne Rouge	0.77 ha

CHAMBERTIN GRAND CRU, GEVREY–CHAMBERTIN

Rossignol-Trapet was founded when the original estate, Domaine Louis Trapet, was split into Domaine Trapet Père et Fils and this estate. When Mado Trapet married Jacques Rossignol, two historic wine families came together: the Trapet family from Gevrey-Chambertin and the Rossignol family from Volnay. For many years, Jacques Rossignol made wine with his brother-in-law Jean Trapet at Domaine Louis Trapet. However, with the arrival of the next generation, Nicolas and David Rossignol, the sons of Mado and Jacques, it was decided that the former Trapet estate be split between Rossignol-Trapet and Trapet Père et Fils. Jacques' sons started the conversion to biodynamic farming and changed the style of the wines: Fruitier, less rustic, more pure, with later harvest timing and more new oak used. The effect of all the changes in the vineyard and cellar really took effect with the 2005 vintage: The wines are now more precise with greater finesse. The Chambertin comes from two parcels that are over 45 years old, with a proportion of vines dating back to 1919. There are now significant proportions of whole bunches included in this wine, varying by vintage, with some, like the 2014, having 50% whole cluster. The three Grands Crus made by the Rossignol brothers are all excellent examples of their appellations. They are extremely fortunate to have more than 1.5 hectares in Chambertin, making them the fourth-largest owner in this exalted Grand Cru, producing over 20 barrels every year. For me, the Chambertin is the most complex and **profound** of the three Grands Crus. This vineyard has a reputation of producing dense, muscular wines, and Rossignol-Trapet's Chambertin fits the mold but without any heaviness or extraction. There is no doubt a firm backbone in vintages like 2015 and 2010, but there is also freshness and minerality to make the wines complete and **harmonious**. Even its 2005, at 13 years old, is too young, so it is difficult to predict how these intense wines will age, but given their depth, taut structure, and **concentrated** flavor profile, I have no doubt they will gain in complexity and beauty with time.

IN THREE WORDS *Complex, vigorous, age-worthy.*

DOMAINE ROULOT

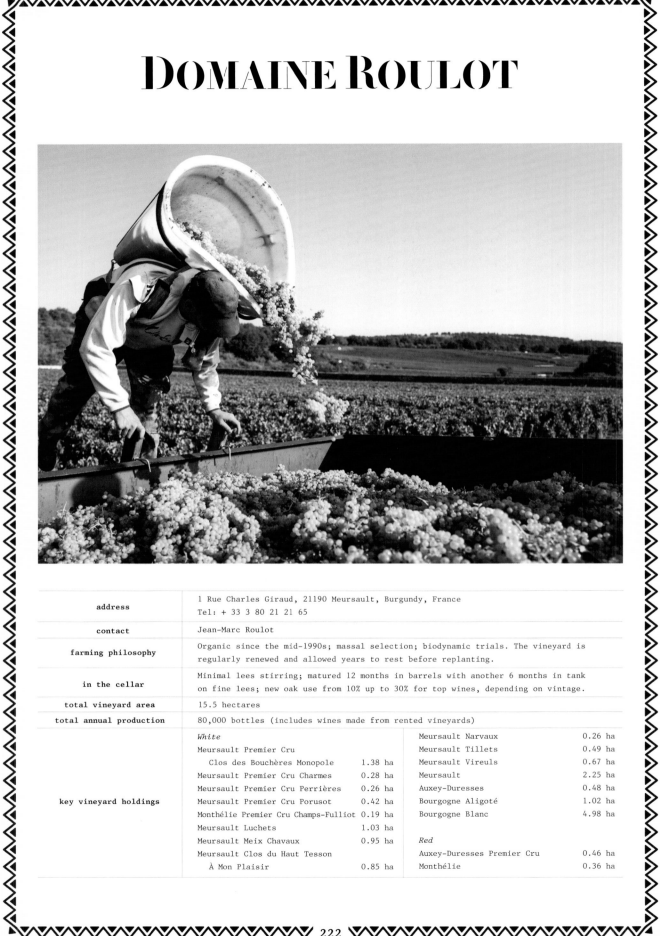

address	1 Rue Charles Giraud, 21190 Meursault, Burgundy, France Tel: + 33 3 80 21 21 65
contact	Jean-Marc Roulot
farming philosophy	Organic since the mid-1990s; massal selection; biodynamic trials. The vineyard is regularly renewed and allowed years to rest before replanting.
in the cellar	Minimal lees stirring; matured 12 months in barrels with another 6 months in tank on fine lees; new oak use from 10% up to 30% for top wines, depending on vintage.
total vineyard area	15.5 hectares
total annual production	80,000 bottles (includes wines made from rented vineyards)

key vineyard holdings

White		
Meursault Premier Cru		
Clos des Bouchères Monopole	1.38 ha	
Meursault Premier Cru Charmes	0.28 ha	
Meursault Premier Cru Perrières	0.26 ha	
Meursault Premier Cru Porusot	0.42 ha	
Monthélie Premier Cru Champs-Fulliot	0.19 ha	
Meursault Luchets	1.03 ha	
Meursault Meix Chavaux	0.95 ha	
Meursault Clos du Haut Tesson		
À Mon Plaisir	0.85 ha	
Meursault Narvaux	0.26 ha	
Meursault Tillets	0.49 ha	
Meursault Vireuls	0.67 ha	
Meursault	2.25 ha	
Auxey-Duresses	0.48 ha	
Bourgogne Aligoté	1.02 ha	
Bourgogne Blanc	4.98 ha	
Red		
Auxey-Duresses Premier Cru	0.46 ha	
Monthélie	0.36 ha	

MEURSAULT PREMIER CRU LES PERRIÈRES, MEURSAULT

Guy Roulot has long enjoyed a reputation as one of the finest Meursault producers, but it is his son, Jean-Marc Roulot, who elevated the estate to icon status. Roulot is tall, with an expressive face that seems ready to break into a smile or song at any moment. He was pursuing an acting career in Paris when his father suddenly died in 1982. He did not return home right away, but the call from the vineyard must have been strong, and in 1989 he returned to manage the family estate. From his father's side, Jean-Marc's ancestors have ties to the vineyard tracing back to the 1820s. The ancestry from his mother's side is equally deep: His mother, Geneviève Coche, is the cousin of Jean-François Coche of Coche-Dury. Jean-Marc has made numerous changes in the cellar and winery: converting to organic farming, expanding the estate, and changing the style of the Meursault from a powerful wine to a finer, edgier one with more precision. All the wines from this estate sizzle with tension and energy. I am a big fan of its Bourgognes, and its Village Meursaults are superior to many other estates'

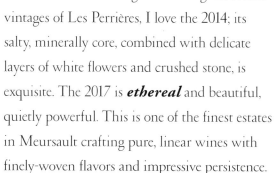

Premiers Crus and Grands Crus. Luckily for Jean-Marc, he is working with many vines that are 50 or more years of age; but it is his attention to detail in every facet that allows the wines from these vineyards to sing. Among the six Village Meursaults, the Clos du Haut Tesson À Mon Plaisir is usually my favorite. This wine always shows the refinement and depth of a Premier Cru Meursault. But the one that makes my heart flutter is the Meursault Les Perrières. This is a wine that has *electrifying* tension, amazing detail, and purity that shows even in its youth. After about 10 years the wine reveals more flavors and depth, without losing its *svelte* figure. Among the recent vintages of Les Perrières, I love the 2014; its salty, minerally core, combined with delicate layers of white flowers and crushed stone, is exquisite. The 2017 is *ethereal* and beautiful, quietly powerful. This is one of the finest estates in Meursault crafting pure, linear wines with finely-woven flavors and impressive persistence.

IN THREE WORDS **Noble, consistent, finely-woven.**

DOMAINE SYLVAIN CATHIARD & FILS

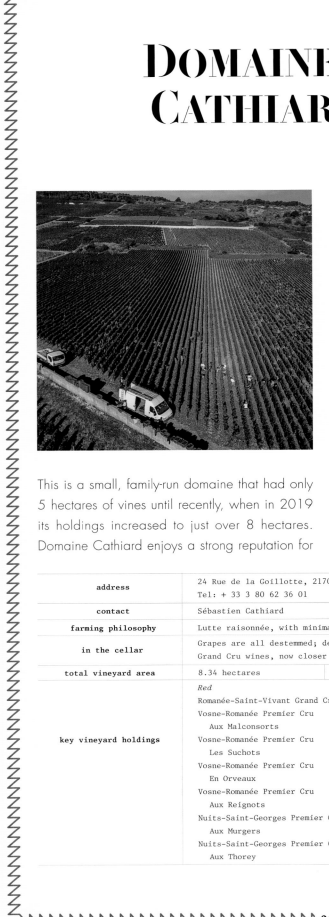

This is a small, family-run domaine that had only 5 hectares of vines until recently, when in 2019 its holdings increased to just over 8 hectares. Domaine Cathiard enjoys a strong reputation for producing some of the most profound wines from Vosne-Romanée. None of the estate's parcels is larger than 1 hectare, except for Bourgogne Hautes Côtes de Nuits; its Grand Cru Romanée-Saint-Vivant vineyard is barely over one-tenth of a hectare. Sylvain Cathiard established the estate with vineyards passed down from his father and grandfather, who worked in the vineyards at DRC and Lamarche. Initially it sold grapes to négociants, but over the years started bottling its own wines. The estate has expanded slowly to include the excellent Vosne-Romanée Premier Cru Malconsorts, purchased in the 1970s, the Romanée-Saint-Vivant, acquired in the 1990s, and most recently the Nuits-Saint-Georges Premier Cru Thorey.

Sylvain has now taken a backseat, while his son Sébastien, who returned to the family

address	24 Rue de la Goillotte, 21700 Vosne-Romanée, Burgundy, France
	Tel: + 33 3 80 62 36 01
contact	Sébastien Cathiard
farming philosophy	Lutte raisonnée, with minimal spraying; plowing, no herbicides.
in the cellar	Grapes are all destemmed; declining use of new oak, formerly 100% for Premier Cru and Grand Cru wines, now closer to two-thirds new.

total vineyard area	8.34 hectares	total annual production	50,000 bottles

key vineyard holdings	*Red*		Chambolle-Musigny Clos de l'Orme	0.43 ha
	Romanée-Saint-Vivant Grand Cru	0.17 ha	Vosne-Romanée	0.85 ha
	Vosne-Romanée Premier Cru		Nuits-Saint-Georges	0.13 ha
	Aux Malconsorts	0.74 ha	Gevrey-Chambertin	0.34 ha
	Vosne-Romanée Premier Cru		Bourgogne Hautes Côtes de Nuits	2.80 ha
	Les Suchots	0.16 ha	Côteaux Bourguignons	
	Vosne-Romanée Premier Cru		Les Croix Blanches	0.10 ha
	En Orveaux	0.29 ha	Bourgogne	0.50 ha
	Vosne-Romanée Premier Cru			
	Aux Reignots	0.24 ha	*White*	
	Nuits-Saint-Georges Premier Cru		Bourgogne Hautes Côtes de Nuits	0.55 ha
	Aux Murgers	0.48 ha	Bourgogne Aligoté	0.13 ha
	Nuits-Saint-Georges Premier Cru			
	Aux Thorey	0.43 ha		

domaine in 2005, runs the estate. It is clear that the Cathiards have viticulture in their blood, and most of their work is focused on the vineyard. The vines are meticulously looked after, and the land plowed to reduce weeds; spraying is kept to a minimum. Sébastien is often found in the vineyard, pruning in the winter, and in the spring removing excessive buds to control yields. With most of its Village and Premier Cru vines at 40 to 50 years old, the yields are already quite low. The result of fastidious work in the vineyard coupled with old vines means small berries that have concentration and depth.

A lot of minor refinements are taking place in the Cathiard cellar. In the past, the Grand Cru and the top Premiers Crus were matured in 100% new oak barrels. In 2014, this was reduced to two-thirds for the Romanée-Saint-Vivant and all the Premiers Crus; the Village wines had 50% new oak. The toasting level, which can add a strong oaky aroma to the wine, has also been reduced.

I have to admit that it is only recently that I have become a big fan of Cathiard wines. In the past I enjoyed the wines, but in their youth found them too oaky, with the toasty notes dominating the wine and detracting from its finer characters. But with Sébastien at the helm since 2011, I have become an admirer. I was very impressed with the stylistic direction of the 2014, 2015, 2016, and 2017 vintages tasted from barrel. There is definitely a lighter touch and greater purity in the wines. Sébastien is headed in the right direction in his pursuit of greater terroir expression and clarity—the Vosne-Romanée Premier Cru Aux Malconsorts is a great example of how this new direction results in elevating an already great wine to an even higher level.

ROMANÉE-SAINT-VIVANT GRAND CRU, VOSNE-ROMANÉE

Romanée-Saint-Vivant is rightly one of the most celebrated, historic Grand Cru vineyards in Burgundy, originally belonging to the monks of the Abbey of Saint-Vivant. With both DRC and Leroy setting high standards for this vineyard, most of the other eight growers, whose parcels are all less than 1 hectare, have succeeded in meeting those standards. Cathiard is one of these, and its main concern is insufficient supply. This is such a tiny parcel that Sébastien is reluctant to let people taste from barrel, as only two barrels, and sometimes only one, are produced per year. The wines are on strict allocation around the world and it is one of the most sought-after Romanée-Saint-Vivants. Of all Cathiard's wines, this one possesses the most refinement, elegance, and exceptional finish. This wonderful parcel, with 75-year-old vines, is consistent year after year, offering flavors that are at once intense and delicate. With at least 8 years of bottle age, this wine becomes *resplendent* with notes of violets, rose petals, and sweet raspberries. The plush palate in its youth becomes silkier and finer with time, gaining depth and complexity. Given the great terroir, the vintage variation is minor, and the *kaleidoscope* of flavors can be expected after a decade in bottle— delicious vintages to approach now include 1995, 1996, and 1999. Vintages that should turn into *stunning* beauties with another decade or two in bottle are the 2009, 2010, and 2015.

IN THREE WORDS *Intoxicating, multifaceted, enduring.*

VOSNE-ROMANÉE PREMIER CRU AUX MALCONSORTS, VOSNE-ROMANÉE

Malconsorts is Sylvain Cathiard's flagship wine, its largest Premier Cru parcel, with three-fourths of a hectare. In this nearly 6-hectare Premier Cru vineyard, which is adjacent to La Tâche, Cathiard is one of the smallest owners. Bichot, Dujac, and de Montille are the three largest, with over 1 hectare each. All six producers of Malconsorts make excellent versions, making this Premier Cru one of the most reliable and among the highest in quality. Cathiard's Malconsorts has inherent *power*, with a stony *minerality* at its core; there is tremendous *complexity* and depth in the wine that warrants a decade of bottle age to bring it to fruition. Vintages that are drinking beautifully now include 1999, 2001, and 2007. Recent vintages will be fabulous in about 10 years' time; I would recommend all the recent vintages from 2012 to 2017. IN THREE WORDS *Deep, seamless, concentrated.*

" There are many ways to the recognition of truth, and Burgundy is one of them. **"**

Isak Dinesen

An abbey cellarer tests his wine, illumination from *Li livres dou santé* by Aldobrandino of Siena, 13th century.

DOMAINE SYLVIE ESMONIN

(FORMERLY MICHEL ESMONIN ET FILLE)

address	1 Rue Neuve, 21220 Gevrey-Chambertin, Burgundy, France Tel: + 33 3 80 34 36 44			
contact	Sylvie Esmonin			
farming philosophy	Organic principles, without certification; no herbicide, insecticide, or fungicide.			
in the cellar	Mainly whole cluster for Premiers Crus, destemmed for Bourgogne and Village; matured 18 months with high percentage of new oak, Clos Saint-Jacques 100% new oak.			
total vineyard area	8 hectares		**total annual production**	35,000 bottles

key vineyard holdings	*Red*
	Gevrey-Chambertin Premier Cru
	    Clos Saint-Jacques
	Volnay Premier Cru Santenots
		
		1.60 ha
		0.18 ha
			Gevrey-Chambertin (including
			    Vieilles Vignes)
			Côte de Nuits Villages
				
				4.40 ha
				0.63 ha

GEVREY–CHAMBERTIN PREMIER CRU CLOS SAINT–JACQUES, GEVREY–CHAMBERTIN

Since the 1990s, this small estate has been led by a remarkable woman: Sylvie Esmonin was one of the earliest female agricultural engineers from Montpellier University, and upon graduation she worked as a consultant until her father urged her to return to the family estate. Sylvie's grandfather had purchased the original 3-hectare vineyard but had never bottled the wine, choosing to sell everything to négociants. One of Sylvie's conditions for returning was her insistence on domaine bottling. She began to work organically and stopped using chemicals in the vineyard, she reduced yields, expanded the estate, and more recently started whole cluster fermentation. In the Clos Saint-Jacques and the Volnay Santenots, it is now more likely that whole clusters make up the majority, whereas in the 1990s the grapes were all destemmed. From the 2002 vintage on, the Clos Saint-Jacques, made with mostly whole bunch, has a different, more complex *aromatic* profile, as well as more **nuances** and depth. From the wonderful Gevrey-Chambertin Vieilles Vignes, with vines that are on average 60 years old, to her fabulous Clos Saint-Jacques, Sylvie's wines are forthright and at the same time beautifully delineated. Her Clos Saint-Jacques plot, like the other four owners of this Premier Cru vineyard, runs the entire length of the slope. There is a beautiful panoramic view of the entire 6.7-hectare vineyard of Clos Saint-Jacques from her backyard. With 1.6 hectares, Sylvie is the second-largest owner, after Rousseau. Many, including myself, consider this vineyard worthy of producing Grand Cru–level wine, as vintages in 2005, 2010, and 2015 prove. The complex geology running down the length of the slope accounts for part of the wine's complexity and **impressive** stature, and the other part is hundreds of good winemaking decisions by a very talented woman.

IN THREE WORDS *Gorgeous, focused, persistent.*

MAZOYÈRES–CHAMBERTIN GRAND CRU, GEVREY–CHAMBERTIN

This estate has been under the radar for many collectors and Burgundy specialists, which has always puzzled me. Romain Taupenot and his charming sister Virginie, who together run the property, represent the seventh generation of growers from Côte de Nuits. Romain's grandfather, Jean Taupenot, who came from a wine family in Saint-Romain, married Denise Merme, who inherited vineyards from the Merme side of the family; thus the union provided the core parcels for this estate, which was then expanded in subsequent generations. Romain is well-spoken and thoughtful, constantly reflecting on how to improve the wines from this estate, which is scattered throughout the Côte de Nuits. The 13-hectare estate is farmed organically but without certification, as Romain prefers to have flexibility in case of emergencies. He does not like the influence of whole clusters and he destems all his fruit, explaining that he prefers pure fruit flavors. There is less and less new oak being used, and in recent vintages such as the 2016, new oak use has been reduced to just 30% for the Grands Crus and much less for the Villages and Premiers Crus. Taupenot-Merme's large range of red wines makes it difficult to generalize its style, but all have good extraction and firm tannins, and are forthright rather than shy. Among its range of seven Premiers Crus, I really enjoy the Chambolle-Musigny Combe d'Orveau and the Gevrey-Chambertin Bel Air; the former for its vibrant flavors and purity, and the latter for its sensual tannins. The Grands Crus are well structured and built to age, and among the three (the minute plot of Clos des Lambrays is not commercially available) I would choose the Mazoyères-Chambertin. Most Mazoyères gets blended into Charmes, which is perfectly legal, so as a separately labeled wine it is special. Taupenot-Merme's Mazoyères is a **standout**—richer, deeper, spicier, and overall more powerful than the Charmes. There is always a ***profound*** depth to this wine, a sense of inner ***strength*** and wonderful length. The 2002 is superb; it's one of my favorite vintages of the Mazoyères, though a few more years of bottle age would make it even better. Among the recent vintages that I would choose for my daughter's cellar are the 2012, 2014, 2015, and 2017.

IN THREE WORDS   *Intense, layered, vigorous.*

DOMAINE TAUPENOT-MERME

address	33 Route des Grands Crus, 21220 Morey-Saint-Denis, Burgundy, France Tel: + 33 3 80 34 35 24
contact	Romain Taupenot
farming philosophy	Organic principles since 2001.
in the cellar	Grapes destemmed; 7-10 days' cold maceration; matured 14 months with minimal new oak, reduced to 20-25% for Villages and Premiers Crus and 30% for Grands Crus.

total vineyard area	13.5 hectares	**total annual production**	80,000 bottles

key vineyard holdings	*Red*		Morey-Saint-Denis Premier Cru	
	Charmes-Chambertin Grand Cru	0.57 ha	Les Pruliers	0.53 ha
	Mazoyères-Chambertin Grand Cru	0.85 ha	Auxey-Duresses Premier Cru	
	Clos des Lambrays Grand Cru	0.04 ha	Les Duresses	0.22 ha
	Corton Grand Cru Le Rognet	0.41 ha	Auxey-Duresses Premier Cru	
	Gevrey-Chambertin Premier Cru		Les Grands Champs	0.31 ha
	Bel Air	0.43 ha	Gevrey-Chambertin	1.64 ha
	Morey-Saint-Denis Premier Cru		Morey-Saint-Denis	0.39 ha
	La Riotte	0.57 ha	Chambolle-Musigny	0.86 ha
	Morey-Saint-Denis Premier Cru		Auxey-Duresses (red and white)	0.71 ha
	La Village	0.06 ha	Saint-Romain (red and white)	2.39 ha
	Chambolle-Musigny Premier Cru			
	La Combe d'Orveau	0.45 ha		

DOMAINE TRAPET PÈRE ET FILS

(FORMERLY JEAN-LOUIS TRAPET)

address	53 Route de Beaune, 21220 Gevrey-Chambertin, Burgundy, France www.domaine-trapet.fr Tel: + 33 3 80 34 30 40		
contact	Jean-Louis Trapet		
farming philosophy	Biodynamic since 1996; certified by Demeter and Biodyvin.		
in the cellar	Mainly whole bunch, depending on wine and vintage; 1 week cold maceration; matured 16-18 months in barrels; reduced new oak use, no more than 40% for Grands Crus.		
total vineyard area	16 hectares	**total annual production**	85,000 bottles

key vineyard holdings	*Red*
	Chambertin Grand Cru 1.85 ha
	Chapelle-Chambertin Grand Cru 0.55 ha
	Latricières-Chambertin Grand Cru 0.74 ha
	Gevrey-Chambertin Premier Cru
	  Clos Prieur 0.21 ha
			Gevrey-Chambertin Premier Cru
			  Petite Chapelle 0.37 ha
			Gevrey-Chambertin 6.00 ha
			Marsannay 0.90 ha

CHAMBERTIN GRAND CRU, GEVREY–CHAMBERTIN

This is a young estate with long, historical ties to its land. The vineyards have been in the Trapet family since the 19th century, expanding its holdings slowly over several generations. But its modern history begins in 1990, when the large Trapet estate was divided into the current Trapet Père et Fils and Rossignol-Trapet. Prior to 1990, the Trapet estate was run jointly by Jean Trapet and his brother-in-law, Jacques Rossignol. Now, Rossignol-Trapet is run by Jacques' two sons, and Trapet Père et Fils is run by Jean's son Jean-Louis. The new generation has invigorated this traditional property, and swift changes were made, starting in the vineyard. First, all chemical sprays were eliminated, followed by conversion to organics, then biodynamics began in 1996. Jean-Louis is convinced that grape quality begins and ends in the vineyard, and for the wine to reach the highest quality level, the soil must be alive and the vines naturally healthy. The grapes are sorted twice, first in the vineyard and again in the cellar. There are no firm rules about percentage of whole bunch used, it varies by wine and vintage. For example, 2015 being a ripe vintage meant the Chambertin had 50% whole clusters, and in 2017, 100% new oak was used. Villages or Premiers Crus would contain less whole bunch, from 20 to 35%, varying by vintage. Trapet is fortunate to have nearly 2 hectares of Chambertin, making it the second-largest owner of Chambertin, just after Rousseau, which owns 2.55 hectares. Trapet's Chambertin is a textbook example of a powerful, muscular Chambertin that easily ages for decades. In recent years the wine has become fleshy and the tannins much more refined. There is no denying its depth, complexity, and class, no matter the vintage. One of the most memorable Trapet Chambertins was a bottle of 1985 that I enjoyed with friends in 2017, when it was 32 years old. It had lost most of its youthful grip, and had evolved into one of the most *seductive*, suave, delicately layered, sensual wines I had ever tasted. The power and *structure* had faded into the background to reveal a *stunning*, complex wine with finesse and an incredibly long finish. Recent vintages such as 2010, 2012, and 2015 have similar depth; these may age even longer and better than the 1985. IN THREE WORDS *Superb, complex, memorable.*

66 **Wine cheers the sad, revives the old, inspires the young, makes weariness forget his toil. 99**

Lord Byron

REPUBLIQUE FRANÇAISE

POSTES·1969

1,00

ROGIER DE LA PASTURE (ROGER VAN DER WEYDEN) Pinx.

PHILIPPE LE BON

B.TEMPS

PULIGNY-MONTRACHET PREMIER CRU LES COMBETTES, PULIGNY-MONTRACHET

This estate is one of the top white wine producers of Burgundy that continues to deliver exceptional wines. The initial 12-hectare property was established by Étienne Sauzet, who propelled it to become one of the top three names in Puligny-Montrachet. Étienne passed on the estate to his daughter Colette, who married Jean Boillot and had three children. The estate was divided among Étienne's three grandchildren: Jeanine and her two brothers, Jean-Marc Boillot and Henri Boillot. In 1975, just before Étienne's death, Jeanine and her husband, Gérard Boudot, took over the estate. Her two brothers left to establish their own highly regarded domaines. In 1991, when Jean-Marc decided to take out his share of the vineyards, there were suddenly gaps in the portfolio. These are now filled by purchased grapes, which can make up one quarter to one third of the total production, depending on the vintage. The fourth-generation family members have decided not to differentiate between domaine fruit and purchased fruit. Thus the label no longer includes "domaine" and the wines are labeled simply "Étienne Sauzet." Recently, after 40 years in the role, Boudot has been stepping aside and handing over winemaking responsibilities to his son-in-law Benoît Riffault and his daughter Émilie Boudot. The estate is now fully biodynamic and the wines have wonderful lightness and greater purity. Among the eight Premier Cru Puligny-Montrachets, Les Combettes is often the most intense and most age-worthy. In vintages like 2014 and 2017, the wines have **stunning** aromas, thrilling acidity, and an **impressive** minerally elegance. Sauzet's Grands Crus are extremely rare, since both the Bâtard-Montrachet and Bienvenues produce just a few barrels each, and the Montrachet produces four barrels in generous vintages like 2017. Puligny Les Combettes, on the other hand, nearly a hectare in size, is more widely available and offers an accessible entrée into Sauzet wines. I had a 1988 just a few years ago, when the wine was 27 years old, and it was glorious. Recent vintages like 2002, 2010, 2014, and 2017 are **exquisite** now but will age beautifully over the coming several decades.

GRAND VIN DE BOURGOGNE

Puligny-Montrachet

LES COMBETTES

Appellation Puligny-Montrachet 1er Cru Contrôlée

Étienne Sauzet

IN THREE WORDS *Detailed, striking, thrilling.*

ÉTIENNE SAUZET

Sarah Butterfield, *Still Life and Seashore, Bandol*.

address	11 Rue de Poiseul, 21190 Puligny-Montrachet, Burgundy, France www.etiennesauzet.com Tel: + 33 3 80 21 32 10
contact	Benoît Riffault
farming philosophy	Organic since 2006, biodynamic since 2010.
in the cellar	Matured 14 months with minimal new oak, up to 30% for Premiers Crus and 40% for Grands Crus.
total vineyard area	15 hectares (including purchased grapes)
total annual production	110,000 bottles

key vineyard holdings				
White			Puligny-Montrachet Premier Cru	
Montrachet Grand Cru	0.25 ha		Les Champs Canet	1.00 ha
Chevalier-Montrachet Grand Cru	0.25 ha		Puligny-Montrachet Premier Cru	
Bâtard-Montrachet Grand Cru	0.14 ha		Les Garenne	0.99 ha
Bienvenues-Bâtard-Montrachet			Puligny-Montrachet Premier Cru	
Grand Cru	0.12 ha		Les Perrières	0.48 ha
Puligny-Montrachet Premier Cru			Puligny-Montrachet Premier Cru	
Les Combettes	0.96 ha		Les Referts	0.70 ha
Puligny-Montrachet Premier Cru			Puligny-Montrachet Premier Cru	
Les Folatières Richarde	0.27 ha		Hameau de Blagny (from 2008)	0.18 ha
Puligny-Montrachet Premier Cru			Chassagne-Montrachet	
La Truffière	0.14 ha		Les Encégnières	0.48 ha
			Puligny-Montrachet	3.52 ha

HENRI JAYER

(UNTIL 2001)

Henri Jayer is a mythical figure for many wine lovers as well as growers—the wines he produced from the 1950s up to 2001 are the most expensive wines at auction in recent years. Even before he passed away from prostate cancer in 2006, at age 84, he was a living legend. He continued to make wine until he was nearly 80, and only in 2002 did he stop completely. For tax purposes, in 1996 he transferred over all his vineyards for his nephew Emmanuel Rouget to manage, but he could not stop working, and up until the 2001 vintage he made about 1,000 bottles of Vosne-Romanée Cros Parantoux for his own pleasure. Those who knew him called him a workaholic; those who loved him called him a perfectionist; those who drank his wines called him a god.

Books by Jacky Rigaux and interviews of the great man indicate that in his heart Henri Jayer was a farmer. He loved the vineyard, he admired nature, and having spent so much of his time in the vineyards with the vines, he instinctively felt their rhythms. He was known to shun chemicals when it was extremely fashionable to use them, just after the war, when increasing volume was the driving incentive.

Henri was born in 1922, and while his two older brothers went to fight in World War II, Henri stayed to look after the family's vineyards. In the 1940s he entered into a share-crop arrangement with Madame Noirot-Camuzet, who had extensive vineyards throughout Vosne-Romanée. This continued up until Jean Méo, the cousin of Noirot-Camuzet, inherited the vineyards and decided in 1985 to reclaim them. Prior to 1985, the Noirot-Camuzet holdings (later called Méo-Camuzet) were leased out to various people to farm, including Henri Jayer, and the wines made were sold in bulk to négociants. Henri made the wines for Méo-Camuzet under its label from 1985 to 1988, until Jean-Nicolas Méo arrived and took over in 1989. He also made and bottled wines for his brother Georges Jayer from 1988 to 2001, and in addition he continued to bottle wines under the Henri Jayer label up to and including the 2001 vintage.

Henri Jayer is the one wine person I wish I had had the chance to meet. All my experiences with his wines were supplied by generous collectors based in Hong Kong, Paris, and New York. If wines could speak, I felt he was talking to me, telling me to listen more carefully to nature, because therein I would find wisdom. Even before I read about his background, his vineyard or winemaking philosophy, I was in awe of his wines.

What made Henri Jayer a legend in the 1980s was his Cros Parantoux, a 1-hectare parcel of land that was not even recognized by the authorities as a prime vineyard site. While farming the Noirot-Camuzet vineyards, which included part of Cros Parantoux, Henri noticed the potential of this neglected small parcel adjacent and similar in soil type to Richebourg. In 1951 Henri acquired his first parcel and spent two years preparing the land before planting vines. Around this time he applied for Cros Parantoux to receive Premier Cru status, which was granted surprisingly quickly. He started to buy up more parcels, finally acquiring 70% of the 1-hectare vineyard, the other 30% owned by Méo-Camuzet.

For the first few decades, Henri sold the majority of his Cros Parantoux production to négociants, keeping only a small amount for himself. It wasn't until 1978 that he bottled the wines under his own name. Henri Jayer was soon "discovered" by the American market, who adored his wines, and credit goes to importers like Alexis Lichine and Martine Saunier, who made sure the wines were tasted by the right palates and listed in the smartest restaurants. In recent years, with "Burgundy fever" catching on in Asia, Jayer wines have become the most expensive and also one of the most faked wines.

address	N/A
contact	N/A
farming philosophy	No fertilizers or herbicides; low yields.
in the cellar	Destemmed grapes, whole berries; nearly 1 week cold maceration pre-fermentation; protracted fermentation in cement tanks; matured in 100% new oak; bottled by hand without filtration.
total vineyard area	6.3 hectares (approximately, as of 1996)

key vineyard holdings, as of 1996	Richebourg Grand Cru (owned by Méo-Camuzet)
	Échezeaux Grand Cru 0.33 ha
	Vosne-Romanée Premier Cru
	  Cros Parantoux 0.72 ha
	Vosne-Romanée Premier Cru
	  Les Beaumonts 0.10 ha
	
	Vosne-Romanée Premier Cru
	  Aux Brûlées (owned by Méo-Camuzet)
	Vosne-Romanée 0.28 ha
	Bourgogne 0.28 ha

RICHEBOURG GRAND CRU, VOSNE-ROMANÉE

Henri Jayer farmed this Grand Cru vineyard for the Méo-Camuzet family until 1987, and in exchange he received half the share to bottle under his own name. My first experience with Henri Jayer wines was the 1978 Richebourg: I was astounded by its sheer power and **seductive** character; it was a hedonistic wine of **opulence** and amazing depth of flavors. This Richebourg was unlike any other Burgundy that I had tasted. It was luscious, persistent, and extremely youthful at 20 years of age. Since then, my experiences with Henri Jayer wines have been a roller-coaster ride—there seemed to be as many fakes as there were authentic bottles. This is extremely worrying, as prices for his wines continue their upward spiral. I have tried many older vintages of Richebourg, mostly from the 1980s, whose authenticity I doubt because they lacked Henri Jayer's distinctive signature—a taut frame supporting an array of luscious flavors with an impossible concentration that has no heaviness or weight. Henri Jayer was a great farmer, first and foremost; regardless of the vintage, he made the best that nature offered him, so any vintage of Richebourg that he made up until 1987, his last vintage of this wine, is to be **treasured** and remembered.

IN THREE WORDS *Unforgettable, sensual, dynamic.*

VOSNE-ROMANÉE PREMIER CRU CROS PARANTOUX, VOSNE-ROMANÉE

Cros Parantoux is what made Henri Jayer famous, and in turn he made this once-neglected vineyard famous. There are only two owners, Méo-Camuzet and Henri Jayer's nephew Emmanuel Rouget, and both are dedicated to making quality wine. I believe I have had authentic bottles of this wine only half a dozen times. Many more were served to me but tasted wrong for the vintage or did not reflect what I knew of Henri Jayer wines. Although my experience with this wine is fairly limited, the bottles I enjoyed during the 1990s and early 2000s were so **superb** that they are etched in my palate memory. First, Henri Jayer wines have incredible intensity, the kind that is so distinctive that one can pick it out in a blind tasting. Henri Jayer is to Vosne-Romanée what Coche-Dury is to Meursault—his style is that singular. Second, Cros Parantoux by Jayer is plush, velvety, with an **alluring** flavor profile and an incredible finish; a complete wine that is poetry in a bottle. A top vintage is the 1990—luscious, intensely concentrated, and **awe-inspiring**. This was six years before Henri transferred his vineyards to his nephew Emmanuel Rouget, who took over his vineyards entirely by 2001.

IN THREE WORDS *Astonishing, rare, distinctive.*

JEAN-CLAUDE RAMONET

(FORMERLY DOMAINE RAMONET)

---

address

4 Place Noyers, 21190 Chassagne-Montrachet, Burgundy, France
Tel: + 33 3 80 21 30 88   Fax: + 33 3 80 21 35 65

contact

Jean-Claude Ramonet

farming philosophy

Lutte raisonnée.

in the cellar

Minimal lees stirring; white wines barrel-matured
12-15 months in 25% new oak for Premiers Crus,
50% new oak for Grands Crus; Montrachet has 100% new
oak; reds destemmed, short pre-fermentation maceration,
aged 15 months in oak with about one-third new.

total vineyard area

17 hectares

total annual production

100,000 bottles

key vineyard holdings

White

Bâtard-Montrachet Grand Cru	0.64 ha
Chevalier-Montrachet Grand Cru	0.09 ha
Montrachet Grand Cru	0.26 ha
Bienvenues-Bâtard-Montrachet Grand Cru	0.45 ha
Chassagne-Montrachet Premier Cru Boudriotte	1.23 ha
Chassagne-Montrachet Premier Cru Cailleret	0.35 ha
Chassagne-Montrachet Premier Cru Chaumées	0.12 ha
Chassagne-Montrachet Premier Cru Les Ruchottes	1.18 ha
Chassagne-Montrachet Premier Cru Morgeot	1.22 ha
Chassagne-Montrachet Premier Cru Vergers	0.54 ha
Puligny-Montrachet Premier Cru Champ Canet	0.33 ha
Saint-Aubin Premier Cru Le Charmois	0.15 ha
Chassagne-Montrachet	1.12 ha
Puligny-Montrachet	0.85 ha

Red

Chassagne-Montrachet Premier Cru Clos de la Boudriotte	1.02 ha
Chassagne-Montrachet Premier Cru Morgeot	0.59 ha
Chassagne-Montrachet Premier Cru Clos Saint-Jean	0.79 ha
Chassagne-Montrachet	1.88 ha

BÂTARD-MONTRACHET GRAND CRU, PULIGNY-MONTRACHET

Ramonet is one of the greatest white wine producers in the world, some may even argue *the* best. The history of the domaine is a classic Burgundian rags-to-riches story: Pierre Ramonet left school at a young age and initially made wine from purchased grapes. His first purchase was the Ruchottes Premier Cru vineyard in Chassagne-Montrachet. A chance meeting with Raymond Baudoin, one of the founders of the French wine publication *La Revue du Vin,* who loved the Ruchottes, led to a meeting with U.S. importer Frank Schoonmaker. Ramonet was one of the first white Burgundies to be imported into the U.S., and once the American market "discovered" Ramonet, its reputation and the demand for the wines took off. Over the decades, it expanded its vineyards to the current 17 hectares. Now Pierre's two talented and equally devoted grandsons run the estate. However, since 2014, the wine has been labeled as Jean-Claude Ramonet, since his brother Noël has partially retired. Ramonet wines define the standards for excellence in Chassagne-Montrachet, although they suffered from premature oxidation in the 1990s (see page 24). I have had too many encounters with premox from 1995 and 1996 Ramonet wines that were disappointing, especially given its reputation and price. It now seems to be under control and I have not come across this problem since the 2000 vintage. Bâtard-Montrachet, with its more ***exuberant*** personality compared to Montrachet, is definitely the brashest Grand Cru in Ramonet's portfolio, though in its youth it can be stoic. Vintages like 2002 and 2005 reveal the energy and incredible power combined with finesse in this wine. I have also enjoyed its older vintages from the 1980s and love drinking them now, especially the 1985 and 1988. After two or three decades these wines are ***opulent***, magnificent, still ***vigorous***, and filled with rich, complex flavors. Ramonet may not be as celebrated as it was in the 1980s and 1990s, but this isn't because they are no longer making great wine, it is that the peak became very crowded, with many producers making terrific white Burgundy.

IN THREE WORDS *Sumptuous, magnificent, formidable.*

MONTRACHET GRAND CRU, PULIGNY-MONTRACHET

Ramonet owns a tiny quarter-hectare parcel in Montrachet, making just over four barrels a year in good years. Clive Coates recounts a humorous story about Pierre Ramonet, who walked into the lawyer's office in 1978 with pockets full of cash to buy this narrow parcel in the exalted Montrachet Grand Cru vineyard. Pierre Ramonet, who passed away in 1994, is a wine legend who was loved and held in high esteem—a true man of the soil; sadly, I never had the fortune of meeting the great man, but everyone seems to have a wonderful story about him and his frugal wife. Ramonet's vineyard strip lies in the Puligny commune and is adjacent to Bouchard's parcel. This is Chardonnay at its most sensitive and nuanced, with a core intensity that is most prominent in the lingering, *unforgettable* finish. Unlike Ramonet's Bâtard-Montrachet, which gains even greater expression and depth with time, Montrachet is complete from its youth. Not that the wine is more expressive or generous, it is the balance that leaves you breathless—great mineral intensity, finesse, delicacy, and length. A young vintage like the 2012 or 2014 is already complete and finely etched, with an impressive presence and *harmony*, but the incredible finish and the way the flavors *crescendo* on the palate are extraordinary. A mature vintage like the legendary 1992, which I have only tasted once, is monumental, sensual, pure pleasure in a bottle. Ramonet's Montrachet is a wine to experience, if you can find it and can afford it, at least once in your lifetime.

IN THREE WORDS *Complete, stunning, monumental.*

> 66 **Ramonet's Montrachet is a wine to experience, if you can find it and can afford it, at least once in your lifetime.** 99

19.

Cornelio. Cornelij Harlemæo
Pictori egregio Xeniolj loco
R:P: Hollzius

Oblecto dulci merentia corda lyęo,
Osor tristicię, leticięß auctor.

C. Schoneus.

JOSEPH DROUHIN

address	7 Rue d'Enfer, 21200 Beaune, Burgundy, France www.drouhin.com Tel: + 33 3 80 24 68 88
contact	Frédéric Drouhin
farming philosophy	Organic since the late 1990s, certified biodynamic since 2006; dense planting preferred, at 12,500 vines per hectare.
in the cellar	Reds mostly destemmed, whole bunch used depending on wine and vintage; several days' cold maceration; minimal use of new oak, up to 30% for Grands Crus. White wines matured about 1 year with minimal new oak, up to 20% maximum. Oak for barrels is purchased and dried for three years by the estate.
total vineyard area	78 hectares
total annual production	Undisclosed (estimated at several million bottles)

key vineyard holdings

Red

Bonnes-Mares Grand Cru	0.23 ha
Chambertin-Clos de Bèze Grand Cru	0.13 ha
Clos de Vougeot Grand Cru	0.91 ha
Corton Bressandes Grand Cru	0.26 ha
Échezeaux Grand Cru	0.46 ha
Grands Échezeaux Grand Cru	0.48 ha
Griotte-Chambertin Grand Cru	0.53 ha
Musigny Grand Cru	0.68 ha
Beaune Premier Cru Clos des Mouches	6.80 ha
Beaune Premier Cru Grèves	0.80 ha
Beaune Premier Cru (various)	1.20 ha
Chambolle-Musigny Premier Cru Les Amoureuses	0.60 ha
Chambolle-Musigny Premier Cru (various)	1.50 ha
Nuits-Saint-Georges Premier Cru Procès	0.40 ha
Volnay Premier Cru Clos des Chênes	0.30 ha
Vosne-Romanée Premier Cru Petits Monts	0.40 ha
Pommard Chanlins	0.40 ha

White

Montrachet Grand Cru Marquis de Laguiche	2.10 ha
Bâtard-Montrachet Grand Cru	0.10 ha
Corton-Charlemagne Grand Cru	0.34 ha
Beaune Premier Cru Clos des Mouches	6.80 ha
Chassagne-Montrachet Premier Cru Morgeot	2.00 ha
Meursault En Luraule	0.50 ha

Chablis

Chablis Grand Cru Les Clos	1.30 ha
Chablis Grand Cru Bougros	0.40 ha
Chablis Grand Cru Les Preuses	0.50 ha
Chablis Grand Cru Les Vaudésir	1.50 ha
Chablis Premier Cru Montmains	1.80 ha
Chablis Premier Cru Secher	1.50 ha
Chablis Premier Cru Vaillons	2.10 ha

MONTRACHET GRAND CRU MARQUIS DE LAGUICHE, PULIGNY-MONTRACHET

This is one of my favorite négociants in Burgundy, because of its consistently elegant wines that are often excellent value, and because of the family members who currently manage it. Founded in 1880 by Joseph Drouhin, the business was passed on to his son Maurice then to his son Robert, who then passed it on to his four children. Currently all four are actively involved in the company with complementary specializations: The eldest, Philippe Drouhin, is responsible for the 78 hectares of vineyards owned by the estate; Véronique is in charge of the winemaking; Laurent is based in New York and looks after its important American market; and Frédéric, the youngest, is the president of the executive board. I have seen all four siblings together in Beaune, and it is wonderful to see such a close family dynamic—each respectful of the others' responsibilities, enjoying each others' company, and each one committed and united toward the same purpose: to preserve the vineyards and the family heritage, to produce the greatest wine possible, and to present it to the right markets and the right people. Tasting with Véronique, I can see how her experience and understanding of her métier translates into the choices she makes in the cellar: She is humble, respectful, and she wants the vineyards to express themselves as clearly and as purely as possible. The wines of Drouhin, from Village to Grand Cru, are elegant, pure, and balanced. What makes Drouhin successful are the people and the care, humility, and pride they show in being entrusted with some exceptional vineyards. They make more than 10 Grand Cru wines, and this is one of the rare estates that makes both red and white wines exceptionally well. The whites are fresh, graceful, and lively, regardless of whether it is a Meursault Village or a Bâtard-Montrachet; the reds are silky, svelte, and beautifully perfumed across the board. There is no heavy hand in the winery, and new oak is kept to less than 20% in most cases, even for the Premiers and Grands Crus. Concentration and intensity from wines like the *magnificent* Marquis de Laguiche Montrachet come from the grapes and old vines, not from any oak, lees stirring, or cellar technique. This special 2-hectare parcel does not belong to the Drouhins, but the wine is synonymous with the name since the family has enjoyed a long-term lease since 1947. I was fortunate enough to try many older vintages from the 1980s, and they are wonderful. The 1989 and 1983 are two of the most *memorable* white Burgundies I have tried, both when they were over 25 years old. Younger vintages that should age equally well or even better are the 2005 and 2010. At its peak, Marquis de Laguiche Montrachet is toasty, intense, and incredibly complex, with an exotic, sweet bouquet. The *magic* in this wine is the way it combines immense concentration with incredible finesse, minerality, and grace.

IN THREE WORDS *Brilliant, remarkable, harmonious.*

MAISON LEROY

In 2018 Maison Leroy celebrated the 150th anniversary of its founding and marked the 63rd year of Lalou Bize-Leroy's leadership. Under Bize-Leroy, Maison Leroy is in the enviable position of setting the standard for what the négociant business in Burgundy can achieve, both in terms of quality and reputation. No other négociant commands the type of prices for its wines nor has the respect of the industry like Maison Leroy.

It is difficult times for négociants now, with prices for grapes rising every year, supply being squeezed due to poor weather conditions for six years in a row since 2010, and spiraling demand for Burgundy wines. Lalou Bize-Leroy says it is not easy to source high-quality wine or even top-quality grapes for her négociant business, and starting in the 1970s and 1980s she saw top-quality supply shrinking and the movement from growers to bottle their own wines. This inspired her to buy vineyards to secure her own supply, and culminated in her purchasing the 12-hectare portfolio of vineyards from Domaine Charles Noëllat for 65 million francs in 1988, thus establishing Domaine Leroy.

The success of Maison Leroy lies in Bize-Leroy's ability to identify quality wines. She is renowned as a skilled quality hound with an excellent palate, and over the years she has used her gift to identify and purchase great wines to bottle under the Maison Leroy label. She always tasted blind and sought foremost the wine's ability to express its terroir. In the 1950s, an era when many women were discouraged from going into the wine business, she was often the sole female face.

Maison Leroy no longer bottles and sells as much wine as it did several decades ago. But one can be sure that if it meets the strict standards of Bize-Leroy and makes it into the market, then the wines will be of outstanding quality. Prices reflect this, so while they are not as expensive as her domaine bottlings, the white-capsule Maison wines command extraordinary prices. A tasting in July 2018 of Maison Leroy's wines from the 1937, 1945, 1947, and 1949 vintages proves the astonishing quality of both red and white Burgundy wines and their ability to age. For mere mortals with budget constraints, I recommend the Bourgogne Rouge from 2009 or 2010, or the Bourgogne Blanc from 2014 or 2016—these are priced around US$50 per bottle.

MAZIS-CHAMBERTIN GRAND CRU, GEVREY-CHAMBERTIN

Mazis-Chambertin is the northernmost Grand Cru in the Côte d'Or, divided into Mazis Haut (upper part of the slope) and Mazis Bas (lower part). Typical of Burgundy, this 9-hectare Grand Cru site is subdivided among 28 owners, with only two having more than 1 hectare. With so many producers at different quality levels bottling Mazis-Chambertin, it is not one of the most reliable Grands Crus if you don't know the producer. Lalou Bize-Leroy's Domaine d'Auvenay owns a quarter-hectare of Mazis-Chambertin, but in the past the wines were often purchased through the largest owner, Hospices de Beaune, and bottled under Maison Leroy. I have been fortunate enough to taste many vintages of Maison Leroy Mazis-Chambertin made in the 1950s, 1960s, and 1970s. Although these wines are now very rare even at auction, I include it in this book because it is worth seeking out. Vintages such as 1955, 1962, 1971, and 1978 are sublime, showing the potential of this vineyard in the right hands. The 1962 left me **speechless** and emotional, with its beauty and ravishing **sensuality**. The 1978 is **perfection** in a bottle. Maison Leroy's rendering offers a quality reference point for all producers of Mazis-Chambertin.

| IN THREE WORDS | ***Ravishing, exhilarating, sublime.*** |

ROMANÉE-SAINT-VIVANT GRAND CRU, VOSNE-ROMANÉE

It was Maison Leroy's Romanée-Saint-Vivant that made me fall madly, irrevocably in love with this Grand Cru vineyard. The 9-hectare vineyard is divided among 11 top growers, each making excellent wine at the highest level. Thus Romanée-Saint-Vivant is consistently one of the most reliable, high-quality Grands Crus from Burgundy. Currently Domaine Leroy owns nearly a hectare of Romanée-Saint-Vivant and makes the best example from this vineyard. Maison Leroy's Romanée-Saint-Vivant, from purchased fruit, is not available in the younger vintages. The rare bottles that come to the market are found mostly from the 1950s and 1960s, and occasionally from the 1940s and 1930s. For me, these mature Romanée-Saint-Vivant bottles, toward the end of their life, offer so much **wisdom**, grace, and depth; they are magical. I love the 1962 and the 1955—both have evolved and aged with style and **poise**. I was impressed by even older vintages, such as the 1947 and the 1937, both of which are delicate and **awe-inspiring**. Everything that I would want in a Romanée-Saint-Vivant—lacy detail, delicacy, finesse, and more can be found in Maison Leroy's wine.

| IN THREE WORDS | ***Delicate, magnificent, graceful.*** |

MAISON LOUIS JADOT

address	62 Route de Savigny, Beaune, Burgundy, France www.louisjadot.com Tel: + 33 3 80 26 31 98
contact	Pierre-Henry Gagey
farming philosophy	Lutte raisonnée, no herbicides or commercial fertilizers; exploring biodynamic viticulture.
in the cellar	Reds destemmed, may include small percentage whole bunch in top wines, depending on vintage; long maceration; matured up to 18 months with 15-25% new oak for Premiers Crus, up to 100% new for Grands Crus; whites undergo slow, long fermentation, up to 3-4 weeks; maturation depends on vintage, appellation, and quality of the wines.
total vineyard area	260 hectares (includes owned and managed vineyards throughout Burgundy, including Beaujolais and Mâcon; 146 hectares in Côte d'Or)
total annual production	10 million bottles

key vineyard holdings

Red (Côte de Nuits)

Chambertin–Clos de Bèze Grand Cru	0.42 ha
Chapelle-Chambertin Grand Cru	0.39 ha
Clos Saint-Denis Grand Cru (Gagey)	0.17 ha
Le Musigny Grand Cru	0.17 ha
Bonnes-Mares Grand Cru	0.27 ha
Clos de Vougeot Grand Cru	2.15 ha
Échezeaux Grand Cru	0.35 ha
Échezeaux Grand Cru (Gagey)	0.17 ha
Gevrey-Chambertin Premier Cru Les Cazetiers	0.12 ha
Gevrey-Chambertin Premier Cru Combe aux Moines	0.17 ha
Gevrey-Chambertin Premier Cru Clos Saint-Jacques	1.00 ha
Gevrey-Chambertin Premier Cru Estournelles Saint-Jacques	0.38 ha
Gevrey-Chambertin Premier Cru Lavaux Saint-Jacques	0.22 ha
Gevrey-Chambertin Premier Cru Poissenots	0.19 ha
Chambolle-Musigny Premier Cru Les Amoureuses	0.12 ha
Chambolle-Musigny Premier Cru Baudes (Gagey)	0.27 ha
Chambolle-Musigny Premier Cru Fuées	0.41 ha
Chambolle-Musigny Premier Cru Les Feusselottes	1.92 ha

Red (Côte de Beaune)

Corton Pougets Grand Cru (Héritiers)	1.47 ha
Corton Grèves Grand Cru	0.44 ha
Pommard Premier Cru Rugiens	0.36 ha
Pommard Premier Cru Clos de la Commaraine	3.75 ha
Beaune Premier Cru Cent Vignes (Gagey)	0.42 ha
Beaune Premier Cru Les Chouacheux (Gagey)	0.67 ha
Beaune Premier Cru Les Chouacheux (Héritiers)	0.37 ha
Beaune Premier Cru Les Bressandes (Héritiers)	0.96 ha
Beaune Premier Cru Les Avaux	1.43 ha
Beaune Premier Cru Clos des Couchereaux (Héritiers)	2.04 ha
Beaune Premier Cru Les Theurons	0.38 ha
Beaune Premier Cru Les Theurons (Gagey)	1.69 ha
Beaune Premier Cru Les Theurons (Héritiers)	1.00 ha
Beaune Premier Cru Boucherottes (Héritiers)	2.52 ha
Beaune Premier Cru des Ursules (Héritiers)	2.75 ha

White

Chevalier-Montrachet Grand Cru Les Demoiselles (Héritiers)	0.52 ha
Corton-Charlemagne Grand Cru (Héritiers)	1.60 ha
Beaune Premier Cru Grèves Le Clos (Gagey)	0.84 ha
Beaune Premier Cru Bressandes (Gagey)	0.93 ha
Chassagne-Montrachet Premier Cru Abbaye de Morgeot	0.44 ha
Chassagne-Montrachet Premier Cru Morgeot Clos de la Chapelle (Magenta)	2.87 ha
Meursault Premier Cru Genevrières	0.29 ha
Meursault Premier Cru Le Porusot	0.14 ha
Puligny-Montrachet Premier Cru La Garenne	0.37 ha
Puligny-Montrachet Premier Cru Les Folatières	0.35 ha
Puligny-Montrachet Premier Cru Les Folatières (Héritiers)	0.24 ha
Puligny-Montrachet Premier Cru Les Referts	0.45 ha
Puligny-Montrachet Premier Cru Clos de la Garenne	1.56 ha
Puligny-Montrachet Premier Cru Champ Gain (Gagey)	0.40 ha
Puligny-Montrachet Premier Cru Combettes	0.14 ha

LE MUSIGNY GRAND CRU, CHAMBOLLE-MUSIGNY

Louis Jadot is synonymous with dependable, high-quality Burgundy wine at fair prices. This company has been a hybrid négociant-domaine since it was founded by Louis Henry Denis Jadot in 1859. Prior to establishing the négociant business, Jadot owned Clos des Ursules, a Beaune Premier Cru that was acquired in 1826. The company remained under the Jadot family management for many generations until, without an apparent heir, it was sold to the Kopf family, owners of Kobrand, Jadot's U.S. importer. There were no dramatic changes when the Kopf family took over; Pierre-Henry Gagey, the second-generation Gagey to lead the company, was appointed its president. Jadot's reputation has always been strong, in the U.S. market and in Asia. Its solid reputation does not mean it is sitting still. Constant refinements and improvements are being made, for decades under the exuberant and talented Jacques Lardière and now under Frédéric Barnier. The farming is sustainable, and biodynamics are being explored, while in the cellar, every vintage writes its own story, but a few things remain the same: natural yeast fermentation, destemming for reds, extended maceration period for about a month to extract maximum color and flavor, and a fairly high percentage of new oak use. Jadot is best known for its red wines, although its whites are excellent too. In their youth, the wines are very tightly knit; not following current fashion, its premium red wines are all built to age. Its huge range of Premier Cru reds from both Côte de Nuits and Côte de Beaune are consistently good. But the best value in its portfolio comes from the Château des Jacques range of top Beaujolais crus, such as Morgon and Moulin-à-Vent; these wines age beautifully and are best at 10 to 20 years old. Jadot produces seven out of the total 24 Grands Crus in Côte de Nuits, and many would warrant inclusion in this book. The white wines are excellent too: I am a big fan of its Corton-Charlemagne and of course the Chevalier-Montrachet Les Demoiselles and Bâtard-Montrachet. Among the reds, Chapelle-Chambertin, Chambertin–Clos de Bèze, and Bonnes-Mares are superb. My top choice is its Musigny, which has recently been consistently *magnificent* year after year. Jadot has a long-term lease for a great parcel, a narrow Grand Cru strip directly adjacent to the plot owned by Roumier. This wine is more muscular and solid than Musigny from Roumier or Mugnier, but its breeding and *nobility* is equally apparent. While older vintages from the 1980s and 1990s have variation, with highs like 1985 and 1993, they are far less consistent than the recent string of *glorious* vintages such as 2005, 2009, 2010, 2012, and 2015. Despite having over 100 wines in its portfolio, Jadot pays attention to every detail, and this is apparent from the Grands Crus to its Village wines.

IN THREE WORDS *Poised, exceptional, classic.*

PIERRE-YVES COLIN-MOREY

address	2 Chemin du Puits Merdreaux, 21190 Chassagne-Montrachet, Burgundy, France Tel: + 33 3 80 21 90 10
contact	Pierre-Yves Colin-Morey
farming philosophy	Lutte raisonnée, no herbicides since 2006; following organic principles.
in the cellar	Whole bunches pressed gently and slowly; indigenous yeast fermentation; no lees stirring; matured mainly in 350-liter barrels for 18 months with 30% new oak; Grands Crus may have 50% new oak, depending on vintage; topped with wax capsules.
total vineyard area	11 hectares
total annual production	90,000 bottles (including wine from purchased grapes)

key vineyard holdings

White

Bâtard-Montrachet Grand Cru	0.10 ha	Saint-Aubin Premier Cru Les Créots	0.50 ha
Chassagne-Montrachet Premier Cru		Saint-Aubin Premier Cru En Remilly	0.65 ha
Les Caillerets	0.20 ha	Saint-Aubin Premier Cru Les Perrières	0.55 ha
Chassagne-Montrachet Premier Cru		Chassagne-Montrachet L'Ancenière	0.40 ha
Abbaye de Morgeot	0.60 ha	Chassagne-Montrachet Houillères	0.25 ha
Chassagne-Montrachet Premier Cru		Chassagne-Montrachet Jornoblots	0.20 ha
Les Chenevottes	0.55 ha	Saint-Aubin Le Banc (Blanc)	0.20 ha
Puligny-Montrachet Premier Cru		Hautes Côtes de Beaune Blanc	2.00 ha
Garennes	0.20 ha	Bourgogne Blanc	0.45 ha
Saint-Aubin Premier Cru Les Champlots	0.65 ha		
Saint-Aubin Premier Cru La Chatenière	0.75 ha	*Red*	
Saint-Aubin Premier Cru Les Combes	0.35 ha	Santenay Premier Cru Gravières	1.10 ha
		Santenay Les Champs Claude	0.30 ha

SAINT-AUBIN PREMIER CRU EN REMILLY, SAINT-AUBIN

The launch of this new estate in 2001 is the coming together of two illustrious wine families with notable reputations for crafting great white Burgundy wines. Pierre-Yves is the eldest son of Marc Colin (based in Saint-Aubin), and made wonderful wines in his family domaine from 1995 to 2005. He married Caroline Morey, the daughter of Jean-Marc Morey, a great Chassagne-Montrachet producer. In 2001, the couple decided to start a négociant business, starting out with just six barrels of wine from purchased grapes. Given its connections and family reputations, the word quickly spread, and by 2005 it had around 35 barrels. By 2006, Pierre-Yves left his family's estate and dedicated himself to building his own estate, bringing with him nearly 6 hectares of vines, which has now expanded to 11 hectares, including rented vineyards. The amount of purchased grapes fluctuates by vintage, given the shortage that Burgundy faced from 2010 to 2016. However, in most years, two-thirds of the wines come from estate-grown vineyards and the remainder is purchased. Colin-Morey does not differentiate between domaine and purchased grapes; Pierre-Yves says that if the grapes are not good enough to be labeled under their estate, he simply won't buy them. The couple has uncompromising standards, and this is clear in all the wines it makes, from the simple Bourgogne to the Bâtard-Montrachet, Bienvenues-Bâtard-Montrachet, and Corton-Charlemagne. Its success meant expanding its winemaking facilities, and in 2015 a new cellar was created at the edge of Chassagne. Pierre-Yves is an intense, exacting individual, and his **devotion** and passion for his craft is palpable. I have always found tasting with him an exhilarating experience, not just because of the high quality of the wines but also because of his energy and focus. All Pierre-Yves Colin-Morey wines are made in tiny quantities, and although the three Grand Cru wines it produces from purchased grapes are stunning, my favorite is its Saint-Aubin. While great Saint Aubin producers such as Hubert Lamy and Marc Colin (Pierre-Yves' family domaine) have done much for this commune, it is Colin-Morey, starting in the early 2000s, which put it on the fine wine map, crafting a range of wines from this appellation that are as **age-worthy** as the best Premiers Crus from Chassagne or Puligny. Among his many Premier Cru Saint-Aubins, I love En Remilly. This parcel is only two-thirds of a hectare, with vines dating back to the 1970s. Recently, the Saint-Aubin En Remilly seems to have increased in **intensity** by another notch, and vintages like 2015 and 2016 are exquisite, complex, and long. I am looking forward to opening them in 10, 15, and 20 years' time to see how they evolve. This is a domaine to follow.

IN THREE WORDS   *Stirring, exquisite, precise.*

VINCENT DAUVISSAT

(FORMERLY RENÉ ET VINCENT DAUVISSAT)

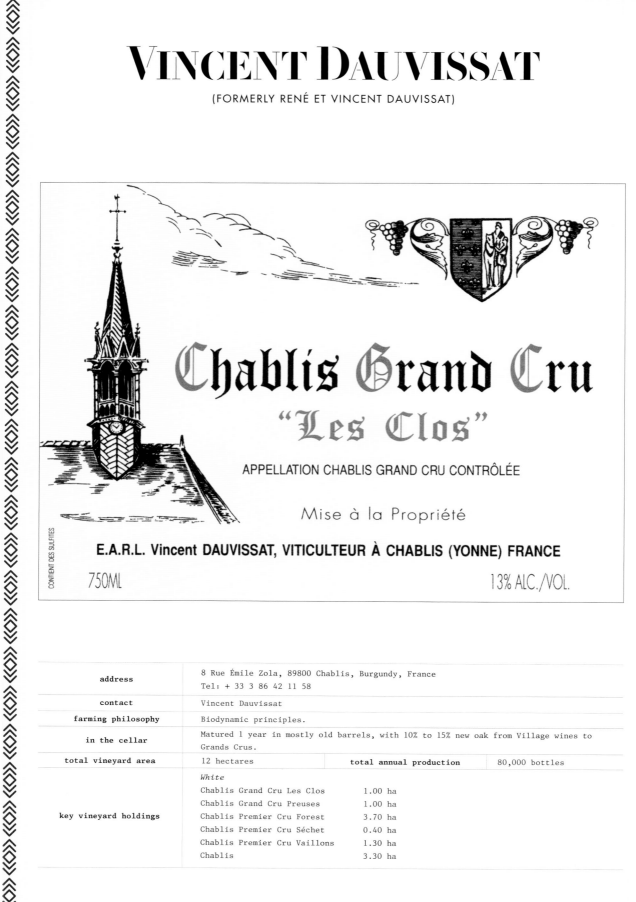

address	8 Rue Émile Zola, 89800 Chablis, Burgundy, France Tel: + 33 3 86 42 11 58		
contact	Vincent Dauvissat		
farming philosophy	Biodynamic principles.		
in the cellar	Matured 1 year in mostly old barrels, with 10% to 15% new oak from Village wines to Grands Crus.		
total vineyard area	12 hectares	**total annual production**	80,000 bottles
key vineyard holdings	*White* Chablis Grand Cru Les Clos 1.00 ha Chablis Grand Cru Preuses 1.00 ha Chablis Premier Cru Forest 3.70 ha Chablis Premier Cru Séchet 0.40 ha Chablis Premier Cru Vaillons 1.30 ha Chablis 3.30 ha		

CHABLIS GRAND CRU LES CLOS, CHABLIS

There are two wine names to know in Chablis—Dauvissat and Raveneau—and these two estates are closely intertwined. Dauvissat was founded in the 1920s by Robert Dauvissat, who began to bottle wines under the estate name in 1931. Robert's sons René and François established the quality and lifted the domaine's reputation worldwide. The mantle was then passed to René's son, Vincent, the third generation of the family to manage the domaine, in 1976. René Dauvissat's sister, Andrée Dauvissat, married François Raveneau, and the couple combined its inherited vineyards to form Domaine Raveneau in 1948. Serious collectors of Dauvissat note that since Vincent started making the wines, vintages from the 1980s onward are increasingly more complex, refined, and profound. I have not had enough Dauvissats from the 1960s and 1970s to comment on this, but I do know that the wines from the 1980s and 1990s are sublime. Those who enjoy a more powerful, intense Chablis experience often prefer Raveneau, whereas those who are looking for cerebral, minerally, **beguiling** Chablis with incredible crystalline purity need look no further than Dauvissat. All the Chablis at Dauvissat are aged in oak, usually old oak, including the traditional small 132-liter casks, for up to a year with a small percentage that are new. The quality and *intensity* come from the vineyard, where the 12 hectares of plots are meticulously farmed under biodynamic principles and yields are kept low. Its Les Clos in its youth is a thrilling experience: The aroma is like the salty air at the edge of a cliff by the ocean, with high waves crashing on the rocks; the palate is crushed stones and slate, with layers of white flowers and citrus; the finish is the *lingering* taste of the sea—salt, seaweed, and ocean rocks brushing past the palate. Great vintages like 2005, 2010, 2012, and 2014 are ones I am keeping in my cellar for my daughter.

IN THREE WORDS *Thrilling, intricate, crystalline.*

GLOSSARY

AOC (APPELLATION D'ORIGINE CONTRÔLÉE)
A French legal term that protects geographically designated wine regions; includes rules for grape-growing and winemaking, and specifies grape varieties allowed, farming methods, harvest timing, yield, and winemaking restrictions. All of Burgundy is under the AOC umbrella, and in principle the regulations help to ensure quality and consistency.

ARDEASEAL
A type of synthetic cork; Domaine Ponsot uses AS-Elite by ArdeaSeal.

ASSEMBLAGE
The blending of wine components to create the final composition.

BARRIQUE
A small barrel, usually 228 liters in Burgundy (225 liters in Bordeaux), made from French oak.

BÂTONNAGE
The stirring of the wine's dead yeast and sediment, also called the *lees*; adds depth and roundness to the wine.

BIODYNAMIC VITICULTURE
A farming system based on Rudolf Steiner's agricultural methods that espouses following the movements of the moon and planets (using a biodynamic calendar) and the use of herbal sprays and composting to enhance soil health and microbial activity. Increasingly popular in Burgundy and throughout high-quality wine regions around the world.

BOURGOGNE AOC WINE
The lowest classification level, under which half the wines from Burgundy fall, indicating that grapes may have been sourced from anywhere in Burgundy.

CÉPAGE
Indicates the grape variety(ies) used.

CHAPTALIZATION
The process of adding sugar to unfermented grape must in order to increase the alcohol content of wine, named for the French chemist Jean-Antoine-Claude Chaptal.

CHARDONNAY
Highly versatile and flavorful, the preeminent white grape of Burgundy, which allows vignerons to make a very wide range of styles.

CISTERCIANS
A strict Christian order that identified quality vineyards in Burgundy, discovered the best variety and soil matches, refined vineyard practices, and was fundamental in laying the foundations for Burgundy's classification system.

CLIMAT
A specific vineyard site that may or may not have AOC classification; used interchangeably with *lieu-dit*, which is more of a geographical rather than a winegrowing term.

CLONAL SELECTION
Vines are replaced using cuttings sourced from a single superior vine, or mother vine; often used to ensure better performance, quality, or disease-free vines.

CLOS
A vineyard enclosed with walls.

CLOSURE
The material used to seal the bottle; the most common being cork, but increasingly alternative cork-based products such as Diam, synthetic material, or screw caps.

COMMUNE
Used interchangeably with *village.*

COOPERAGE
A place or company that produces barrels used for aging wine.

CORK TAINT
See *TCA.*

CÔTE
French for "slope."

CRU
French for "growth"; usually refers to the level of wine, such as *Grand Cru* or "great growth," and *Premier Cru* or "first growth."

DÉBOURBAGE
Decanting; settling the wine to remove coarse lees and sediment.

DÉLESTAGE
The act of racking and bringing the wine back up to the top of the vat during fermentation to ensure good extraction for red wines. Also known as *devatting*.

DESTEMMING
The removal of stems prior to fermentation via destemmer machines. Also known as *égrappage*.

DEVATTING
See *Délestage.*

DIAM
A technological closure made from ground natural cork that has been cleaned to ensure it is TCA-free (see *TCA*). Used by a growing number of top domaines, especially for white wines, including Bouchard, Benoît Droin, William Fevre, Lafon, Leflaive, Louis Jadot, and Domaine de Montille.

DOMAINE
Another term for estate or winery in Burgundy; this is in contrast to *négociant* or *maison,* in which the grapes for the wine are usually purchased rather than directly farmed.

ÉGRAPPAGE
The act of removing grapes from the stems.

EN PRIMEUR
Unfinished wines offered to the market prior to release. For Burgundy, this is the earliest time that customers can purchase the wines and usually occurs in January, about 16 months after harvest.

FERMAGE
A tenant farming agreement in which a grower rents land from the owner and is responsible for all related expenses and owns the entire crop. This differs from *métayage,* in which the arrangement is share-cropping rather than payment.

FERMENTATION
The winemaking process that turns grape juice into wine; yeast converts grape sugars into alcohol and releases carbon dioxide.

FILTERING
The act of pushing the final wine through a screen or pad to remove unwanted particles. This practice is shunned by many quality red Burgundy winemakers, who believe that it strips flavors from the wine.

FINING
A technique to clarify wine using egg whites, bentonite (powdered clay), or other fining agents to settle particles and make wines limpid.

FINISH
A key factor in determining quality in wine; how long the taste or flavors linger in the mouth after being tasted. Great wines should have long, lingering finish.

GOÛT DE TERROIR
French for "taste of the soil," referring to the positive distinguishing aspects (often earthy, non-fruity flavors) of how a wine reflects the place from which it originates.

GRAND CRU
French for "great growth"; in Burgundy, the highest quality designation given to a vineyard.

HECTARE
Equivalent to 10,000 square meters, or 2.47 acres.

HECTOLITER
Equivalent to 100 liters, or 26.4 gallons. In Burgundy, yield is measured in hectoliters per hectare.

INAO (INSTITUT NATIONAL DE L'ORIGINE ET DE LA QUALITÉ)
A powerful French government body, part of the French Ministry of Agriculture, that regulates agricultural products such as wine, including defining AOC status, its regulations, and demarcation.

LEES
The dead yeast and other solids found during and after fermentation. Fine lees sediment can add depth and body to wine.

LENGTH
See *Finish.*

LIEU-DIT
A vineyard place-name that is often confused with *climat.* Used as a geographical term for a specific vineyard site.

MACERATION
The steeping of grape skins and solids with the juice pre- and post-fermentation to extract color, *tannins,* and desired aromatics.

MALOLACTIC FERMENTATION (MLF)
The process following alcoholic fermentation in which malic acid is converted into softer lactic acid; occurs naturally for red wines but is an option (often controlled) for white wines.

MASSAL SELECTION
A replanting practice in which new vines are taken from cuttings of the best vines in a vineyard, rather than using clones from a nursery.

MÉTAYAGE
A vineyard crop-sharing rental agreement in which the rent for farming is paid as an agreed percentage of the vineyard yield, often one-third or one-half. This differs from *fermage,* in which rent is paid in cash rather than a share of the crop.

MILLÉSIME
See *Vintage.*

MIS EN BOUTEILLE AU DOMAINE
French for "bottled at the domaine."

MONOPOLE
A defined AOC vineyard that is owned by one estate (e.g., Clos de Tart, La Tâche, and Romanée-Conti).

NÉGOCIANT
A wine merchant or shipper who sources grapes from farmers and bottles and markets it under its own brand.

NEW OAK
The use of new barrels for the first time, when it has the biggest impact on the wine, by allowing more oxygen ingress and imparting cedar, toast, and vanilla flavors. This impact varies by barrel preparation and toasting level prior to use.

OLD VINES (VIEILLES VIGNES)
There is no legal definition, but usually refers to wines that are 50 to 100 years of age.

ORGANIC WINE
Wines that follow organic principles (no synthetic chemicals, low intervention, and lower sulfur use), certified by a local governing organization, with requirements that differ by country.

OXIDATIVE WINEMAKING
Winemaking steps that intentionally expose the wine to oxygen, chosen to stabilize the wine.

PEAK
A subjective assessment about the optimal time to enjoy a wine; varies from a few years to a few decades for top Burgundy.

PERFUME
The aromatics or the smell of a wine.

PHENOLICS
Compounds found in red wine that originate mainly from the skins, which add to the wine's color, taste, and aroma; seeds, stems, and oak can also add phenolics to a wine.

PHYLLOXERA
Destructive tiny aphids that attacked vine roots and wreaked havoc in vineyards across Europe and the U.S. from the late 1800s until the 1980s.

PIÈCE
A 228-liter Burgundy barrel.

PIGÉAGE
Punch down; an extraction method for red wines that involves punching down the cap of grape skins and seeds to extract color, tannins, and flavors.

PINOT NOIR
Thin-skinned and extremely finicky, this preeminent red grape of Burgundy loves limestone soils.

PREMATURE OXIDATION
An issue with white Burgundy wines becoming prematurely oxidized, resulting in deep amber-brown color, flavors devoid of vibrancy and freshness, and prematurely advanced overall; identified as a serious concern starting with the 1996 vintage and continuing to the present day, although incidences are less common than when first identified in the early 2000s.

PREMIER CRU
French for "first growth"; in France this term usually indicates the best, but in Burgundy it falls below *Grand Cru.*

PUMP OVER
See *Remontage.*

PUNCH DOWN
See *Pigéage.*

RACKING
Separating the clear wine (may be in a vat or barrel) from any sediment, such as dead yeast cells, to clarify and aerate the wine.

REMONTAGE
Pump over; an extraction method for red wines that brings the grape juice from the bottom of the vat to the top, submerging the cap of grape skins and seeds to extract color, tannins, and flavors.

SKIN CONTACT
The practice of allowing the grape skins to have contact with the juice or fermenting must, to extract desired color, tannins, and flavors.

SORTING
A quality check procedure, from the vineyard harvest to the cellar, in which the best grape bunches and/or berries are sorted manually or by machine.

SOUTIRAGE
See *Racking.*

SUR LIE
Aging wine on the *lees* to increase depth, complexity, and harmony; very common in Burgundy for whites and reds.

TANNINS
Phenolic compounds found in grape skins and seeds (also in stems and oak) that add dryness, bitterness, or astringency to red wines; the winemaker's goal is to find the right amount of tannins that will contribute the most desirable balance of flavors and aging potential to the wine.

TARTRATES
Benign crystal deposits that form during fermentation or bottle aging that can be found in white wines.

TASTEVIN
A very shallow saucer the size of a small cup, traditionally made of silver, used by sommeliers and wine merchants centuries ago to taste wine in dim light.

TCA (TRICHLOROANISOL)
A chemical compound that causes a damp, musty, or dirty smell in wine and strips it of flavor; the source is usually from the cork, thus TCA-tainted wine is referred to as "corked" wine.

TERROIR
The sum of a complex combination of factors that contribute to a wine's uniqueness, including the soil, topography, climate, culture, and the people who farm the land.

VERTICAL TASTING
A tasting of multiple vintages of one wine.

VIEILLES VIGNES
See *Old vines.*

VIGNERON
A winegrower who farms the vineyard, makes the wine, and also matures and bottles the wine.

VILLAGE WINE
A Burgundy wine classification that is above the regional Bourgogne level but below Premier Cru and Grand Cru.

VINE SPACING
The distance between rows of vines; the best vineyards in Burgundy have higher density plantings, close vine spacing of well over 10,000 vines per hectare, or one vine per square meter.

VINIFICATION
The process of winemaking.

VINTAGE
The year the grapes are harvested.

WHOLE BUNCH/WHOLE CLUSTER
The use of whole grape bunches or clusters during fermentation for making red wine, instead of destemmed berries; popular among top estates.

YIELD
The quantity of fruit or wine from a given vineyard, measured by weight or by volume, with strict limits in Burgundy according to *appellation* laws.

VINTAGE GUIDE

A vintage guide can offer general guidance, a broad look at how wines fared across appellations and quality levels, from generic Bourgogne to Grand Cru–level wines. A vintage rating is the average of thousands of producers, so it does not always reflect how good a specific wine may be in that vintage. In most years, the best growers often exceed the vintage assessments, crafting glorious wines in even weaker vintages. But challenging vintages such as 1977, 1981, and more recently 1994, were difficult even for the best estates, so don't expect the same level of concentration or aging potential in these weaker vintages. In that sense, the vintage guide is useful, to help us understand the weather conditions that provided challenges and to point us in the right direction.

Burgundy has been both extremely lucky as well as unlucky over the past few decades: It was fortunate to not have any terrible vintages—even 2004 and 2013, which were both very challenging climatically, offer pretty, early-drinking wines. The region has unfortunately suffered an onslaught of climatic impediments during the past decade, mostly in the form of hail punctuated by frost or mildew. Supply has been short since 2010, and it is only with the more generous 2017 and 2018 vintages that yields are back to normal levels.

Following is a reference for the red and white wines of the Côte d'Or to provide buyers a sense of how the region fared.

5 STARS ***
An outstanding vintage that usually occurs only a few times a decade, with great wines across communes and classification levels.

4 STARS **
An excellent vintage for the majority of the producers.

3 STARS *
A very good vintage but not homogenous, with top growers making excellent wines.

**2 STARS **
Good to challenging vintage in which top producers likely exceeded the vintage assessment.

1 STAR *
Difficult vintage for which knowing the grower and the vineyard are key.

NO STARS
A vintage that requires very careful selection; majority are weak or thin.

REDS

2017 **
Juicy, fresh, balanced wines that may not have immense concentration but offer delicious approachability and balance.

2016 **
A challenging vintage for vignerons, due to frost, hail, and mildew, with low yields and uneven quality; however, top estates made concentrated, beautiful wines with firm acidity for long-term aging.

2015 ***
Glorious, fleshy vintage for reds, with modest yields from healthy, ripe grapes without excess.

2014 **
An excellent vintage, with vibrant flavors, good concentration, and firm acid backbone; leaner and higher in acidity versus 2015.

2013 *
A heterogeneous vintage due to uneven ripening and challenging weather conditions, but a dry September helped to produce a small crop of ripe fruit.

2012 **
While the weather was erratic and challenging, leading to low yields, the wines from the top estates are impressive, with succulent flavors with good intensity.

2011 *
A charming, light vintage with modest alcohol and good freshness; better for whites than reds, and most producers had to chaptalize (see Glossary).

2010 ***
A magnificent vintage, with firm acidity as well as excellent ripeness and flavor concentration; modest yields mean volumes are lower than in 2009.

2009 ***
A textbook great vintage, with a dry summer and no hail or challenging weather conditions, creating sumptuous, delicious reds that will enjoy a wide drinking window.

2008 **
A polarizing vintage: climatically challenging, with rot and hail creating havoc in the vineyard; despite the challenges, wines are fresh, vibrant, and pure with well-defined flavors.

**2007 **
Initially dismissed due to high rot and challenging weather, this light vintage was successful in producing delicious, balanced, mainly early-drinking wines.

2006 ***
An uneven vintage, with some wines performing well despite the poor summer weather, and others being astringent and light; best to go for top producers.

2005 *****
An excellent vintage that has lovely "crunchy" fruit, ripe, generous, supple tannins, and wonderful freshness and purity.

2004 *
Light, early-drinking vintage, with a green, unripe character detectable in many wines, but there are some exceptions. Choose carefully.

2003 ***
Uneven: Depending on how growers managed the heat and the timing of harvest, some wines are luscious and plush, while others are too chunky with dense, dry tannins.

2002 *****
A great, charming vintage with wonderful freshness. An ideal summer—dry and warm, not hot, with scattered light rains that were beneficial.

2001 ***
Another difficult vintage, following 2000, with a difficult summer, resulting in a wide variation in quality; top vineyards produced light, pretty wines.

2000 ***
A challenging vintage, with the constant threat of rot through the late summer and harvest; mainly early-drinking wines, but some producers outperformed the vintage.

1999 *****
Fantastic vintage that combines intensity and concentration with precision. Long aging potential.

1998 ***
Challenging vintage with variable results; some wines are concentrated and gorgeous while others are chunky and dull.

1997 ***
A pretty, light vintage with good balance—not homogenous, but top estates and wines are surprisingly delicious.

1996 *****
An excellent vintage combining precision and depth, the result of a cool August and warm September.

1995 ****
A very good vintage with a dry, hot summer that produced concentrated wines that have aged gracefully.

1994
Rain and rot plagued the vineyards during harvest time and late summer, resulting in uneven and modest quality; a small number are charming, but they should be consumed soon.

1993 *****
Rich, balanced wines that have good color and intensity. Top wines drinking well now, even in their mid-20s.

1992 *
Charming, forward wines that suffered from rain in late August and during harvest.

1991 ****
Frost and hail reduced yields but not quality. Intense wines that were austere in their youth but are now at their peak.

1990 *****
Ripe, lush, aromatic with great intensity and concentration. A wonderful vintage that is still drinking beautifully now.

1989 ****
Warm, dry summer produced concentrated grapes with ideal ripeness. Top wines are delicious now.

1988 ***
A warm September allowed the small crop to ripen well; though the summer was not ideal, top estates produced classic, age-worthy wines.

1987 *
Light-bodied, mostly early-drinking wines from a challenging summer that resulted in uneven ripeness.

1986 *
Rain and rot were a constant challenge, but the last month of good weather saved the vintage and some were able to make good, though not great, wine.

1985 *****
Homogenous vintage at every level, producing fine wines that are elegant and sweet; many are still going strong.

1984
Cold, wet vintage, with mostly unripe grapes; avoid.

1983 **
A challenging vintage, though some growers made surprisingly good wine; however, most are past their peak.

1982 *
A huge crop with ripe, fruity wines mostly for early drinking. Top growers made concentrated, ripe wines that are well past their peak.

1981 *
Rain during harvest diluted the grapes, producing weak wines for early drinking.

1980 ***
A vintage filled with surprises with some top vineyards still showing well; a warm September saved the vintage.

1979 *

An uneven crop, with some fruity wines as well as weak ones that are well past their prime.

1978 *****

Ideal weather in August and September meant ripe, intense, age-worthy wines. Top vineyards from the best estates are still going strong.

1977

Rainy summer that turned in September but not enough to save the vintage; avoid.

1976 ***

A dry, warm summer saw good concentration and ripeness producing balanced, fruity wines. Most wines are now past their prime.

1975

Rainy August and September, the third weak vintage in a row; avoid.

1974

Rainy and cool September meant dilute, less-than-ideal grapes; avoid.

1973

Heavy rains during the summer months with weak, mainly insipid wines; avoid.

1972 *

Unexciting vintage, with a long growing season and a cool summer but no heavy rains. Select very carefully.

1971 **

Cool growing season with fresh, light wines for early drinking.

1970 *

Large crop, mostly early-drinking wines. Select only top estates and vineyards to enjoy now.

WHITES

2017 ****

A charming vintage with fresh, light-bodied, pure white wines that are detailed and filled with sweet ripe fruit. Expressive even in its youth. Quantities returned to normal levels after seven small vintages.

2016 ****

Elegant, delightful wines with good structure and intensity. A vintage filled with balanced, attractive white wines that have good potential to age.

2015 ****

A fabulous vintage—two in a row—with the 2015 being the more generous, riper and rounder compared with the 2014. Great quality across the board.

2014 *****

Chiseled, sleek white wines, intense and taut from high acidity; top wines have great mineral concentration and aging potential.

2013 ***

Fresh, minerally, with a racy backbone. Another small crop due to hail, with a wide variation in style depending on harvest and fruit selection.

2012 ****

More fleshy and intense than the 2011, this is a small vintage with good intensity and purity of flavors.

2011 ***

A heterogenous vintage with pretty, svelte, light-bodied whites that are balanced and delicious but lack concentration; still better than the reds in this vintage.

2010 *****

Well-defined, precise wines with lifted, delicate aromatics. Higher acidity than 2009, with longer aging potential.

2009 ****

Fleshy, opulent, and ripe, with modest acid backbone, reflecting the warmer vintage conditions. Good concentration from healthy grapes.

2008 *****

High acidity gives the wines a racy frame and lovely tension. Top producers made excellent whites built for long-term aging.

2007 ****

Pure, elegant whites that lack concentration but compensate with balance and charm.

2006 ****

Delicious, elegant wines that were saved by the improved weather in September.

2005 *****

A gorgeous vintage for whites and reds. Concentrated, intense, well-defined flavors with firm, ripe tannins and good acidity.

2004 ****

Very high acid levels make these whites austere and bracing, but those who like lean, racy whites will enjoy this vintage.

2003 *

A challenging year due to the immense heat, even when harvested early. Acidity tends to be low and the flavors broad rather than defined. Select carefully.

2002 *****

A fantastic year with excellent growing conditions. Wonderful fruit concentration plus good acidity levels.

2001 ***

A wet, quite cool year with thin, light-bodied whites, except for a handful that made lovely, delicate, finely etched wines.

2000 ★★★★
Another large crop, following the generous 1999, with some excellent whites with good concentration and freshness; others were simple, upfront, and fruity.

1999 ★★★
A large vintage, with pleasant whites with good fruit; acidity is modest due to the warm weather in late summer.

1998 ★
An uneven vintage with rain and mildew in September, but some estates successfully made good wines.

1997 ★★★★
Pretty, balanced, light-bodied wines for fairly early consumption; they are harmonious, with the backbone to age.

1996 ★★★★★
Two phenomenal vintages in a row with wonderful ripeness, depth, and purity of flavors as well as good concentration.

1995 ★★★★★
An exceptional vintage offering elegant, focused, intense whites with tension and finesse. Small crop overall.

1994 ★
Better than reds in this vintage, but grapes suffered from rain during harvest, so there is only modest concentration.

1993 ★★
Taut and elegant with light, pretty wines that were early-maturing. Rain during harvest diluted the grapes.

1992 ★★★★
A wonderful vintage for whites with lovely fruit, precision, and detailed flavors, especially impressive at the top vineyards and estates.

1991 ★
A mixed vintage, with most whites being light and charming but lacking in concentration.

1990 ★★★★
Another gorgeous vintage but with less acidity than 1989. Generous, ample wines with good depth and intensity.

1989 ★★★★★
A phenomenal vintage with opulent, expansive wines that benefited from a warm, dry summer.

1988 ★★
A light-bodied, lively vintage without much concentration.

1987 ★
Simple, light, balanced white wines, now past their peak.

1986 ★★★★
Gorgeous wines that are less homogenous than 1985, but delightfully fresh, vibrant, with good intensity.

1985 ★★★★
Wonderfully balanced, filled with ripe flavors that are generous and still quite concentrated.

1984
Simple, acidic wines destined for early consumption; avoid.

1983 ★★★
High variation in quality, with many that suffered from dilution or rot; some managed to overcome the challenges and make balanced wines.

1982 ★★★
A large crop with fruit that were ripe, round and delicious to enjoy young. Most are well past their peak now.

1981
Rainy, challenging vintage; avoid.

1980
Large, dilute crop; wines are past their peak now.

1979 ★★★★★
Concentrated whites, with a handful that are still hanging on. For most whites, this is a better vintage than 1978, which was better for reds.

1978 ★★★★★
Great harvest weather conditions contributed to ripe, generous whites that had excellent concentration.

1977
A rainy vintage that produced wines for early consumption.

1976 ★★★
A hot year that was a relief after a string of lackluster vintages. Big, generous whites that are mostly well past their peak.

1975
Poor vintage; avoid.

1974
Difficult vintage, with the wines well past their peak.

1973 ★
A large crop that produced respectable, light-bodied white wines with a few pleasant surprises.

1972
Lean, thin whites that are well past their peak.

1971 ★★★★
An excellent vintage for whites, with good concentration and balance. The best whites are still alive though they are sadly past their peak.

1970
A poor vintage for whites; avoid.

RECOMMENDED MERCHANTS

LISTED IN ALPHABETICAL ORDER BY COUNTRY

CHINA

RUBY RED FINE WINE
Room 101, Block A, Building 3, Shanghai Fashion Hub,
1718 Tianshan Road, Changning District, Shanghai
https://www.rubyred.com.cn
+86 21 6234 3031
info@rubyred.com.cn

INSIDE THE VINES GROUP
15/L, Huamin Empire Plaza, 728 Yan'an Road,
Changning District, Shanghai
+86 21 5238 5488
sales@insidethevines.com

FRANCE

CAVES DES HOSPICES
15 rue Monge, 21200 Beaune
+33 (0)380 22 69 44
http://www.cavedeshospices.com

CAVEAU DE CHASSAGNE
7 rue Charles Paquelin, 21190 Chassagne Montrachet
+33 (0)380 21 38 13
http://www.caveaudechassagne.com
info@caveaudechassagne.com

CAVEAU DE LA TOUR
Z.A. Les Champs Lins, 3 impasse des Lamponnes,
21190 Meursault
+33 (0)380 21 66 66
http://www.cdlt.fr/
contact@cdlt.fr

CAVEAU DE PULIGNY-MONTRACHET
1 rue de Poiseul, Puligny-Montrachet
+33 (0)380 21 96 78
http://www.caveau-puligny.com
contact@caveaudepuligny.fr

DES METS DES VINS
20 rue d'Aligre, 75012 Paris
+33 (0)144 68 22 94
http://www.desmetsdesvins.com
dmetsdvins@gmail.com

GRANDS BOURGOGNES
Z.A. Le Saule, 21220 Brochon
+33 (0)380 79 29 90
https://www.grandsbourgognes.com
info@grandsbourgognes.com

LA GRANDE EPICERIE DU BON MARCHÉ
24 rue de Sèvres, 75007 Paris
+ 33 (0)144 39 80 00
https://www.lagrandeepicerie.com
relationsclientelegep@la-grande-epicerie.fr

LAVINIA
3 blvd de la Madeleine, 75001 Paris
+33 (0)142 97 20 20
https://www.lavinia.fr
laviniafrance@lavinia.com

LEGRAND FILLES ET FILS
1 rue de la Banque, 75002 Paris
+33 (0)142 60 07 12
https://m.caves-legrand.com
info@caves-legrand.com

S CAVES AUGE
116 blvd Haussmann, 75008 Paris
+33 (0)145 22 16 97
http://cavesauge.com
cavesauge@cavesauge.com

LES CAVES DE TAILLEVENT
13-15 rue Lamennais, 75008 Paris
+33 (0)144 95 15 00
https://taillevent.com
contact@taillevent.com

MON MILLÉSIME
54 rue du faubourg Madeleine, 21200 Beaune
+33 (0)380 22 92 71
http://www.monmillesime.com
info@monmillesime.fr

PLACE DES GRANDS CRUS
20 place Carnot, 21200 Beaune
+33 (0)380 22 62 89
http://www.placedesgrandscrus.com
contact@placedesgrandscrus.com

VINOBOAM
4 rue d'Alsace, 21200 Beaune
+33 (0)380 21 43 58
http://www.vinoboam.com
contact@vinoboam.com

HONG KONG SAR

ALTAYA
Lyndhurst Tower, 20th Floor, 1 Lyndhurst Terrace,
Central, Hong Kong
+852 2523 1945
http://www.altayawines.com
info@altayawines.com

ASC FINE WINES
Two Harbourfront, 11th Floor, Units 1101-02 & 1112-13,
22 Tak Fung Street, Hunghom, Kowloon, Hong Kong
+852 3923 6700
http://www.asc-wines.com
ascpohk@asc-wines.com

BERRY BROS. & RUDD
Pacific House, 2nd Floor, 20-20B Queen's Road, Central,
Hong Kong
+852 2511 2811
https://www.bbr.com/hk-home
hkenquiries@bbr.com

BURGUNDY WINE COMPANY
Nam Wo Hong Building, 3rd Floor, 148 Wing Lok
Street, Sheung Wan, Hong Kong
+852 9542 6686
https://www.burgundywinecompany.com
office@burgundywinecompany.com.hk

CONNOISSEUR
Yau Tong Industrial City, Block A One, Unit A21-25,
5th Floor, 17 Ko Fai Road, Yau Tong, Kowloon,
Hong Kong
+852 2772 3670
https://www.connoisseur-wines.com.hk
orders@connoisseur-wines.com.hk

CORNEY & BARROW
Unit D, 6th Floor, 9 Queen's Road, Central, Hong Kong
+852 3694 3333
http://corneyandbarrow.com.hk
export@corneyandbarrow.com

EAST MEETS WEST FINE WINES
Kam Sang Building, 18th Floor, 257 Des Voeux Road,
Central, Sheung Wan, Hong Kong
+852 3955 1583
https://www.emw-wines.com
info@emw-wines.com

E VINTAGE (FAR EAST)
Hong Man Industrial Centre, Room 1208, 2 Hong Man
Street, Chai Wan, Hong Kong
+852 2896 6108
http://finevintage.com.hk
info@finevintage.com.hk

FINE WINE EXPERIENCE
Shop A (entrance on Chiu Kwong Street),
165-166 Connaught Road West, Sai Ying Pun,
Hong Kong
+852 2803 0753
http://www.finewineexperience.com
sales@finewineexperience.com

GINSBERG + CHAN
Loke Yew Building, 6th Floor, 50-52 Queen's Road,
Central, Hong Kong
+852 2504-2221
https://ginsbergchan.com
sales@ginsbergchan.com

GLOBAL WINE CELLAR
Wong's Factory Building, 4th Floor, 368-370 Sha Tsui
Road, Tsuen Wan, Hong Kong
+852 2543 6339
http://www.gwcellar.com
sales@gwcellar.com

GOEDHUIS & CO.
On Hing Building, 9A, 1 On Hing Terrace, Central,
Hong Kong
+852 2801 5999
https://www.goedhuis.com/hong-kong
hksales@goedhuis.com

JUSTERINI & BROOKS
The Centrium, 15th Floor, No. 5B-6A, 60 Wyndham
Street, Central, Hong Kong
+852 3628 3627
https://www.justerinis.com
justhongkong@justerinis.com

KERRY FINE WINES
Kerry Centre, 20th Floor, 683 King's Road, Quarry Bay,
Hong Kong
+852 2169 7700
https://www.kerrywines.com
info@kerrywines.com

LINKS CONCEPT
The Sun's Group Centre, 18th Floor, 200 Gloucester Road, Wan Chai, Hong Kong
+852 2802 2818
http://www.linksconcept.com.hk
wine@linksconcept.com

L'IMPERATRICE
Hollywood Centre, 8th Floor, 233 Hollywood Road, Sheung Wan, Hong Kong
http://www.imperatricewine.com
+852 2850 5544

OMTIS FINE WINES
Admiralty Centre Tower 1, 28th Floor, 18 Harcourt Road, Admiralty, Hong Kong
+852 3748 3748
https://www.omtisfinewines.com
sales@omtis.com

PEARL OF BURGUNDY
Central Building, Level 10, 1-3 Pedder Street, Central, Hong Kong
+852 3975 2798
https://www.pearlofburgundy.com
info@pearlofburgundy.com

PONTI
Ground Floor, 18A Stanley Street, Central, Hong Kong
+852 2739 7678
https://pontiwinecellars.com.hk
central@pontiwinecellars.com

SOTHEBY'S WINE
One Pacific Place, 5th Floor, 88 Queensway, Hong Kong
+852 2886 7888
https://www.sothebyswine.com/hk
howard.lee@sothebys.com

WATSON'S WINE
Watson House, 1-5 Wo Liu Hang Road, Fo Tan, Shatin, New Territories, Hong Kong
+852 2606 8828
https://www.watsonswine.com
info@watsonswine.com

JAPAN

DAIMARU
1 Chome-9-1 Marunouchi, Chiyoda, Tokyo 100-6701
+81 3 3212 8011
https://www.daimaru.co.jp

ENOTECA
5-15-27 Minami-azabu, Minato-ku, Tokyo 106-0047
+81 1 2081 3634
https://www.enoteca.co.jp
support@enoteca.co.jp

HIRAOKA
Rakuten Crimson House, 1-14-1 Tamagawa, Setagaya-ku, Tokyo 158-0094
+81 8 4862 4431
https://item.rakuten.co.jp/hiraoka
hiraokahana@mx41.tiki.ne.jp

ISETAN
3-14-1, Shinjuku, Shinjuku-ku, Tokyo 160-0022
+81 3 3352 1111
https://isetan.mistore.jp
iclub@isetanmitsukoshi.co.jp

KATSUDA
8507-2 Kuriharacho, Onomichi, Hiroshima 722-0022
+81 8 4825 3838
http://www.katsuda.co.jp
support@katsuda.co.jp

TAKASHIMAYA
5 Chome-24-2 Sendagaya, Shibuya, Tokyo 151-0051
+81 3 5361 1111
https://www.takashimaya-global.com
tokyo@ad.takashimaya.co.jp

TOKYU
2 Chome-24-1 Dogenzaka, Shibuya-ku, Tokyo 150-0043
+81 3 3477 3582
https://www.tokyu-dept.co.jp
home@tokyu-dept.co.jp

UMEMURA
2 Chome-6 Zaimokucho, Okazaki-shi, Aichi-ken 444-0057
+81 5 6422 0263
https://www.rakuten.ne.jp/gold/umemura
umemura@eurus.dti.ne.jp

VIN-SUR-VIN
1 Chome-7-6 Toranomon, Minato, Tokyo 105-0001
+81 3 3580 6578
http://www.vsv.co.jp
info@vsv.co.jp

SINGAPORE

ARTISAN CELLARS
390 Orchard Road, B1-01 Palais Renaissance,
Singapore 238871
+65 6838 0373
www.artisan-cellars.com
sales@artisan-cellars.com

DOMAINE WINES
24 Sin Ming Lane, 04-97 Midview City,
Singapore 573970
+65 6589 8745
http://domainewines.sg
cm@domainewines.sg

GRAND VIN
18 Boon Lay Way, 08-139 Trade Hub 21,
Singapore 609966
+65 6465 3081
http://grandvin.com.sg
info@grandvin.com.sg

VINTAGE
49 Jalan Pemimpin, 01-13 Loading Bay, APS Industrial
Building, Singapore 577203
+65 8511 2972
https://www.thevintageclub.sg
order@thevintageclub.sg

VINUM
Level 1, Unit 1, Pacific Tech Centre, 1 Jalan Kilang Timor,
Singapore 159303
+65 6735 3700
http://vinum.com.sg
sales@vinum.com.sg

WINE CLIQUE
168 Jalan Bukit Merah, 12-01 Surbana One, Singapore
150168
https://www.wine-clique.com
info@wine-clique.com

WINE CULTURE
897 Bukit Timah Road, Singapore 589617
+65 6463 3888
https://wineculture.com.sg
sales@wineculture.com.sg

SOUTH KOREA

CRYSTAL WINE COLLECTION CO. LTD.
18th Floor, Daekyo Tower, Boramea-ro 3-gil 23,
Gwanak-gu, Seoul
+82 2 6912 4859
http://www.crystalwinegroup.com/sub/index.php
info@crystalwinegroup.com

ENOTECA
3rd Floor, Samkyung B/D, Nonhyeon-dong, 34 Eonju-ro
150-gil, Gangnam-gu, Seoul
+82 2 3442 1150
http://enoteca.co.kr
importkorea@enoteca.co.kr

HANDOK WINE
3503 Trade Tower, 159-1 Samsung-dong, Gangnam-gu,
Seoul
+82 2 5516 874
http://handokwine.com
handok@handokwine.com

MARILYN WINE 365
B1, 138 Seochojungang-ro, Seocho-gu, Seoul
+82 2 3478 0365
https://www.instagram.com/marilynwine365
wine0365@naver.com

SHINDONG WINE
Shindong Building, 726-164 Hannam-dong,
Yongsan-gu, Seoul
+82 2 794 4531
http://www.shindongwine.co.kr/
wine@shindongwine.com

SSG WINE
442 Dosan-daero, Cheongdam-dong, Gangnam-gu, Seoul
+82 2 1588 1234
http://store.emart.com/branch/list.do?brtg=food

VITIS
100-161 Unam Building, 3rd Floor, 4-2 Bongrae-dong
1-ga, Jung-gu, Seoul
+82 2 752 4105
https://blog.naver.com/vitis_pn
wshan@dhlflour.co.kr

WINE & MORE
84 Dokseodang-ro, Hannam-dong, Yongsan-gu, Seoul
+82 2 2794 5329
http://www.facebook.com/wineandmoressg

TAIWAN

ATHERTON
22 Section 3, Zhong Shan North Road, Taipei
+886 2 2592 5252 -2280
http://www.wine.com.tw
prowine@wine.com.tw

DOMAINE
383-B1 Section 4, Ren'ai Road, Da'an District, Taipei
+886 2 2776 0066
https:/domaine.com.tw
service@domaine.com.tw

ESLITE
135/137-B1 Section 2, Jianguo North Road, Zhongshan District, Taipei
+886 2 2503 7687
http://www.eslitewine.com

UNITED KINGDOM

ARMIT WINES
5 Royalty Studios, 105 Lancaster Road,
London W11 1QF
+44 (0)20 7908 0655
http://www.armitwines.co.uk
info@armit.co.uk

AVERYS OF BRISTOL (ONLINE)
4 High Street, Nailsea, Bristol BS48 1BT
+44 (0)3330 148
http://www.averys.com
208sales@averys.com

BERRY BROS. & RUDD
63 Pall Mall, London SW1Y 5HZ
+44 (0)20 7022 8973
http://www.bbr.com
orders@bbr.com

CHARLES TAYLOR WINES
11 Catherine Place, Westminster, London SW1E 6DX
+44 (0)20 7821 1626
http://charlestaylorwines.com
office@charlestaylorwines.com

DAVY'S
161-165 Greenwich High Road, Greenwich,
London SE10 8JA
+44 (0)20 8858 9147
https://www.davy.co.uk
info@davy.co.uk

FIELDS, MORRIS & VERDIN
24-34 Ingate Place, Battersea, London SW8 3NS
+44 (0)20 7819 0360
http://www.fmv.co.uk
order@fmv.co.uk

FLINT
16 Stannary Street, London SE11 4AA
+44 (0)20 7582 2500
http://www.flintwines.com
info@flintwines.com

FORTNUM & MASON
181 Piccadilly, London W1A 1ER
+44 (0)20 7734 8040
https://www.fortnumandmason.com
customer.services@fortnumandmason.co.uk

GOEDHUIS & CO.
5 & 6 Elm Court, 156-170 Bermondsey Street, London SE1 3TQ
+44 (0)20 7793 7900
http://www.goedhuis.com
wine@goedhuis.com

HANDFORD
105 Old Brompton Road, London SW7 3LE
+44 (0) 20 7589 6113
http://www.handford.net
wine@handford.net

HARRODS
87-135 Brompton Road, London SW1X 7XL
+44 (0)20 7730 1234
https://www.harrods.com
help@harrods.com

HAYNES, HANSON & CLARK
7 Elystan Street, London SW3 3NT
+44 (0)20 7584 7927
http://www.hhandc.co.uk
london@hhandc.co.uk

HEDONISM
3-7 Davies Street, London W1K 3LD
+44 (0)20 7290 7870
http://www.hedonism.co.uk
drink@hedonism.co.uk

HOWARD RIPLEY
18 Madrid Road, London SW13 9PD
+44 (0)20 8748 2608
http://www.howardripley.com
info@howardripley.com

H2VIN
Southbank House, Black Prince Road, London SE1 7SJ
+44 (0)20 3478 7376
https://www.h2vin.co.uk
info@h2vin.co.uk

JEROBOAMS
6 Pont Street, London SW1X 9EL
+44 (0)20 7288 8888
http://www.jeroboams.co.uk
sales@jeroboams.co.uk

JUSTERINI & BROOKS
61 St. James's Street, London SW1A 1LZ
+44 (0)20 7484 6400
http://www.justerinis.com
justorders@justerinis.com

LAITHWAITE'S
Customer Services, One Waterside Drive, Arlington
Business Park, Theale, Berkshire RG7 4SW
+44 (0)33 3014 8168
http://www.laithwaites.co.uk
customerservice@laithwaites.co.uk

LAY & WHEELER
Holton Park, Holton St. Mary, Suffolk CO7 6NN
+44 (0)14 7331 3300
http://www.laywheeler.com
sales@laywheeler.com

LEA & SANDEMAN
51 High Street, London SW13 9LN
+44 (0)20 8878 8643
http://www.leaandsandeman.co.uk
barnes@leaandsandeman.co.uk

LIBERTY
6 Timbermill Way, London SW4 6LY
+44(0)20 7720 5350
http://libertywines.co.uk
order@libertywines.co.uk

MONTRACHET
11 Catherine Place, London SW1E 6DX
+44 (0)20 7821 1337
http://www.montrachetwine.com
office@montrachetwine.com

THE WINE SOCIETY
Gunnels Wood Road, Stevenage, Hertfordshire, SG1 2BT
+44 (0)14 3874 1177
https://www.thewinesociety.com
memberservices@thewinesociety.com

THORMAN HUNT
4 Pratt Walk, London SE11 6AR
+44 (0)20 7735 6511
https://thormanhunt.co.uk
info@thormanhunt.co.uk

UNITED STATES

ARLEQUIN WINE MERCHANTS
384A Hayes Street, San Francisco, CA 94102
+1 415 863 1104
https://www.arlequinwinemerchant.com
info@arlequinwine.com

ASTOR WINES
De Vinne Press Building, 399 Lafayette Street,
New York, NY 10003
+1 212 674 7500
https://www.astorwines.com
cs@astorwines.com

ELDEN SELECTIONS (ONLINE ONLY)
+1 855 315 1761
https://www.burgundywinecellars.com
info@eldeneselections.com

BURGUNDY WINE COMPANY
143 West 26th Street, New York, NY 10001
+1 212 691 9092
https://www.burgundywinecompany.com
info@burgundywinecompany.com

CHAMBERS STREET WINES
148 Chambers Street, New York, NY 10007
+1 212 227 1434
https://chambersstwines.com
office@chambersstwines.com

CRUSH WINE AND SPIRITS
153 East 57th Street, New York, NY 10022
+1 212 980 9463
https://www.crushwineco.com
offers@crushwineco.com

FLATIRON WINES AND SPIRITS
929 Broadway, New York, NY 10010
+1 212 477 1315
https://flatiron-wines.com
info@ flatiron-wines.com

JJ BUCKLEY
7305 Edgewater Drive, Suite D, Oakland, CA 94621
+1 510 632 5300
https://www.jjbuckley.com
info@jjbuckley.com

KERMIT LYNCH
1605 San Pablo Avenue, Berkeley, CA 94702
+1 510 524 1524
https://www.kermitlynch.com
info@ kermitlynch.com

K&L WINE MERCHANTS
3005 El Camino Real; Redwood City, CA 94061
+1 650 364 8544
https://www.klwines.com
customerservice@klwines.com

MORRELL AND COMPANY
1 Rockefeller Plaza, New York, NY 10020
+1 212 688 9370
https://morrellwine.com
info@morrellwine.com

NORTH BERKELEY WINES
1601 Martin Luther King Jr. Way, Berkeley, CA 94709
+1 510 848 8910
http://www.northberkeleyimports.com
retail@northberkeleyimports.com

SOMMPICKS
548 Market Street, #89930, San Francisco, CA 94558
+1 415 294 0622
https://www.sommpicks.com
info@sommpicks.com

THE SAN FRANCISCO WINE TRADING COMPANY
250 Taraval Street (at Funston), San Francisco, CA 94116
+1 415 731 6222
https://www.sfwtc.com
mail@sfwtc.com

TRIBECA WINE MERCHANTS
40 Hudson Street, New York, NY 10013
+1 212 393 1400
https://www.tribecawine.com
info@tribecawine.com

VINFOLIO
644 Hanna Drive, Suite E, American Canyon, CA 94503
+1 800 969 1961
https://www.vinfolio.com
service@vinfolio.com

WALLY'S
447 North Canon Drive, Beverly Hills, CA 90210
+1 310 475 0606
https://www.wallywine.com
customerservice@wallywine.com

WOODLAND HILLS
22622 Ventura Blvd., Woodland Hills, CA 91364
+1 818 222 1111
https://www.whwc.com
wine@whwc.com

ZACHYS
16 East Parkway, Scarsdale, NY 10583
+1 866 649 5181
https://www.zachys.com
cs@zachys.com

ABOUT THE AUTHOR

Jeannie Cho Lee is the first Asian Master of Wine (MW), an award-winning author, wine critic, judge, and educator. Currently a professor at Hong Kong Polytechnic University, where she helped launch the Master of Science program in International Wine Management, she is also a consultant for Singapore Airlines since 2009. For three years, Lee co-hosted a popular weekly wine TV program, *In Vino Veritas,* in Hong Kong for TVB Pearl, the leading English-language TV broadcaster. Jeannie is the former publisher of *Le Pan,* a wine lifestyle publication she launched in 2015, and she is currently a monthly wine columnist for *Robb Report* China. Her two books, *Mastering Wine* and *Asian Palate,* have won numerous awards, including the Gourmand Award for Best Food and Wine Pairing Book in the World and the International Association of Culinary Professionals (IACP) award. Lee is co-chair of the Decanter Asia Wine Awards in Hong Kong and the Burgundy chair for the Decanter World Wine Awards in London. She also holds a Certificat de Cuisine from Le Cordon Bleu institute, and she is a Certified Wine Educator with the UK's Wine & Spirits Education Trust and the U.S. Society of Wine Educators. She holds a Bachelor of Arts degree from Smith College as well as a Master's degree from Harvard University.

BIBLIOGRAPHY

Coates, C. (2011). *The Wines of Burgundy.* Berkeley, USA: University of California Press.
Curtis, C. (2015). *The Original Grands Crus of Burgundy.* New York, USA: WineAlpha.
Hanson, A. (1995). *Burgundy.* London, UK: Octopus Publishing Group Ltd.
Kramer, M. (1990). *Making Sense of Burgundy.* New York, USA: William Morrow & Company.
Landrieu-Lussigny, M.-H. & Pitiot, S. (2016). *The Climats and Lieux-Dits of the Great Vineyards of Burgundy.* Beaune, France: Éditions du Meurger.
Meadows, A. (2010). *The Pearl of the Côte: The Great Wines of Vosne-Romanée.* California, USA: Burghound Books.
Morris, J. (2010). *Inside Burgundy: The Vineyards, the Wine & the People.* London, UK: Berry Bros & Rudd Press.
Nanson, B. (2012). *The Finest Wines of Burgundy.* London, UK: Aurum Press Ltd.
Norman, R. (2011). *Grand Cru: The Great Wines of Burgundy Through the Perspective of Its Finest Vineyards.* New York, USA: Sterling Publishing Co., Inc.
Norman, R. & Taylor, C. (2010). *The Great Domaines of Burgundy: A Guide to the Finest Wine Producers of the Côte d'Or.* London, UK: Octopus Publishing Group Ltd.
Philippe, P. (2013). *Nine Centuries in the Heart of Burgundy: The Cellier aux Moines and Its Vineyards.* New York, USA: Assouline Publishing.
Pitiot, S. & Servant, J.-C. (2012). *The Wines of Burgundy.* Beaune, France: Collection Pierre Poupon.

ACKNOWLEDGMENTS

Writing a book is a long journey, and I have numerous people to thank for their advice, inspiration, feedback, support, and love.

In Burgundy, I would like to thank all the *vignerons* who make the wonderful wines that we are privileged to enjoy and are mentioned in this book—this book is for and about them. A special thanks to the growers, many of whom have become friends, who have patiently spent numerous hours educating me about the region: Pierre-Henri Gagey, Véronique Drouhin, Étienne de Montille, Jacques Devauges, Cyprien Arlaud, Jean-Claude Boisset, Cécile Tremblay, François Millet, Aubert and Bertrand de Villaine, Dominique Lafon, Jean-Marie Fourrier, Jeremy Seysses, Bernard Hervet, Isabelle Raveneau, Jean-Marc Roulot, Romain Taupenot, and Anne Parent. I am grateful for the support and assistance provided to me by Cécile Mathiaud and her team at BIVB; also to Stevie Bobes who has always been helpful; to Adrienne Saulnier Blache for sharing her enthusiasm and thoughts on lesser-known, up-and-coming growers; and to Arnaud Orsel for keeping me up to date with the latest happenings in the region.

I especially want to thank Sylvain Pitiot, whose numerous books on Burgundy and his dedication to sharing the details and intricacies of this fascinating region continues to inspire me. A huge thank-you to Jasper Morris MW, whose tome *Inside Burgundy* is every Burgundy lover's reference book (and door-stopper); thank you also for your guidance, encouragement, and friendship! I also want to thank Becky Wasserman for the time she spent with me—she is a wealth of knowledge and insight on the region and the people. The first book I read on Burgundy was by Serena Sutcliffe, *Guide to the Wines of Burgundy*, and I want to thank her for writing the book that turned me on to this region and its seductive wines.

Among all the people in Burgundy who have inspired me, moved me, and made me fall madly in love with the wines, the most influential person has been Madame Lalou Bize-Leroy. It was her incredible wines that first moved me, but after getting to know her, it was her philosophy, her dedication and love for her vines that made me understand a bit better what Burgundy is all about. I am honored and thankful to be able to spend time with her whenever I am in Burgundy to gain the immense amount of wisdom and experience she has to share.

In Hong Kong, I have a long list of people to thank for their generosity, friendship, and support: In brainstorming this book, I am especially indebted to the inimitable, generous John Chow, a true gentleman of wine who has done more to spread the wine gospel in Hong Kong than anyone I know. I want to thank Fred Yeung, a collector who puts most wine professionals to shame with his sheer depth and breadth of knowledge, matched only by his wine collection; to Kevin Chan, a true Burgundy lover and collector, who patiently reviewed the first draft of The 100 list with me; and to Wood Chen in Taipei, who only drinks Burgundy, and shared his insights and thoughts with me as I was whittling down the list to just 100.

This book would not be possible without many very generous friends who opened their cellars to share great bottles with me. I want to especially thank N.K. and Melina Yong, Edmund Cheng, Jonathan Slone, Peter Lam, Fred Ma, Vincent Cheung, Michelle and Chris Chan, Ming San Lee, Whang Shang Ying, Joy Hu, and many others who wanted to remain anonymous.

In Hong Kong's thriving and competitive wine market, a handful of outstanding wine professionals stand out, and I want to thank them for their friendship and acknowledge them for their dedication to wine, especially to the great wines of Burgundy: Eric Desgouttes, Paulo Pong, Mandy Chan, Jay Ginsberg, Antonio Koo, Mike Wu, Linden Wilkie, Pierre Legrandois, David Wainwright, Julian Froger, Andrew Bigbee, David Ben Yair, and Eli Shoshani (the latter two only partly based in Hong Kong). To David and Eli, thank you for sharing your wonderful photos of Burgundy!

For great friendships sealed over great wines, I want to thank my WPT wine group: Gene Reilly, Mika Sugitani, Morgan Sze, Bobbi Hernandez, Riana and Savio Chow, Brian Gu, Wenisa Ma, and Nancy and X.D. Yang. Thank you for always accommodating our tastings and dinners around my crazy schedule!

In every city I travel to, I am fortunate to have generous friends who share my love for Burgundy wine. In Korea and Japan: Johnathan Yi, Nicholas Park, J.D. Lee, K.P. Eun, and Kenichi Ohashi MW; in Europe and America: Gérard Sibourd-Baudry, Jeremy Cukierman MW, Jeff Zacharia, Charles Curtis MW, Spence Porter, Christy Canterbury MW, Amy Ray, Tom Mason, and Bijan Jabbari.

For my wonderful girlfriends who provide essential emotional support and bring me so much joy, I want to thank: Betty Cheung, Mable Chan, Sarah Kemp, Margareth Henriquez, Jaime Araujo, Véronique Saunders, Sylvie Cazes, Riana Chow, Jane Lee, and my sister-in-law (aka female soulmate) Aimee Lee.

This book would not be possible without the efforts of the talented, dedicated, and professional team at Assouline. It has been a pleasure working with Esther Kremer, who is the Editor-in-Chief but still has time to review the book with me every time I visit New York City, and Prosper Assouline, who has been supportive of this project from the beginning. A huge heartfelt thanks goes to Amy Slingerland, my editor, who has made this book so much better in every way with her meticulous editing and sound advice. The beautiful design and layout of the book can be credited to the entire art and design team at Assouline, including the art directors Jihyun Kim and Shreya Razak, and the photo editors Elizabeth Eames and Andrea Ramirez, who have transformed the book into an art piece—thank you!

Finally, and most importantly, I want to thank my incredible family who have given me the love and support to pursue my dreams. I can only do what I do because of them. To my husband, Joe, my rock and anchor; my daughter Katherine, who leaves me bursting with pride; my daughter Lauren, who never ceases to amaze or challenge me; my daughter Christina, who makes me smile and laugh; and my baby daughter Julia, whose kind heart and generosity inspires me to have faith in humanity. And to my father, who stands strong for me despite being lost without my mother.

Mom, this book is for you.

Jeannie Cho Lee

CREDITS

Special thanks to the following individuals for their contributions to the book: Michel Baudoin; Julie Carpentier, Baghera Wines; Juliette Charvet; Yuri Chlebnikowski, Nicks Wine Merchants; Kevin Day; Jillian Edelstein; Hallie Freer, Sotheby's; Thomas Haggerty, Bridgeman Images; Ken Johnston, Art Resource; Michel Joly; Katelyn Kraunelis, Christie's; Cécile Mathiaud, BIVB; Maria Fernanda Meza, Artists Rights Society; Mick Rock, Cephas; Michael Shef, Morrell; Eli Shoshani, Pearl of Burgundy.

© 2019 Assouline Publishing
3 Park Avenue, 27th floor
New York, NY 10016, USA
Tel.: 212-989-6769   Fax: 212-647-0005
www.assouline.com

Creative director: Jihyun Kim
Designer: Shreya Razak
Editorial director: Esther Kremer
Editor: Amy Slingerland
Photo editor: Elizabeth Eames
Assistant photo editor: Andrea Ramírez Reyes
Printed in China.
ISBN: 9781614288084

10 9 8 7 6 5 4 3 2

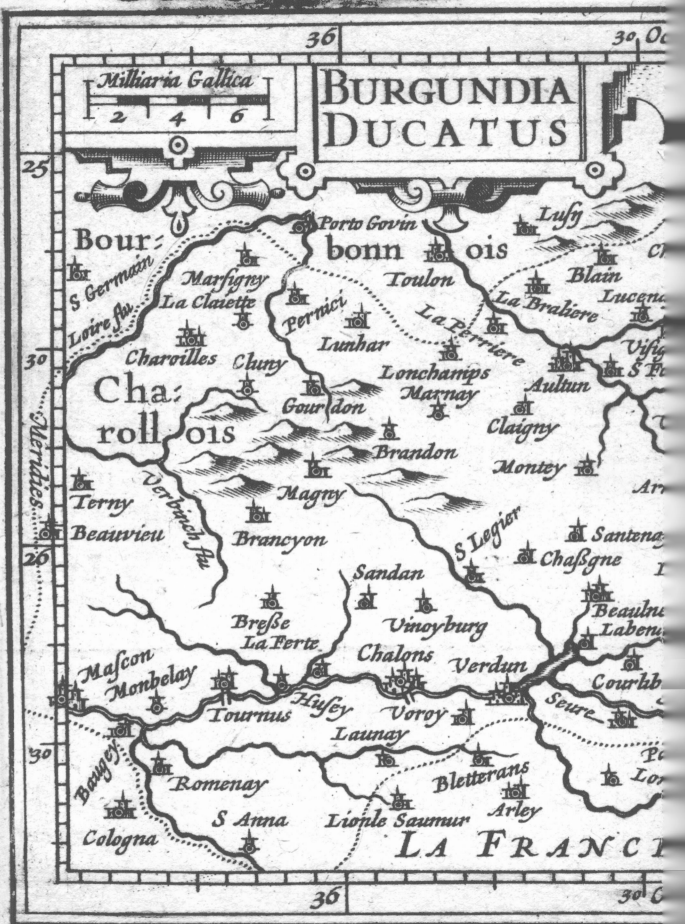

BURGUNDIA DUCATUS

Milliaria Gallica
2 4 6

36

30 Oc

25

Bour=
S Germain
Loire fu.

bonn ois
Porto Govin
Toulon
Lusy
Blain
Lucena
La Braliere

Marsigny
La Claiette
Pernici
Lunhar
La Perriere

Charoilles
Cluny
Gourdon
Lonchamps
Marnay
Aultun
Visig
S Fe

Cha=
roll ois
Brandon
Claigny
Montey

Terny
Verbinch fu.
Magny
S Legier
Santena
Ar

Beauvieu
Brancyon
Chaßgne

26

Sandan
Beaulu
Labenu

Breße
La Ferte
Vinoyburg
Chalons
Verdun
Courbb

Mascon
Monbelay
Tournus
Husey
Voroy
Seure

Baugey
Launay

30

Romenay
Bletterans
Po
Lor

S Anna
Lionle Saumur
Arley

Cologna
LA FRANC

36

30